A WARRIOR'S ODYSSEY

A Life Transformed

ROBERT SANABRIA

Best Wishes

Robert Sanabria

Library of Congress Cataloging-in-Publication Data

Sanabria, Robert

A Warrior's Odyssey: A Life Transformed / Robert Sanabria.

p. cm.

ISBN: 978-1-54398-031-8 (print)

ISBN: 978-1-54398-031-8 (ebook)

1. Sanabria, Robert. 2. Mexican American-Biography. 3. Enlistment--USAF, 4. Basic training--US Army 5. Officer Candidate School--Ft. Benning, GA. 6. 45th Inf. Division--Korea. 7. Platoon Leader--3d Inf. Division, Korea. 8. TB Hospitalization--Denver, CO. 9. Advisor--MACV, Vietnam. 10. Intelligence Officer, 1st Bigrade, 101st ABN, Div.--Vietnam. 11. Intelligence Officer, Pentagon, Washington, DC.

First edition

Also by
Robert Sanabria

Stewing in the Melting Pot
Capital Books, Inc. 2001

The Last Califórnio
Paraguas Books 2011

Dedication

To my late son, Robert II, to my daughter, Suzanne,
to my granddaughters,
Alina and Olivia,
to my late son's wife, Anne,
and finally, in remembrance,
to my late wives, Audrey and Sherry.

Acknowledgements

I owe debts to writers including John Rolfe Gardiner, who has guided my work in the past and keeping me in the right direction once again; and also, Richard Haddock and Sandy Overbey for overseeing and guiding my writing for clarity.

Not all persons mentioned in the text are actual names.

Contents

Prologue

A WARRIOR'S ODYSSEY: A LIFE TRANSFORMED

———————◆———————

WITH THE RESPONSE OF THE UNITED STATES TO NORTH Korea's sudden invasion of the South in 1950, I am among the many thousands of young men about to be taken into military service. Rather than let the Army do what it will with me, I enlist in the U.S. Air Force--a four-year commitment. Assigned to a disappointing low-level duty of cleaning stored weapons, I soon regret the choice. Faced with remaining more than three years of this, I jump at the chance for a commission in the US Army. If successful, I'm still expected to serve in Korea, but more importantly I can be discharged in less than 18 months. I feel it's a chance worth taking.

In 1953, successfully competing in Officer's Candidate School, I'm commissioned a second lieutenant and, as expected, order to Korea. While out of the country on pre-embarkation leave, an Armistice stops the fighting in Korea, and I miss the chance for an early discharge. It leaves me committed to nearly two years of service, including nine months in Korea. The surprising circumstances following will keep me in the Army for more than 22 years, and including my eventual combat in Vietnam.

One day in the late 1980s, remarried and unpacking after moving into a new home in Virginia, I sort through my belongings. Among them I come on a leather zippered case I'd put together years before, while as a patient at Fitzsimons Army Hospital near Denver, Colorado. In it, I've maintained important documents acquired during active military service through years to retirement. Here are these years-worth of official orders, directions to military assignments in the U.S. and abroad, promotions and decorations. Looking through them rekindles memories long forgotten; and some I still have tried to forget. By now, many of the paper pages have become old and brittle; the yellowing is a warning they will eventually decay into unreadable fragments. Suddenly, my first reaction is compelling to rescue them. Then I realize I can use them as sign posts recalling to tell the tale of my brief period in the U.S. Air Force, and following in the longer story of my life in the U.S. Army. It results in a memoir entitled, *A Warrior's Odyssey: A Life Transformed.*

Rather than mainly a war story, this is an account of my life altered by service in the U.S. Army. A life transforming a confused and frightened young Mexican American into a confident resident, even if still scarred. At last I become a man with self-regard, and a full citizen in the eyes of fellow Americans.

Chapter I

TO BE A SOLDIER

————◆————

"BANG, YOU'RE DEAD!" THE RAUCOUS CRY SQUAWKS across the open yards. A single chicken feather in his headband, the dying "Redskin," rises, clutches the vital area of his heart, crumples and bites the dust.

It's likely boys ever dream of being a warrior, and I've had those dreams, too. In the early 1940s, the action is happening at the Sierra Madre Children's Home, a southern California orphanage, where I'm growing up. The other eleven boys and I vent our aggressive instincts by battling each other as imagined Indians and cowboys. For variety, we switch to the likes of the broadcast and movie heroes of Tom Mix, the Lone Ranger, or deputy sheriffs bringing outlaws to justice. Gifts and donations for birthdays and Christmas might yield a cap pistol, a Cowboy's hat, even a lariat and a pair of chaps, though even used and old still much valued. Otherwise we arm ourselves with handmade wooden six-shooters, slingshots, bows and arrows. We even secretly fashion forbidden spears of bamboo cut from the thickets growing on the property. Duly armed, we choose up sides and race around the ample grounds, or lie in wait among the shrubs to launch attacks on one another. We take turns playing good guys and bad. On Saturday at the town's only theater ten-cent matinees with heroes and bad guys, provide our scenarios. If one starts boring us, there is always the next Saturday's matinee to reframe the fight.

All this changes on December 7, 1941, ...*a day of infamy,* our President Roosevelt calls it. Japan's sneak attack on Pearl Harbor grips my ten year-old-mind with dread. It spreads anxiety through all the children in our small town of Sierra Madre. Our ignorance of Pearl Harbor's place on the world map only magnifies our fears. It's enough to know our country is at war with Japan, Germany and Italy. Now, they are our real enemies. Instead of cowboys fighting Indians and outlaws, we're now GIs battling Japanese and German soldiers. Bows and arrows give way to hand-made wooden rifles and bayonets. Apples and oranges, if we can filch them, can become our hand grenades. As more and more of our citizen soldiers march off to war, we act out battlefield bravery and heroism, giving little thought facing soldiers to the real war's maiming and death.

But awareness of the actual consequences of distant war is unavoidable. The graphic battle scenes pictured and described in the *Los Angeles Herald Express*, the newspapers I sell every weekday afternoon, except Sunday, and those I see in newsreels are frightening, if are still remote. Now, the Japanese have attacked our country, and there can be no hiding from reality. Living near California's Pacific Coast, we know Japan just lies beyond the Pacific Ocean, "out there somewhere below the horizon." A greater sense of vulnerability sets in. Could our town, located closer to our enemy, can be bombed? A great dread arrives, when, for the first time just before the year-end, air-raid sirens fill the night air with their ominous wail. This means "blackout!" Darkness might hide us but not protect us.

With the sudden warnings, we don't know if it's practice or the real thing. If sirens sound and we're at our Sierra Madre Elementary School, we all dive under our desks for protection. For us at the Home, we lunge under our beds serving as bomb shelters. We strain to hear the sound of approaching bombers; even the rumble of exploding bombs. When these don't arrive and fail us to retain high anxiety it turns to boredom, and sometimes to mischief. We can make a game out of almost anything and despite our fretfulness the urge for some fun takes over. Down in the boys' dormitory, until our matron stops us, we may pretend to be anti-aircraft gunners, calling out the number of enemy airplanes shot down. In the dark, one belly-crawling boy will sneak up on another to deliver a pretended stab, and declare him dead. But after the first few air raid alerts, eventually, our response to the sirens become routine. Tired of making believe, we just turn out the lights, stumble around in the dark, or go to bed and burrow under the covers to sleep.

Our small, Mount Wilson foothill town of Sierra Madre, California joins the rest of the country in the war effort. When I hear the war might go on for years, my first thought is some day, when I've grown taller and put more weight on my skinny body, I may be able to volunteer. But as time passes, the reality of lost fathers and sons will temper my enthusiasm. As truth bores into my imagination, my boyish ideas gradually change to a hope I won't ever have to serve. By the arrival of the New Year 1943, three former Homeboys, once lived in our orphanage, have enlisted in the army. In March, a 17-year-old previous Homeboy shows up excitedly waving a letter in front of us. It's first shown to his father asking for permission to enlist in the Army Air Corps. With the knowledge, the rest of us we're proud some of us Homeboys are "in."

We're quick to absorb the country's war fever, with its rousing music, and nationalistic sentiment pervasive on the radio. At school, we learn and sing patriotic music, especially the fight songs of the army, navy, marines and the coast guard. Virulent propaganda in all media teaches us the monstrosity of the enemy soldiers--The Axis. "Sink the Rising Sun!" "Smash the Axis!" say posters depicting rats and snakes with the heads of Hitler, Hirohito and Mussolini. We are moved again to a ferocious patriotism and a new yearning to get into uniform.

Letters from our enlisted Homeboys fuel more excitement. A letter from one with an infantry division in the Pacific tells us of heroic fighting against the Japanese. Two others write regularly but can't say where they are, or what they're doing. We're thrilled when there are visits by former Homeboys returning in uniform. They're still our heroes, even if they've yet to shoot at or kill an enemy soldier.

As boys we're eager to get into the fight; afraid again the war won't last long enough. Instead, we collect any military paraphernalia we can lay hands on. And with those fragments of gear, we imagine ourselves at war. As the fighting wears on and more brothers, uncles, even fathers are drafted or join up, more war trappings find their way down to us. Kids show up at school with unit identification patches, or sergeants' stripes, a helmet liner, a cartridge belt, even a real rifle bullet! These treasures pass reverently from one awed boy to another. Later, genuine souvenirs from the war zones begin to show up. Our school's shop teacher's son, fighting in Europe, sends things he's taken from a captured German. It includes a grotesque wallet made from the tanned skin of a woman's breast, including the nipple. As impressive boys, this strikes us more as an awesome curiosity than it should provide proof of barbaric behavior.

Determined to be part of the war effort, we make models of German and Japanese warplanes. We then study their silhouettes, ready to help air-raid wardens identify them, even if only in our imaginations.

While the economy improves, even my mother and stepfather have established a successful Mexican restaurant in Los Angeles. I'm also excited about the possibility of helping to work in it during the summer vacation, as their business succeeds.

Even as the war enters its third year, our support never flags. Now pulled out of the Great Depression, the country's work force reaches full employment. Though there's still rationing and shortages of all kinds it takes a toll on America's morale. The government can't keep the reality of death and destruction from our people; newspapers and newsreels bring it home in graphic form. Gold Star Flags hanging in homes' windows mark the loss of sons, brothers, husbands and fathers. Their numbers grow relentlessly; our boyish understanding of war can no longer ignore their truth. And as time passes, the reality of loss tempers my enthusiasm. My boyish ideas gradually change to hope I won't have to serve at all.

Yet, there are racial currents clouding our home front unity. The newspapers I sell carry articles about Mexican-American zoot-suiters, called *Pachucos*. As a Mexican American I'm troubled by the bad press they're making. I try not to pay attention. My mother says they're no-goods. Yet there's no ignoring them, especially on one Friday night when on shore leave sailors drive into East Los Angeles. It's the home of many Mexican Americans, where sailors try to pick up their girls. The zoot-suiter boyfriends fight them off in a nasty battle ensuing. It continues through the weekend, as the sailors are reinforced by hundreds of soldiers and civilians.

When my mother and stepfather visit us the following Sunday, they're fearful and reluctant to talk about what is happening in the city. They even feel as threatened as I do. At school the next Monday morning, I'm intimidated with my self-confidence failing. At recess, I join a small group of the usual friends. When the conversation drifts to the weekend rioting, one of my buddies blurts: "Boy, we really showed those dirty Mexicans!" He suddenly realizes what he's said in my presence, looks at me and tries to apologize, saying he didn't mean me. But from the moment on, I'm feeling wounded and lessened among these peers.

Yet, I know Mexican Americans are in all the services and doing their part. A short time later, I can take some satisfaction when I learn Mexican Americans have earned more medals of honor than any other ethnic group. But this can't dispel my sense of feeling of second-class status and not fully appreciated as an American.

By the spring of 1945, the tide of the war in Europe has turned in our favor. Victory in Europe Day, or VE Day, arrives on May 7th. The allies accept the unconditional surrender of Nazi Germany, and the end of its Third Reich. Understood by even among the youngest of us, it's an exhilarating time, an event never to be forgotten.

But there's still the war with Japan to finish. It continues on for a few more months. With the focus shifted to the war in the Pacific, there's no hiding the news of death and destruction there. The Battle of Okinawa, the largest amphibious assault in the Pacific war, rivets our attention for 82-long days, from early April to mid-June. By then, also on mind is my final departure from the orphanage after my seemingly endless ten-year stay. I prepare to leave it in late June to live in Los Angeles with my mother and stepfather.

In early August, atomic bombs devastate Hiroshima and Nagasaki and, more importantly, Japan's will to resist. A week later, the Nippon's surrender ends the war and with it the wartime rationing and short-ages. In the evening, my parents and I join the throngs at Long Beach already in a victory celebration. With a collective sigh of relief, the coun-try's thoughts turn to the recovering effort. It hasn't lasted long enough for me to join in and I can't really say this bothers me. Newsreels and movies, deliberately held back to avoid destroying the country's morale, now confirm the terrible wounds of returning servicemen. We learn of their struggles to adjust they're drastically changed and profoundly damaged lives. I may not have been old enough to enlist, but I'm old enough to realize war is not a game, and for some death would have been more merciful than maimed survivors.

Less than five years later, as I'm graduating from high school, trouble is erupting in another far-off place I know nothing about. In the fall of 1949, I begin classes at Los Angeles City College, planning to study for a career as an electrical engineer. Then in June of the next year, North Korea attacks the South. President Truman hardly hesitates to commit the country to the defense of South Korea. Many men, barely resettled in civilian life, find themselves recalled to duty and, along with new draftees, hustled off to the fighting. As an 18-year-old, I've registered for the draft as required. Now, along with my buddies, I worry about actually being drafted. Two of my friends, who've enlisted in the 40th Infantry Division, California's National Guard, are surprised ordered to duty. WWII being over when they joined, they've only signed up mainly to make a little extra money. They're assuming the division having fought during the war will never have to fight again. But now discovering how they are so mistaken.

By then, unable to juggle classes, a night job and a girlfriend, I drop out of college. With the wartime draft still in place, and facing the reality of induction myself, I realize my enthusiasm for becoming a warrior of any kind has long since evaporated. With the growing possibility of being called up, instead I enlist in the U.S. Air Force. My mother and stepfather, having experienced the Mexican Revolution War, try to talk me out of an enlistment of any kind. In the end, they at least take some comfort by realizing I'm not going to combat and possibly die in Korea.

Chapter 2

PORTAL TO A NEW LIFE

THE DOOR TO MY TEENAGE CLOSES ON JANUARY'S THIRD day of 1951. It's a chilly Wednesday morning, as I ride in the drive with my mother to Union Station in downtown Los Angeles.

Before we leave, she asks my stepfather, "Felipe, aren't you coming to the station with us? Roberto is leaving home, and who knows for how long." My Mother's pained expression tells him what she expects.

"No, *Querida*," he disappoints her. "Downtown L.A. is in the wrong direction. I do want to go there with you, but if I do, it'll take another hour drive back to Hermosa Beach and I won't get the restaurant open on time." Except on Tuesdays, *Tortilla Flats*, our Mexican restaurant placed on the strand, after two hours of preparation cooking, opens for business each morning at eleven.

I hope he comes with us, I'm thinking, but I can't argue with his reasoning. He and I get along well enough, but I suspect he doesn't see my leaving as big an event as mother and I do. He wants me to become a partner in the restaurant with them, but I've had enough of it and decline. I know he assumes I'd join them, yet he never bothers first to consult me about it. Now I suspect I've upset his plans by enlisting earlier than I might actually need to. Besides, by now he knows I'm going into the US Air force, while his son, Ricardo, a year younger than I am, is already in the Army. Stationed on Guam, he can be sent into combat in South Korea at any time. My chances of combat now will be slim at the most, exactly as I've planned. Two of my high school buddies, Ray Pacheco and Dave Stevens calculated a tradeoff of 18 months in the Army as opposed to four years in the Air Force. It may seem uneven, but in the Army, we might find ourselves in combat in Korea within six months. On the other hand, enlisting in the US Air Force would mean no combat, though it'll be four years of service before I'm be back in civilian life. Those forty-eight months seem like a good tradeoff for staying alive, uninjured and whole.

Though I've often passed by it, this is my first time in the Los Angeles Union Station itself. Right now, the loading platform is already teeming with other anxious parents, shepherding their own respective young recruit or draftee with his suitcase in hand. I see for some others the whole family has turned out. The cold air turns the crowd's breath into clouds merging with the idling train's steam to form a haze overhead. On every side we see and hear emotional farewells, the forced smiles disguising tearful goodbyes. The sight of others snapping photos to commemorate the leave-taking reminds my Mother she'd forgotten our camera. So, we'll have no visual record of this life-changing moment, after all.

After locating my assigned passenger car, I look around for the two buddies with whom to join up I've agreed. With the war in Korea going badly, and facing the draft, we all three decided to join the Air Force. It was their idea and they succeeded convincing me. Our plan is to go through basic training and serve out the four years of our enlistments together. At the signing and oath taking, the recruiting officer promised us the same departure date. If the promise has been kept, they should be here with me on the platform. But so far, neither of them is anywhere in sight. Actually, I have to admit I'm not disappointed. Maybe I'll get along just as well without them. The choice I've made is more than having their company. I'm sure enlisting in the U.S. Air Force makes more sense than being drafted, quickly shipped off to the fighting in Korea and plunged into combat. The Army's loss of territory and high casualties by now are well known and not a little terrifying. Unlike during WWII, there's no holding back on the bad news on this war.

Mother, who knows both of my friends, blames them for my impending departure. After awhile, I give up the search for them thinking its as much their responsibility as mine is to find each other. I don't know it now, but suspect I'll never see either one of them again.

A sergeant, showing up in what is now in the new Air Force blue uniform, is start getting the departure moving. His uniform is far more attractive, I'm thinking, than the Army's olive drab. In fact, blue is my favorite color; I think I should look good in it. A clipboard in hand, the sergeant sounds off names and compartment assignments. I wait for the esses.

"Sadler! Sadler, Allen!"

"Uh, I'm here," a wavering voice answers.

"Compartment 28."

"San, uh. Snabra?"

"You mean, Sanabria?" I shout back.

"Yeah, sorry. Robert, right?"

"Right."

"OK. Compartment 28, too. I mean also."

Until my name is called, Mother has maintained her stoic posture and kept her emotions in check. But hearing "Sanabria," realizing I'm really going to leave, she inhales a sudden breath and seems to wilt. Then there's a torrent of tears; she's wailing she'll never see me again. But her reaction is no surprise. It's why I wanted my stepfather to come with us. For a moment, I stand staring at her and then wrap her in my arms. She buries her face in my chest and clings to me.

"*Hijo*, they'll hurt you," she cries.

"No, they won't. Don't worry, I'll be home on leave in a few months," I say, patting her back and kissing her forehead. Then holding her face in my hands, I look into her tear-welling eyes and add, "I'll write to you at least once a week, I promise." Then to distract her, I add, "There is something you can do for me while I'm gone."

"What is it?" She asks, as she wipes away a tear.

"Make sure that brother-in-law of mine takes care of my car."

"Did you tell Gilbert he could use it?" she asks.

"I did, but only enough to keep the battery charged and the engine oiled."

She nods, her expression changing, "I don't know if you can depend on him. He's a new father and your sister...," her voice trails off. Then, returning to the reason for her unhappiness, she says, "You shouldn't go, Roberto. You're hardly an adult, too young for the service. They'll hurt you," she repeats.

"Mother, I'm nineteen and you know I had to join, or be drafted. At least I'm not going to Korea. We've been through this already. Anyway, I've signed up and it's too late for me to back out." I take a deep breath and add, "Now, I have to go," I say, unpeeling her arms from me, and turn to leave.

"Wait, here take this with you," she says, handing me the brown paper bag she's been clutching. "So, you'll have something to eat on the way."

"Oh, you didn't have to do that," I smile, "they do have to feed us, you know. But thanks, that's very thoughtful."

Giving her a final hug and taking my small suitcase and the brown bag in hand, I follow others already climbing into the passenger car, find my compartment and settle at a window seat. While the loading finishes, Mother and I stare at each other through the window. I'm impatient, while she's dabbing her tears, but I try to keep smiling and urge whispering the train to get moving.

At last, with a blast of its whistle, the locomotive engine bellows and starts creeping forward, its wheels gaining purchase on the rails, and we begin to move. Finally, asserting its motion, the train starts to pull away. My Mother and I wave at each other. She remains anchored there on the platform as we pick up speed. The train makes a turn, and soon she's out of sight. I know she'll stay where I've left her, until the last car has passed from view and disappears. My emotions are in turmoil. Leaving home for the uncertainty of a chosen new life is both frightening and exhilarating, as I'm facing independence from my troubled home.

It has been only fifteen years since she left me at the orphanage. And now, I can't help but recall that leave-taking, too. She'd parked my siblings and me there for a decade, while she went about living her own life. This time, I'm leaving her to live mine. I wonder if her show of caring is related to her sense of guilt recalling the orphanage to her mind, too. Even if so, I doubt she sees the irony. This time it's I who can blame for my leave-taking on circumstances. Now I'm separating from a place and its people. And in my absence, I will change and they will, too. I wonder if I'll ever to return in search of them.

The trip is not only my first by train, but also an overnighter. I share the compartment with five other guys, all of whom appear to be about my age. Despite feigned bravado, anxiety mixed with excitement are obvious on all their faces, and probably on mine, too. For a while, we all avoid eye contact, pretending to listen to the train's wheels click-clacking below us.

"You ever flown before?" The kid sitting next to me asks, finally breaking the silence, his eyes shining wide.

"Nope," I say. "Is why you joined?"

"My dad was a crew chief in the Army Air Corps during World War II and thought it was great. I told the recruiter it's what I want to do, too."

I nod. "Hope you get your wish." For a moment, I'm about to tell him I've joined because I don't want to get shot in Korea. But just then, a kid in the seat across from us speaks up and says it for me. An honest man, I think. The ice, now broken, others also begin to talk. It soon becomes clear their reasons for enlisting, like mine, have more to do with a wish to stay alive and remain in one piece than to fly airplanes.

The warmth from the brown bag Mother has given me finally draws my attention. From inside comes the enticing odor of two still-warm burritos, wrapped in wax paper. I feel a lump form in my throat, the full realization of leaving home. With only a scant breakfast in my belly, I want to eat them right away. But it doesn't seem polite to do so in front of others, and there isn't enough to go around. Determined to enjoy my going-away gifts, anyway, I end up munching the burritos standing in space between the two passenger cars at the end of the aisle. Careful to keep their ends closed to prevent the contents from oozing out and dirtying my clothes; the last thing I need is returning to my seat with brown bean mush dribbled down my shirtfront.

We're headed for Texas, where I'd been born, but left when I was barely a four-year-old, the probable age of first memory. I have little to revisit in mind. My mother never has anything good to say about it. Now, our destination is to a place outside of San Antonio, where the Air Force trains recruits like us. Lackland Air Force base will be home at least for the next eight weeks.

Before long, our chatter suddenly stops when another sergeant sticks his head into our compartment to check off our names again. This done, he smiles and tells us the direction of the dining car, and the schedule for meals. The friendliness, gives the illusion the Air Force is glad to have us, but it'll likely to be quickly dispelled the next morning.

Chapter 3

NEW VISTAS

FITFUL SLEEP MARKS MY FIRST NIGHT AWAY. THE MIXTURE of clacking train wheels, excitement and insecurity keep me in restless wakefulness and imagining about what awaits us in Texas. In the long trip we don't arrive until the following afternoon.

In a mixed cloud of steam and smoke, the train jerks to a squealing stop. From the compartment window through the haze I see no sign of San Antonio; the station sitting vast beyond its city limits. We're in a huge train yard, filled with railroad cars passing for a station, nothing memorable in sight. Nevertheless, my pulse is up with anxiety and anticipation, with my breathing shallower.

A sergeant in gray-green fatigues comes storming through the aisles of our Pullman car snapping us out of our anxious reveries.

"Grab your stuff and line up outside!" He yells, repeatedly. Uncertainty makes for slow reactions and our hesitation brings the angry commands from this noncommissioned officer. And we're stunned for the moment.

"Come on, move it, MOVE IT!" He yells, louder and louder to get us moving faster out of the car and onto the platform.

With the launch of the war in Korea, we're told the basic training population at the base has burgeoned. Even as we detrain, there's no surprise encountering the platform swarming with hundreds of other young men like me. The scene is like a madhouse of milling bodies, while noncoms can be heard repeatedly yelling demanding orders. Acrid diesel fumes from the nearby row of idling trucks are hardly a welcoming atmosphere to Texas. I'm overtaken with a sense of loneliness, abandonment, yet somehow still also excited I barely notice the chill of the overcast January morning.

Our sergeant, has us lined up, and bellows for our attention.

"When I call your name, pick up your luggage and load onto the trucks behind me," jerking a thumb over his shoulder as he speaks. "Starting with the lead vehicle, sixteen men per truck, luggage in your lap." We stand shivering until the recruit list finishes and its members once released. Then follows the formation bursting in the scrambling to load.

A short rumbling trip later, the convoy pulls-up outside a line of barracks; old two-story wooden structures coated a smoky gray from years of coal-fired boilers. We're told they were built to house air cadets and pilot trainees during the Second World War. Now they're for basic trainees like us. We tumble clumsily from the vehicles, line up again, and listen for our names, this time with an assigned building and a bunk number.

Inside the barracks, a corporal, obviously enjoying his bit of authority, bellows still more instructions.

"Put your personal stuff in the lockers at the foot of the bed, suitcase underneath." The combination padlock I've brought along gives me some sense of security assurance for my few belongings. We have about five minutes to do as directed before the corporal is back at us with an order. "Fall out-on-the-double." Fall Out? On-the-double? The terms are new, but their meaning is clear soon enough.

For the next eight weeks, days begin with a rousting from our bunks at 4:45 AM, or 0445 hours. Cold dark hour reeking of burnt coal is shock enough leaving its blackened presence on our upper lips and around our nostril openings. Still in our civvies, looking anything but military, we're herded half-awake to breakfast. The mess hall, a cavernous building outfitted with benches at long tables, is not unlike penitentiary scenes in old black and white movies. But at least it's warm. Besides fruit and coffee, a steaming serving line offers rubbery, reconstituted scrambled eggs, and its oatmeal tends to resist a spoon's penetration. There's greasy bacon and a mound of a thick, hot creamy-white something poured on toast, remarkably similar to what I'd often eaten at the orphanage: creamed chipped beef on toast, now known as SOS, or *shit on a shingle*. Despite its deplorable name, it's filling, and what's more, I like it.

Except for an issued fatigue cap, during our first two weeks we live in the clothes we've brought with us; Air Force logistics, overwhelmed by the influx of recruits, can't even issue us underwear--the daily worn pair nightly rinsed out-- much less boots and uniforms. The absence of uniforms is also discouraging.

It falls to a corporal in charge to teach the 40 men of our group, known as a 'flight,' to stand at attention, face left, face right, also turn halfway around, or about face. In between spitting tobacco juice, his angry demands call for instant obedience. The bellowed orders are followed by a nose-to-nose chewing-out of those reacting too slowly, or unable to tell their left from right. He appears to be in a perpetual, red-faced state of rage. As a reminder of which hand is which, he orders a few men to carry rocks in their right hand. Livid in his deep Georgia accent, he screams, "Yaw utha raht! Herman!" It takes nearly the entire next two weeks to understand by "Herman," he means "Airman."

Once he has us under reasonable control, we start the day with a half hour of physical training, or PT. He then moves to the next level of close order drill, having us marching in formation. And march we do, from one appointment to the next: To the barbershop for close shearing, head-shot photos for ID cards, the dreaded dispensary for an array of painful shots, orientation on the Uniform Code of Military Justice, followed finally to chow. By lights out each night at 2200 hours, or 10 PM, we're thoroughly cowed, sore, and exhausted. I'm thankful all my tramping is being done around in my favorite crepe-soled shoes, instead of a new, stiff, blister-producing pair of boots.

This latest routine, in many ways like at the orphanage, has a predictability makes it bearable. Kitchen Police, or KP, duty and other extra chores add to the routine of keeping the barracks ordered and clean. By the end of the third week, we're finally issued boots and fatigues and fitted for blue uniforms and billed caps. The uniforms at least give us a sense of belonging to the Air Force. But it's learning to shoot a .45 caliber pistol and a .30 caliber carbine that bring back some of the enthusiasm for military service I imagined as a boy. Eight weeks of "Basic" seems like a long stretch, but it keeps us so busy and constantly on the move, time never drags.

Until now, I've kept pretty much to myself. As a group we tend to self-segregate according to from our States, or cities of origin, the first commonality we find in each other. Small buddy groups coalesce, but that's as far as friendships develop. And as at the orphanage, these friendships are short-lived, mainly due to the constant turnover among us. Similarly, there's a change here in our group's composition. Some new arrivals are men held back from preceding flights, some are departing due to sickness or injury. Surprisingly, and, though I can't imagine where they could go out into the prairie, a number of them go absent without leave, known as AWOL, and simply disappear.

Despite having shared the trials of basic training with nearly forty other men, I tend to avoid befriending anyone. As one of the youngest in the group, my instinct makes me wary, not only of the possibility of being robbed, but of awkward confrontations. Preoccupation with the rigorous training schedule has little time for fistfights. Rare, but tensions among over-tired men living in cramped quarters could bring arguments and shoving matches. My caution amplifies a sense of solitude and loneliness. I find I do miss the buddies who'd talked me into joining the Air Force; supposedly we were to be doing it together, and wonder if they've managed to remain in contact. Maybe or maybe not, considering the military's propensity to order by alphabetizing. Yet, our surnames each beginning with letters weren't all very far apart in the alphabet, and if they were here, we'd have met by now. With or without them, the four years lonely future ahead seem like an eternity.

As the end of basic nears within sight, rumors are rampant about where next we'll be posted. I expect to be sent to a school of some sort, but I won't know what might be until I arrive at a permanent assignment. As it turns out, I don't have to wait very long to find out. My next home will be at Walker Air force Base in New Mexico. The prospect of leaving Texas for a new state has a certain appeal; at least New Mexico will be somewhat closer to home.

Graduation, near the end of March, is much welcomed, the affair to be attended by very few parents. I wished mine would show up, yet I know they can't. Now a full-fledged Airman, I'm eager to see what's next in store for me. The following day, my suitcase and duffle bag loaded into the belly of a Greyhound bus, I settle in for the overnight 600-miles to Roswell, New Mexico.

Chapter 4

OPEN PLACES

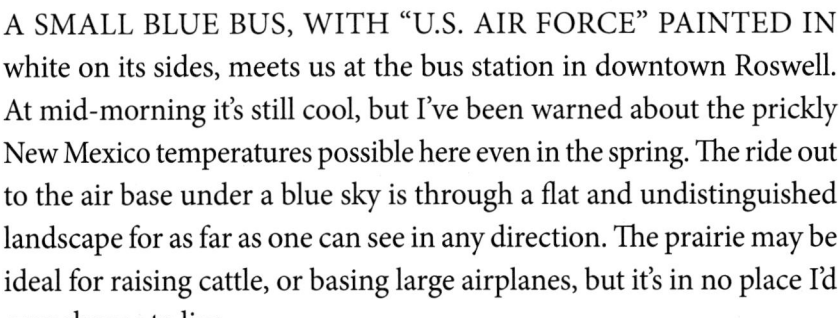

A SMALL BLUE BUS, WITH "U.S. AIR FORCE" PAINTED IN white on its sides, meets us at the bus station in downtown Roswell. At mid-morning it's still cool, but I've been warned about the prickly New Mexico temperatures possible here even in the spring. The ride out to the air base under a blue sky is through a flat and undistinguished landscape for as far as one can see in any direction. The prairie may be ideal for raising cattle, or basing large airplanes, but it's in no place I'd ever choose to live.

The squadron commander, a Captain, makes a short welcome speech and turns us over to a tall serious-looking Chief Warrant Officer. A man of few words, he, too, hands us off to a noncom, who then leads us on to our barracks. It's housing one of a group of unattractive, long, one-story, low concrete-block buildings, each in rows of double-tiered bunks. With the showers and latrines at each end, the buildings give the distinct aura of a prison--but at least its without bars.

In this early April, I stow my belongings in a locked trunk turned in to the unit supply building for storage, and board a bus in downtown Roswell for a ten-day leave at home. The trip, a constant day and night travel of 1,000-miles each way, will eat up nearly four days of my short furlough. Still, six days at home are better than none at all. This, my first leave, puts off for a while longer having to get acquainted with my new bunk and work mates.

During my three-month absence from home, I find little has changed. I look pretty sharp in my new uniform, at least my mother thinks so, and I stand for a number of photographs with my parents and younger siblings. But, the novelty of my new status is quickly set aside, and I'm put back to work in the restaurant. Surprisingly, I'm comfortable with it.

In the spring of the previous year, it has been my job to re-paint the signs on the front and above of our restaurant. Intervening months of wind, rain and salt air have done their damage fading the painted letters. *Tortilla Flats,* the restaurant's name really now needs repainting, as well as its definition and colors.

This done, amidst familiar cooking odors, I work along beside my parents waiting on customers, bussing tables, even cooking, things I'd been doing with them for a few number of years on weekends. But this, my visiting weekend, I spend calling on my older sister and, Anthony, her new baby boy. As promised, Gilbert, my brother-in-law has taken care of my car, a front-fender-less '34 Dodge coupe, though somehow he's managed to burn out the used radio I'd installed. My six days of leave quickly evaporate. Though I badly wanted this home leave, I find heading back to duty in New Mexico turns out to be a measure of relief.

My new airbase, named after Medal of Honor winner, General Kenneth Walker, is impressive for its role and its history. As a Strategic

Air Command base, it houses B-29 bombers, which can conduct heavy bombing missions anywhere worldwide. During WWII to 1948, the airbase on land acquired from a rancher, has been known as the Roswell Army Air Field, only three miles south of the town of Roswell's small business district. But according to some residents the base they feel is entirely too close to them. Its vast empty prairie in all directions around the base and the town give both a sense of isolation.

The major military unit at Roswell trains pilots and bombardiers for the B-29 Super Fortress, the same type of aircraft had dropped atomic bombs each on Japan's Hiroshima and Nagasaki. Bombing and gunnery ranges are also located only a few miles south of the airfield. But there the bombers only drop sand-filled practice bombs, not just to save cost, but also to avoid bomb blasts upsetting local civilians, and frightening grazing cattle.

On my return from leave, I learn I'm to be trained as an armorer; I'm told it's a step or two up from the majority of assignments enlisted men receive. The name itself has a certain drama and excitement and for a while intrigues me. In a war zone, armorers fuse bombs and rockets and load ammunition for the machine guns on fighters and bombers. No doubt a necessary critical activity. But when I meet the other six men with whom I'm to be attending the course, I learn the truth from a corporal named Marty, the oldest in the group.

"Yeah, we'll learn more about fuses and ammo than we'll ever use," he tells us. "But once on the job, we'll be filling dummy bombs with sand." Hardly an appealing job description, I'm thinking, and work held in such low regard I doubt will hold my interest either. The armorer's school at Lowery Air Force Base is near to Denver, Colorado. At least it will be in a new state, close to an interesting city, and I'll be gaining another new experience.

It's only mid-April and already I'll be taking my second train ride on the way to Denver. Marty, a man in his late twenties has decided to take my nineteen years of age under his wing. I'm wary, thinking I'm sure I can and prefer fending for myself.

He tells me, "To be one of the guys, you should buy a half pint of Canadian Club whiskey, like the others are doing."

"Marty, but I'm under age," I tell him. Without any hesitation, he agrees to buy it for me and, of course, I'll repay him.

I've tasted beer and wine in my parents' restaurants and didn't care for either of them. After leaving the orphanage to return to live with my mother and stepfather, I'd seen how their heavy drinking could make life be frightening and precarious. Ever since, being around people who are drunk, or even likely to become so, I soon experience anxiety. Yet, here I am about to indulge, too.

"Marty, I'm not a drinker," I tell him.

"Don't worry, you'll like the CC's smoothness, as you'll see why all the guys prefer it." Later, when I take a whiff, the sweetish smell seems agreeable enough. Next, Marty produces a deck of cards and gives me some quick lessons in poker, the game our little group will be playing, when the trip gets underway. I give little thought to the fact I'll be wagering my half-month's advance pay of twenty-one dollars.

In the late afternoon, we shortly settle in our Pullman car and get used to the comforting of the clacking of the train's wheels. The poker game next then gets organized and underway. I watch for a while to get the hang of it, trying to understand the play with the essentials Marty has taught me. After a while, when one of the players drops out, Marty invites me to sit in the open place. Cautious, at first, I fold hands I later learn they could have won. Then, confidence rising, it occurs to me maybe I'm being suckered in to keep me playing, only to be cleaned out later. Yet, my luck holds, and if dinner doesn't interrupt, I'm confident it will continue. Meanwhile, though the whiskey takes some getting used to, I've been nipping at the Canadian Club all along with everyone else.

I've planned to stop playing after dinner. But when the game resumes, the others cajole me into giving them a chance to get their money back. While it doesn't make sense occurs to me, but for the sake of buddy-ship I play on anyway. No one can believe my continuing luck: I win one hand after another; except for the ones I have the good enough sense to fold. I attribute my success first to beginner's luck, but then could it also be a growing skill?

By about ten o'clock, I'm pretty drunk and announce I can hardly see straight. With my head spinning, collecting my winnings I leave the game and all but crawl to my lower berth, lie down fully dressed and pass out. Sometime during the night, my stomach decides to get rid of what's left remnants of the alcohol and everything else in my stomach. I'm only vaguely aware of someone standing in the aisle watching me vomit. Through bleary eyes, I see the disgusting mess I've made on the aisle carpet and, next to the remains of my dinner, the porter's shoes. The vague image comes with sound; he's cussing me nonstop. But too far-gone to care, I turn away into my bunk and go back to sleep.

The next morning, sick enough to want to die, I discover I've been rolled for all the money I'd won as well as my half-month's advance. Mine is now a very pale face, a crushing headache and nausea, as they turn out, will stay with me for the next three days. I'm flat broke and the payday is a full two weeks away. I wonder if I've been robbed by the porter, or more likely by one of the guys in our group. But lacking any evidence, I keep my suspicions to myself. When he learns what has happened, if indeed he doesn't already know, Marty asks the other guys to pitch in for me. The small collection nets eight dollars, which I'll have to nurse for two weeks. I swear I've learned a lesson. From then on, the mere smell of Canadian Club, or any other whiskey, I'm sure will trigger instant nausea. But fortunately, I haven't been turned away from poker.

The six weeks of munitions school at Lowry are unlike my basic training at Lackland. Knowing its aim, the class work is serious and interesting. I like learning to assemble and how to arm fuses. But nonetheless, I don't feel particularly challenged. Marty says, if this training is ever to put to use, I'll be sent to Guam or Japan; neither of which are thought to be bad postings.

With weekends free, one of my classmates, a guy named Harvard-- call me Harvey, he insists--and I explore downtown Denver, where the large City Park Lake becomes a favorite hangout. I've heard it's a good place to pick up girls, and each of us succeeds in attracting one each time we go there. But with no wheels and little money, there is no follow-up. Fortunately, at lakeside a lot of first-class free entertainment, like Stan Kenton's big band, is there on weekends for everyone's enjoyment.

A Chicagoan, Harvey has decided my being from L.A. makes me hip. It's enough credential for him to confess he shares my passion for *George Shearing's Quintet*, then enjoying national popularity. At one of the bus stops close to Denver, he discovers a jukebox with a variety of Shearing's recordings. We're both short of cash, and the jukebox, at a dime a pop, is a source for our cheap entertainment.

The Shearing sound is intoxicating, and so far, I'll always associate it with that season of my military career. No matter what piece George and his group perform I have to stop and listen. At the time, "September in the Rain" is his biggest hit, and we play it with his other selections, over and over. Harvey, who has played piano in the past, explains the unique Shearing sound is based on a technique known as *voicing*.

"It's a type of melody block chord, with a fifth note doubles the melody an octave lower," he explains. I have to admit I don't entirely understand, but the Shearing sound is instantly recognizable and it certainly speaks to me. While we're there, we're really excited when the Shearing Quintet makes a visit to Denver. Thankfully, we're able to scrape up enough money for admission to see and hear the group live.

In Harvey, I find a kindred spirit, which for a time does a lot to dispel my sense of loneliness. I know our acquaintance will end with the conclusion of the course. And when it does, with a handshake and sincere best wishes we go our separate ways, never to meet again.

Chapter 5

DIGGING IN

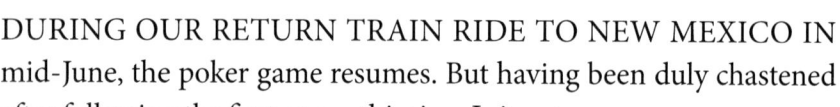

DURING OUR RETURN TRAIN RIDE TO NEW MEXICO IN mid-June, the poker game resumes. But having been duly chastened after following the first game, this time I sit out.

Scorching, sun-glaring days and sweaty nights greet us in our return to Roswell. The concrete block walls of the fully occupied barracks soak up the sun's heat during the day, and radiates it all through the night. Large floor fans at both ends of the barracks only move in air from the outside and shift it about inside the building and then out again. There's no escaping the unrelenting temperature. For most of us getting to sleep is only possible by lying in our skivvies under a water-soaked bed sheet. The fan-moved air is supposed to evaporate the moisture and cools enough to let us drift off to sleep. As for the new assignment, thankfully, Marty's prediction that we'll spend our days shoveling sand into dummy bombs turns out to be wrong. But what it also reveals are such chores might not have been any worse than those in my actual new assignment.

Following a successful performance in the munitions course, I'm awarded an Airman's stripe on my return to Roswell. It also means a small increase in my pay, a briefly passing pleasure. Yet, despite having done well in the armorer's classes, to my disappointment I'm inexplicably reassigned from my Armament and Electronics squadron to a supply and housekeeping unit. It's a deplorable step down, as my barracks mates are quick to point out.

The Author is the fourth an enlisted Airman standing from the left, with another Airman with a hand on my chest at Walker U.S. Air Force base, Roswell, New Mexico in 1952

The logistics unit includes a six-man workshop charged with restoring a seemingly endless quantity of pistols and carbines taken out from storage. At the end of WWII, the weapons were encased in Cosmoline, a thick, dark-brown grease to preserve and keep the small arms from rusting. Now, our job is to disassemble them, remove the grease, put them back together, oil and then re-pack them for shipment. This means hand-washing the weapons in a large vat of solvent, a nasty and possibly toxic task. Dizzying fumes from the potent liquid leave us light-headed and headachy, the skin of our hands reddened, dried out and burning for a time afterwards each day. Without a ventilation system in the low-ceiling workroom, we have to take turns for frequent breaks outside the shop to clear our heads.

The other five men in the workshop have all served in the Second World War and since either stayed on at the war's end, or are reservists recalled to active duty. They make no secret of it, they're just serving out enlistments, or their years to retirement. All of us really loathe the chore we're doing and are in no hurry to set any records, nor does the staff sergeant in charge push us to work any faster. Being assigned to a job like this says a lot about how the Air force values our service, or our individual skills. All of these men seem to understand their lower status; most evident in growing beer bellies and the stained one-piece fatigues in which they arrive for work each day.

Disillusioned by the assignment and feeling punished—-for what I can't imagine, I nonetheless try to do my share. I'm the youngest member of the crew, and after work each day I assume they're inviting me to hang around with them, as a friendly gesture. But it could more likely be they just want an innocent young mind to listen to their imagined war stories.

Besides a movie theater, in which the feature changes twice a week, the diversions on the base include a library, a swimming pool, a bowling alley and a German-style beer garden. One after another I try out all five. In the end my favorite is the beer garden in which I soon develop quite a taste for beer, despite recalling the drunks often at my parents' restaurants. Before long, I fall into the group's routine of beer-garden nights. While sharing pitchers of beer, I listen to the group's complaints and exaggerated war stories until the garden closes at 11 PM each night. In the mornings we're usually hung over and uninspired. To sleep it off during the workday, we take turns napping in the loft above the shop.

Though I really feel guilty about this, I manage to shrug it off, telling myself I'm just following the behavior examples of my seniors.

Our immediate boss is the Chief Warrant Officer we met on our arrival from Lackland. He usually shows up at the shop two or three mornings each week on a predictable schedule. On those days, no one naps until after the Chief has dropped by for his inspection. But, if I imagine this could end in disaster, I would be right. On a day when I'm in a particularly bad shape, taking my turn in the loft, what I've imagined it actually happens. I suspect it's a cruel joke when the others fail to warn me. Though the Staff Sergeant in charge later claims the Chief showed up on an odd day, it was on purpose to catch the shop unaware. With only six men to account for, the absence of even one is glaring. When the Chief asks where I am on this day, rather than a cover story the Staff Sergeant simply tells him, "He's asleep up in the loft." Now, how's that for a buddy?

Angry and disgusted, the Chief orders me down from the loft, to leave the shop and report to his office. Groggy and certain I'm in deep trouble, I fully expect to be read the riot act and given punishment of some sort. Yet, he does neither. After ordering me to stand and sweat for a while in his office, he directs me to take a chair across from his desk. Then, instead of dressing me down, he begins questioning me.

"What did you do before you enlisted?" he asks, in a stern but calm tone.

"I went to college for a while," I tell him, "worked nights and tried to keep up with a girlfriend." I explain how this left little time to study, and eventually, I have to drop out.

"What was your major?"

"Electrical engineering," I tell him.

"And then what did you do?"

"A friend got a job for me in a factory that produces capacitors."

"OK, that's at least in the field, but what was your job there?"

"At first, I worked on the production line, dipping the raw capacitor tubes in jigs into a thick liquid silver bath. I described how the capacitors were then dipped in liquid ceramic and after dried, placed in longer jigs and moved on to the painting station. He seemed interested, so I went on explaining how the capacitors were painted by rolling tubes each containing different colors to indicate their respective capacities. Because the heights of the capacitors weren't even, I told him how I'd identified the glitch in the coloring system and offered a solution for fixing the problem. And how this had led to my promotion as an assistant supervisor.

"Really?" he's impressed. "Go on, tell me about your solution."

"When I'd seen and understood the problem," I relate, "I made scale drawings. They showed how the notched wheel of each paint cartridge, under light spring tension, could ride freely over the uneven tops of the raw capacitors held in the jig. In that way, they could all get paint-coded and none of them bent in the process."

"So how did you get your drawings to the head office." he asked.

"I gave them to my supervisor," I continued, "and, maybe because he didn't understand them, he took them directly to the owner, who immediately called for me. He wanted to know more about my background. When I told him about dropping out of college, he surprised me by promoting me on the spot to an assistant supervisor, and asked I alert him to any other ideas I might have."

Whether impressed by my tale, or just to keep an eye on me, the Chief sets me to creating a large organizational chart of the numerous units under his control. I do it gladly and apparently to his satisfaction, since he finds other similar tasks to keep me busy. I can see he actually needs an assistant, and his assignments at least keep me from returning to the deplorable weapons shop cleaning job.

Once out of the workshop and away from its crew, I know the spent drinking beer with my former shop mates has been a waste of time. Now with more free time in the evenings, I explore other base facilities. On the weekends, then I see what the town of Roswell might have to offer. Its main attractions are a movie theater and numerous bars. At our arrival briefing we were warned to avoid the latter; hardly a night passing without some Airman is being thrown out of one, maybe beaten senseless or ending up in jail.

While exploring the town, I learn Roswell is divided north and south by Main Street, and east and west by Second Street. East of Main is a small community of Mexicans. On Second Street, a short distance from Main, I find a *bodega*, a small Mexican grocery, where I meet the owner's daughter, Victoria, who works at the store summers and on weekends. In repeated visits, I buy fruit or other items I really don't need, but with patience I finally get her to talk to me. She's very pretty and about my age, with long beautiful auburn hair and fascinating green eyes. She's also light-skinned and buxom, and the latter I always appreciate. Right away, I'm very taken with her, but at the same time I can tell my interest is not mutually. She's obviously wary of me, no doubt used to an endless stream of other Airmen trying to approach her, seeing themselves as her would-be lovers.

Persisting, I try to convince her to go out with me. She finally agrees to see a movie, but only if we meet at the theater. I'm sure she sees me more as an Airman than a fellow Latino, and doesn't want me to meet her family. If I were, that might mean I'd be courting her for eventual marriage, the farthest thing from my mind. Keenly aware of her reticence, during the show I make no attempt to put an arm around her or even to hold her hand. But afterwards, I try to make the evening last a little longer.

"Would you like to have a soda and something to eat?" I ask.

"No thanks," she says, "I promised my parents I would come straight home."

"Well, maybe next time," I say, hopefully. "But look, it's pretty dark out. I'll walk you home, OK?" She agrees to allow me to escort her to what passes for her home's front gate.

She lives in the town's southeast quadrant, the Mexican quarter, I call it, defined by Main Street on the west and Second Street on the north. Once past those primary streets, even in the dark, the impoverishment of her neighborhood is evident. Main Street and those to the west of it are paved, complete with curbs and illuminated concrete sidewalks. But east of it, except for Second Street, the roads are not paved, but graveled, rutted, unlit and entirely without sidewalks. I'm thinking it's why she wanted to meet at the theater during still daylight. Her house, like the rest I can see, is a small frame building, without a lawn and shrubbery. One or two of the others nearby have vehicles parked on what might have been lawns, and some are up on concrete blocks. Trees abound and provide some shade, but only squirrels seem really enjoy them.

"What's it like living here?" I ask, her.

"Oh, I so wish we could move," she answers, sighing and then quickens the pace of her talk that continues with surprising intensity.

"Is it really that bad? Your family has a business and it seems to be doing all right."

Ignoring my question, she says, "We are Hispanos."

"I'm sorry, I don't know what it means," I reply.

She looks at me for a moment, and explains, "Hispanos are descendants of the Spanish who settled parts of the southwest of the U.S. in the 18th Century. We were here long before any Anglos ever showed up," bitterness in her tone is detectable.

"And you don't get the respect you believe deserve?"

"Hardly. The Anglo community considers us as Mexicans and treat us poorly."

Knowing something of prejudice, I stifle my own defensiveness and bite my tongue. Instead of challenging her comment, I ask, "Well, in what way?"

"We're not allowed any role in running the city, if you can call it. And you can see the poor conditions here. We're only slightly better off than the few Negroes who live even farther out." She can hardly wait to get away from here, she says.

Any romantic notions I might have now vanish with the next movie date, when I walk her home and try for a goodnight kiss. I'm left wondering how many more of these dates would it take for her to allow it? I can't begin to guess. Well, so much for romance!

Chapter 6

A BREAKOUT

FOR TWO WEEKS IN CALIFORNIA THIS TIME, I'M GRANTED another leave in mid-September. With more time to kill, I spend much of it visiting friends, and even include a trip to my childhood orphanage in Sierra Madre, where I've spent so many years of my life. During the war, the head matron, Miss Elsie Gibson--we called her Gibsie-- had been very proud of the Homeboys who'd served in the military during World War II. For the whole lengthily time I lived there, I was never a favorite of hers. Now I'm thinking my showing up in uniform might change her attitude. But upon arriving, almost immediately I can see on her unsmiling face there's no such luck. At best, once again in her presence, I feel some tolerated but hardly welcomed. Regina, now grown to be one of the younger matrons and still serving there, she and I had once had a few loving secret meetings in the furnace room for brief sessions of kissing and fondling. But this time as now a fully grown adult she apparently has decided to avoid any renewing of our formerly expressions of affection.

Though I do need a break from duty, the fifteen days at home with my folks still gives me too much time on my hands. Feeling surprisingly a little estranged, I spend little of it working in the restaurant. Instead of welcoming, this trip home is leaving me disgruntled. When I depart it again there's little sense of disappointment and I'm even beginning to realize I'm outgrowing our home.

Returning to New Mexico makes me see how ineffectual and unsatisfied I'm feeling about my present status in life. Especially, serving in the Air Force has been a real disappointment. Not even a promotion to Airman First Class in early-December does much to dispel a sense I'm wasting my young life. I suspect it's the Chief's hand in my promotion, at least for which I'm grateful. But what I want most now is to get through the three remaining years of my enlistment, get out, go back to school, and make a fresh start for my life.

At first, some events when they occur seem ordinary and inconsequential. Yet, later when I think about them, one of them especially, I recall being caught napping in the weapons workshop loft. But then it's when I realize it has actually been a lucky break. It has saves getting me out from the drudgery of the dead-end cleaning weapons job, and forces me to start thinking about the need to improve my situation. At about this time, an opportunity comes along sooner than I might even expect.

At breakfast in early December, a buddy, equally unhappy with his Air Force service life, tells me he has some really great news.

Noting his cheerful attitude, I ask, "You getting married, or something?"

"Hell no," he retorts, "but, I've just learned we can transfer to the Army. They're looking for infantry platoon leaders, you know, second lieutenants," he says, ending with a big smile.

"I thought you had to be a college graduate even to qualify," I say.

"You were right and it has been true, but not anymore," he says, shaking his head. "Because of the war in Korea, the Army needs a lot more junior officers. Now, high school graduates, if they can pass certain tests, can enter their Officers Candidate School."

"Wow! That's really great news," I tell him. "Are you planning to try for it yourself?"

"Damn right! And you should consider it, too," he says, waving as he walks away.

I'm left really intrigued, but my self-confidence has long been damaged, especially for living in an orphanage and it's leaving me sensing as being second-class. I've been struggling against those feelings of myself for a long time. And now, since after assigned to the cleaning weapons workshop it also seems to reinforces those lower senses of myself.

I've never ever thought of the possibility of becoming an officer. Yet, if there's a chance I could make it through the six-month course, I'd be commissioned an infantry second lieutenant and, more importantly, I'd also have less time left to serve. I know there are drawbacks. Given their high casualty rates in Korea, infantry "2d Looies" aren't referred to as cannon fodder for no reason. On the other hand, even if I were to wash out, though I would remain an infantry enlisted man and still be cannon fodder, I'll only have little more than a year left on my enlistment. With my youth's sense of invulnerability, I then decide to go ahead and apply.

A week later in the sprawling, hot dusty City of Albuquerque, I check in with six other guys from Walker at the U.S. Army Recruiting Station. For most of a day, we take a number of tests and are told, if our scores are high enough, we'll be discharged from the Air Force and, then without delay, sworn into the Army. Though I have no way of knowing, I still feel like I've done well on all the tests. And a few days later, I'm thrilled to learn I've made the grade. I'm then ordered to report back to Albuquerque in a matter of days later.

On January ninth of 1952, a year and six days after joining the US Air Force, I go to sign out of the squadron headquarters. My commander, the captain, who had so briefly greeted us when we arrived, calls me in to meet him personally for the first time.

"Airman, you know the Air Force has also reduced its education requirement for a commission," he says. "Did you know?"

"No sir, I never heard anything about it," I reply, thinking at the same time he's made no effort to see we were informed of it.

"Well, maybe you can still apply for pilot training, if you're interested."

"Sir, if I'd known about it in time, I really would have considered doing so," I say, trying not to sound sarcastic. "But, now it's too late. I've been tested and have already qualified to try for a commission in the Army, and I'll soon be on my way to Fort Benning, Georgia."

He stares at me for a moment or two before returning my salute. "Well, I wish you luck," he says, his head slightly shaking from side to side, probably thinking about the fighting in Korea into which I'll soon be thrown.

In Albuquerque later with my luggage in hand, an Army Major, during a brief ceremony, swears in the eleven us as Privates in the U.S. Army. Ignoring my Air Force equivalent rank of Corporal, the Army requires I start over again at nearly the bottom. But even despite the demotion, crossing this first hurdle successfully makes me feel I'm changing my self-image. And especially learning I've tested with a high IQ gives a real boost to my self-confidence. The Major hands us orders to report to Fort Sill, Oklahoma, home of the Army's Artillery Training Center being the nearest center for processing. After we arrive there, fatigue uniforms and the Army's version of combat boots are to be issued to us. Meanwhile, we also receive partial pay for our travel expenses.

Sworn in with me is a stocky, gregarious guy named Sam Calder, who's from Little Rock, Arkansas. We'd seen each other around Walker, but had never spoken. I guessed he's also near my age in his early twenties. Recognizing me, he comes over and introduces himself.

"Hey, I'm Sam," he says. "How're you planning to get to Fort Sill?"

"I guess I'll take a bus," I tell him. "Isn't how you're going there, too?"

"Oh no, I'm looking for someone to share the drive getting there with me. It's a long way to drive alone. Would you be interested?"

"Sure," I say, "What kind of car are you driving?"

"A new Ford coupe," he says with a big grin. "I just got it as a going away present from my folks."

"Wow! That's some gift. They must have wanted you to go away in style. Do you have any idea what you'll charge?" I ask. "I can only afford the money I've just been given for bus fare and living expenses."

"Actually, I'm thinking more about sharing the driving, and maybe half the cost of the gas and a motel," he says. "Would that be fair?"

"Hell, yes, it is," I tell him, not caring for the prospect of a long lonely bus ride. Yet, I do wonder briefly why he hasn't asked any of the other guys. But with little effort I put the question out of my mind. Without further hesitation, instead I stick out my hand and we shake.

At a gas station a short while later, as he fills the Ford's tank, I buy a map and plot the 550-mile route to Fort Sill, Oklahoma, where we're due in four days. The route will take us east through the Texas Panhandle, to Oklahoma City, then north to Lawton, the town outside of Fort Sill, the Army's artillery center. Driving all day and well into each night will get us there, and give us time to get to know more about each other's backgrounds.

During having plenty of driving time we each begin to learn about who we are. Sam begins sounding proudly while I learn he's the only child of wealthy parents, who apparently have given him everything he's ever wanted. With such a history, I wonder why he isn't in college or at least already an officer. Without asking, he continues telling me he dropped out of school and joined the Air Force to avoid being drafted into the Army. I conclude he must not have been doing well in school, either, and, like me, had become eligible for the draft. When I tell him, I'd joined up for the same reason, he smiles and sticks out his hand to shake. Neither of us needs to discuss why changing to the more hazardous Army is a better idea.

Once on the road, as we exchange our personal histories, I find he's fun to be with and enjoy his company. We'd both played football and had some popularity among our respective high schools' girls. I couldn't match his "scoring" with them, since I'd only gotten past "first base" and then with only one. Listening to Sam's numerous escapades, it isn't long before I sense he tends to be a little wild, something I think he'll have to rein in to make it through OCS. As we put miles behind us, it also becomes obvious "having a good time" has been his main effort in life and eventually what has become his undoing in college.

In the early morning, we arrive at Fort Sill on Saturday the 12th. It leaves us at loose ends until the reception center opens at 0800 hours on Monday morning. Rather than in a motel, we're able to save a few dollars by bunking in the Fort's enlisted barracks and even get issued soap and towels. Oklahoma is a dry state, and we can't even find a place to have a beer in Lawton, the nearest town of any size. I think it's just as well, so we won't have a chance to get into trouble. Despite the war going on in Korea, there's an unwelcome atmosphere in Lawton, much like I experienced in Roswell. We find a place to eat, and take in a movie. Otherwise, there isn't much else to do there and we'll be happy to leave the place.

After a week of processing, accompanied by the constant distant booming of artillery--the source of which we never see--we receive orders sending us onward to The Infantry School at Fort Benning, Georgia. This time it's a journey of over 700 miles and within only a week to get there. I'm thinking, the most direct route we can take will put us through Little Rock, where Sam could visit his parents. But my suggestion to do so only stops him. He takes a long look at me before saying anything.

Then he tells me, "I really do like my parents, understand, but it hasn't been all that long since I've last seen them." Continuing, he says he'd rather not stop there, and tells me, "Anyway, I've got a better idea."

Chapter 7

GOING EASY IN THE CRESCENT CITY

———•◆•———

EVEN THOUGH IT WON'T BE A NEW EXPERIENCE FOR HIM, Sam still wants to stop in New Orleans on our way to Georgia, anyway. He's been there twice before with his parents, and I can tell by the look on his face he's really eager to go there again, but especially this time without them. Briefly, I silently have to wonder why?

"I can tell you really must have liked it," I say to him.

"Liked it? Are you kidding? I love it," he says, "and so will you. It'll be a chance for me to see it again, but this time without my parents hovering and watching my every move. I simply want to do the place without my chaperones."

It isn't hard to guess what he implies, but I put it aside for the moment and again take on the role of our navigator. According to the map, I estimate driving directly to New Orleans by following a coastal route to Georgia will add another 400 miles to the trip.

"Hey look," I say, and making no secret of my concern, "we'll have to drive at least ten or twelve hours each day to have any time left in the city, and still arrive on time at Fort Benning. Its only seven days from now, you understanding what I'm saying?"

Sam literally waves off my concern, arguing that we can make it to Fort Benning in plenty of time. I keep my doubts to myself, but we both know if we're late, we not only won't get into OCS, but even worse, we'll be AWOL. Faced with a risk, I have to decide whether to continue with him, or catch a bus and go on alone, though it's hardly a thrilling prospect. Still, I'm thinking so far, he's been a responsible driver, and each day we'd been making better time than we've expected. In the end, the chance to see a fabled place like the Crescent City wins out.

To get an early start on our seven-day push on to Fort Benning, as early as we can to get signed out and on the road, we leave Fort Sill. It's well before noon on a Friday, and for the next two days we take turns driving well into each night. This could put us in New Orleans with almost five days to spare. Figuring we could also drive all night to get to Columbus, Georgia, it will then leave us three days to spend for exploring the Crescent City's charms.

It's late Sunday night by the time we finally roll into New Orleans, and we're nearly exhausted. Sam tells me Mardi Gras is only two weeks away, and visitors will already be flooding into town for the celebration. The evidence is the famous Basin Street it's already alive with people pouring from the bars. The cacophony of happy voices and the blaring sounds of Dixieland jazz and Blues fill the air. Just hearing it, we're immediately revived from the strain of our three days of driving. We park the Ford and join the contagious excitement of revelers moving along sidewalks, vying for space with vehicles on the roadway. I have to admit Sam's right. New Orleans is impressive, exciting and, for the moment, I'm enchanted and happy to have decided to come along.

"Bob, what you're experiencing here is a Creole culture," Sam tells me, while watching me stare at all the Blacks and Whites roaming the street together. As he continues telling me about the city's relaxed way of life, I'm sure I can already feel it.

While stopping for gas and food in Texas and Oklahoma, I've been shocked by the "White Only" signs on bathrooms and drinking fountains. Though I knew they were directed at Negroes, they were for me still unnerving and making the stops feel hostile. Every place we've pulled in to eat each also announced the same exclusion. The segregation in Arkansas and Louisiana was even more blatant. There were signs read, "If you're White, you're alright. If you're Brown, hang around. But if you're Black, stand back." Here, at least, in New Orleans the races are mixing freely and clearly having a good time of it. I'm beginning to realize how the trip so far has really been such an educational experience and for me even more so about our country.

Though both of us are worn out, Sam still wants to bring in the new day by exploring the bars. We start with entering a couple of "drinking holes," as he calls them. The loud blaring music makes talk difficult, and exhaustion begins to sap my enthusiasm. I finally have to tell him he can do as he wishes, but not until after we find and check into a motel. I absolutely must have to sack out.

Late the next day we return to roam the French Quarter, the oldest and most popular part of New Orleans. Sam explains, in the past both the Spanish and French have ruled the place and left their mark on the architecture and its unique culture. He doesn't actually know much about New Orleans' history, but he can rave about its unique food, and does so. And while we're here, I'm eager to get a look at the rare city as much as we can see and do in our short time.

With his parents' past tutoring, Sam seems to know all about the restaurants.

"I have to tell you I'm short of cash," I tell him.

"Hey, that won't be a problem," he says, "I know of one or two places where we can get lots of authentic food without emptying our wallets. I know you like spicy Mexican food; Cajun cuisine here will suit you perfectly."

So far, after eating all the junk food we've been surviving on, I sure hope he knows what he's talking about.

Dinner later night proves Sam right. But as our meal progresses, I can see he's becoming impatient and even anxious.

"OK," he says, suddenly, "Are you about finished?"

"No," I say, "not yet," looking up. "And what's the rush? I didn't think we were in a hurry."

"Well, you're right, we aren't," he says, "but it's just, well, I'd like to get back to prowling the bars and taking in the music on along Bourbon Street."

"OK, OK. Relax, we'll do it," I say, nodding, "but we'll still have all night," I tell him. "So, take it easy." Sam is normally easygoing. But right now, his edginess is obvious, and I finally have to ask about it. "What're you so jumpy about? I can see something's really bothering you."

He glances quickly at the people at nearby tables and then leans in towards me. "You don't think I've come to New Orleans just for the food, the music and to see the sights, do you?" he says, in a low voice. Leaning closer still, he adds, "Man, I've come here to get laid!"

I've already guessed what he meant earlier by not having his parents' watching his every move. Getting laid is no doubt one of the things his parents had kept him from achieving, at least here. During the trip, he'd let me know he'd long since lost his virginity, thanks to a high school girl, or two. Now, he's decided the moment has arrived with fully grown women to add to his experience. And I can see he isn't going to put it off any longer, or let me stop him, either.

"So, what do you think about it?" He challenges, eyeing me eagerly.

"Well yeah, it's intriguing," I say, grinning to cover my anxiety, already feeling slightly breathless. With my answer he's assuming I have something similar in mind. Since such a "service" isn't advertised, I wonder how to find out where to go.

"Do you know someone to tell you where to find what you want?" I ask. "A cab driver, maybe?" He doesn't answer, except for his head shaking slightly. And his grin tells me it's no mystery for him.

A little later, on a bartender's recommendation, we drive to a quiet residential area searching for the address we've been given. Driving around slowly, we find it in an old neighborhood it was once an area of stately houses, now the semi-darkness hiding their deterioration. The building we're about to enter is an ancient two-story of tall windows in a dark quiet lane. The street lamps outside it glow eerily through trees swathed with hanging Spanish moss, just now slightly swaying in a gentle breeze.

Once inside the old house, the scene could be right out of a movie set for the brothel it really is. The high-ceilinged dimmed lights seem to pulse with a dangerous energy, speeding up my heartbeat, my breathing now more shallowly. The also candlelit roomful of beautiful young women in various states of undress, mostly white-skinned, but also of shades from lightly olive to black, lounge on overstuffed furniture arrayed around the front room, its pink walls draped in red velvet. In an alcove area of the room a couple of other men are talking softly to two of the women. Impressing me most is the interior's opulence suggesting prices well beyond the meager reach of my wallet. A sweeping glance around decides me I won't even ask. Sam, on the other hand, hesitates only long enough to scan the feminine offerings. After a quick appraisal, he chooses one of the young beauties and disappears with her up the stairway, leaving me to fend for myself.

As I watch them depart, I'm increasingly nervous. The remaining women are already shifting their focus on to me. With a pounding in my ears, I try to maintain a façade of worldly nonchalance. Even knowing I'm fooling no one, I force myself to give the "ladies" a casual once over, and then yet again. They, in turn, are evaluating me, some looking expectant, others curious, and a few, already having figured me out, have lost interest. With my heart racing, I'm thrilled, embarrassed, and scared all at the same time, anything but aroused. After a few more minutes, an older woman heavily made up and extravagantly dressed, whom I guess her to be the Madam, approaches me.

"Don't you see someone you'd like to be with?" she asks, in a husky voice.

This puts me in a quandary. To claim I don't find any of them desirable--each of them an obvious beauty--will make me look a fool. I consider asking about prices but, considering my near empty wallet, know I will only humiliate myself further. Almost out of breath, I can't even answer. The experience is simply too much: I mumble an unintelligible excuse and, trying to keep from running, I leave the house and return to sit waiting in the Ford outside.

Later, a shiny-eyed Sam rejoins me and learns I've ducked out. He has the decency not to mock, nor judge me. Instead, sounding the worldly *aficionado*, he's excited about how the beautiful girls here are clean, good and experienced. He says it's a chance I shouldn't miss, even though he knows I can't afford it. Nonetheless, the next night, our last, I decline his offer of a loan for an encore. The experience only leaves me feeling regretful, inadequate, and glad to leave New Orleans.

With our arrival on time at the Infantry School, we check in to our student troupe, and things start to happen fast. The 160-man company is divided into four platoons of candidates. Mine includes those with surnames beginning with the letter "R" through "Z". Included in the group puts me on the barrack's ground floor.

Two Second Lieutenants, known as "Tac Officers," control each platoon. Decked out daily in freshly starched khakis, the bottoms of their trouser legs are tucked and bloused into the tops of their combat boots. They're all spit and polish, an example we're expected to emulate.

How to accomplish it is detailed in a handbook spelling out requirements covering standards, our conduct and every aspect of life in and out of the company. Foremost is a strict regimen for keeping oneself, one's clothing and equipment clean, neat and in precise order. Daily inspections check the rolled and folded clothing in our open footlockers, and a bed's cover blanket tucked so tightly a dime bounces when dropped on its center. The area around and under each bed has to be clean, waxed, polished, free of lint and even clear of the tiniest grain of the sand found everywhere outside on the Post's grounds. The latrine, also our responsibility, has to be ready for daily inspection. A failure in any of these and other areas will accrue demerits, which added in sufficient quantity can mean extra drill time and confinement to the barracks area on weekends. Taken to the extreme, a sufficient number of bad marks can, *horror of horrors*, lead to an expulsion.

But I'm pleased to discover I'm well prepared for this environment, giving a boost to my self-confidence. I've had years of similar demands forced on me at the orphanage. Together with the pressure of military classes, little sleep, and the strenuous physical demands, many candidates, who've never made a bed, ever picked up after themselves, scrubbed and waxed a floor, or put a hand in a toilet to clean it, have a hard time keeping up. Almost from the start, men begin dropping from the ranks; as the regimen is exactly designed to weed out. The morning formation before marching off to class is the time for culling. If a candidate is called out and ordered to remain behind, the chances are very likely, upon our return to the barracks, his bedding will be gone, the mattress rolled up, his clothing absence and he never to be seen again. We're well aware it could happen without warning to any one of us.

At one such morning formation in our third week, a number of us who've transferred from the Air Force are ordered to stand fast. At rigid attention, heart sinking, I search my memory for any infraction might be the cause. But instead of reprimand or dismissal, we're being held back, because the Army has decided with only eight weeks of Air

Force basic training behind us it's unlikely we'll meet the demands of the OCS course requirements.

There is evident truth in it. I've already been experiencing some difficulties, like not knowing how to disassemble, clean, and re-assemble the M-1 rifle, an infantryman's basic weapon. And there are other problems, in which find most of us lagging.

As each of us is called out of ranks, we're handed orders reassigning us to Fort Jackson, South Carolina. There, we're to complete sixteen more weeks of Army basic training and four weeks of leadership school. Afterward, assuming graduation from the latter, we'll return to The Infantry Center and Officer's Candidate School. We're all disappointed, but determined to meet the new requirements.

On the road once again, Sam and I drive the 300 miles south directly to Columbia, South Carolina. This time, he doesn't propose anything other than each of us taking turns at the wheel and driving straight to Fort Jackson. There will be no deviation enroute for some good times. We're facing two more hurdles, and either one could be our undoing.

Chapter 8

SOUTHERN INHOSPITALITY

———•◆•———

BEING REASSIGNED TO FORT JACKSON FOR A BASIC TRAIN-
ing re-run is a real setback. This place, of course, has also been stirred
up to meet the military demands of the Korean War, and there's the
same high level of activity here I'd found both at Lackland and Fort
Benning. Like a number of others, this Fort is named for another Civil
War general, this time it's for Andrew Jackson, a native son and the
seventh President of the United States. Located a few miles outside of
Columbia, the state capital, the Fort was established there at the start
of the First World War. Then, patriotic citizens gladly donated the land
on Fort Jackson now occupies.

When I arrive, its present home for the 8th Infantry Division, devoted
since 1939, to training young men in basic infantry for combat. We're
assigned to wooden, two-storied barracks, which were hurriedly built
supposed to temporarily house soldiers training for the First World
War, and it really looks like it. Continuous use since then has taken its
toll, evident in flaking paint, worn floorboards, misfunctioning coal-
fired furnaces and reeking latrines. There's nothing inspiring about the

barracks, even less welcoming than those have been at Lackland Air Force Base and Fort Benning.

Apart from housing, two other differences are immediately obvious and somewhat shocking: In July 1951, following President Truman's order, the Army has begun to integrate White and Colored troops. Now here, without actually counting, I guess about one quarter of the recruits in our company are Negroes. While their presence is unusual, I'm surprised their number doesn't raise overt hostility among the White soldiers, especially those from the southern states. My guess, in this military environment they're afraid to express the hostility they may be really feeling.

The other major difference in our ranks is the presence of draftees. The airmen at Lackland and the candidates at The Infantry School are all volunteers and have at least graduated from high school. But here, the education gamut ranges from the nearly illiterate to college graduates, many of the latter making no secret of their bitterness at being drafted. The mix of backgrounds and attitudes makes for low morale and sluggish performance. There's also an obvious shortage of NCOs.

On our arrival, in charge of our 38-man platoon is a corporal. But within days, having been ordered to Korea, now he's gone. The next ranking man, a Negro Private First Class, named Jimmy, is drawn from the ranks, made the platoon leader and placed in charge. From the start, it's clear he has trouble controlling the platoon. Rather than race his being the problem it's simply his ignorance. He obviously hasn't an inkling of how to get the platoon from one place to another, much less how to keep order in the barracks. There's also a sense of latent resentment among the White draftees. And even though Jimmy is an American, his southern-accented English for me, and probably for others, is nearly incomprehensible.

After suffering two weeks of his stressed bumbling, I decide, with Sam's encouragement, I should give Jimmy a hand by taking over the platoon myself. Though he usually hangs out with the other Negro soldiers, I have to call him aside one evening.

"Look here Jimmy, you're having a lot of trouble trying to manage the platoon, isn't that right?" At first, he just stares at me and then slowly nods.

"OK, so listen, I want you to know I've already had a year of Air Force service and I'm actually a corporal. How about if I take over the platoon while you learn to handle it? In the meantime, you could be the leader of the third squad?" Again, he says nothing but finally nods. Though I expect some resistance or confrontation from him, instead he seems relieved and makes no effort to resist the change. Without any announcement to the men, I simply position myself in front of the next platoon formation and assume command. At first, there's little reaction among the men. But as days go by and I continue as platoon leader, some of them seem accepting, while others appear disgruntled. Some have accepted my leadership, since I seem to know what I'm doing, but a couple of older men challenge my assuming power. And though it carries no actual authority, I pull my Air Force rank of corporal and make it known I'm also one of those headed to Officers Candidate School. With Sam and a few others backing me up, this seems to settle the question. I ask Sam to take over the first squad and two other OCS-bound privates the other two remaining. Meanwhile, Private First-Class Jimmy seems happy enough to be appointed leader of an all-Negro squad, where he feels better understood.

With someone in charge who seems to know what he's doing; the company First Sergeant tacitly agrees to leave me in control. The company commander, nominally a first lieutenant, is never seen, if in fact he exists. To my satisfaction, it isn't long before the grumbling stops in the ranks. And, as the days go by, the platoon actually begins to show a bit of *esprit d' corps*. With the help of the new squad leaders, I also set about to get the barracks, especially the latrines, in shape, carrying out inspections and meting out punishments to those who won't do their share or won't seem to shape up. After the day's requirements, I impose physical penalties, like pushups and runs of a mile or more carried out at night. Because I perform the penalties along with the delinquents, not only assures they're carried out, it also makes me and the punishments seem fair. Soon, even the most flagrant "fuckups" knuckle down and show some pride in the platoon. As time goes along, I discover, like children, they crave order and welcome discipline.

Whether I like it or not, being in charge often requires my involvement in personal problems. One day, when a squad leader tells me one of his men, a big, good-natured draftee from Tennessee, is giving away his issued underwear. Baffled, I call the man over to hear his explanation. He assures me one pair of underwear is really all he ever needs at home. To be friendly, he is giving away what he considers his unneeded "extras." His explanation can only mean one thing: The recruit simply isn't bathing. His odor should have been enough to confirm what I already suspect. I ask him to bend over so I can get a closer look at his scalp. Sure enough, the skin on the top of his head is gray with dirt. The stench of it forcing me to take a step back. I tell the squad leader to have some of his guys take the bewildered man to the showers, strip him and scrub him down from head to toe. And afterwards, make sure he showers daily and he regularly changes his underwear.

As the days go by and temperatures rise, Fort Jackson lives up to its reputation for hot muggy summers full of bugs. Unlike my Air force experience, I learn infantry basic emphasizes physical training and endurance. Road marches of increasing distances eventually weighed down with combat loads are regular events, which nobody likes. As the late spring weather warms toward the humid heat of summer, the training day starts earlier as a precaution against to heat exhaustion. In the sparse shaded area, there are two or more large Lister bags of iced, watered and salted grapefruit juice. Frequent drink breaks are scheduled to keep us sufficiently hydrated as the heat rises. Still, some men find the concoction is too distasteful. It's not surprising how frequently men are prostrated by the higher temperatures and carried off to the aid station, even sometimes to the hospital.

Worse than the South Carolina heat are Chiggers. Since they're most active in afternoons, we're told, is another reason our field training exercises are held in the earlier, cooler morning hours. Even so, there is no guarantee we won't be bitten anyway. The "Good Ole Boys" in our ranks claim to have remedies for these bugs, which they say burrow under the skin, drink blood and die. The southerners among us here tell us applying lighter fluid, bleach, alcohol, turpentine or salty water can kill them. If any of this is true, once bitten, none of it helps at all.

When irritating red bumps show up on my ankles, I know Chiggers have burrowed in. Within hours, the itching is so badly I can't help resisting savagely scratching the swelling welts. This produces sores only making the condition worse. The sores can quickly become infected, and last for days. My infestation is mainly on my ankles, where the itching is maddening and my scratching is so extreme, I have to be restricted to the barracks for a time, my ankles wrapped in bandages and dosed with medicated salves. The sores finally begin to heal, but for some of us the infection lasts for weeks. If I miss more than two weeks of the training, I could be set back to the next basic training cycle. And should it happen, I'd miss the start of the next OCS class I'm scheduled to attend. So, I decide to force myself returning to training despite the condition of my ankles, and suffer it silently. Luckily, the sores are finally healing.

Along with fitness, Army training here emphasizes weapons, small unit tactics and learning to work together as small teams. We spend hours on the rifle range with our M-1 Rifles, firing in prone, sitting and standing positions. The goal is to become Expert, or at least to become a Marksman, the lowest level of qualification. My accuracy at the greater distances leads to talk about my later training as a sniper. In the following weeks, we graduate to firing weapons requiring teams of two to four men. Learning their use makes me feel more like a soldier. I prove adept with the .30 caliber machinegun, though I hate to be the team member who has to carry it. I find the mortars and their parts intriguing but also are even heavier to carrying them around. I also fear I may be losing my hearing from the roar along with the back-blasts of rocket launchers and recoilless rifles.

As a boy, the most thrilling military activity I'd seen were soldiers parading in formation, unit flags flapping in the breeze to the sound and cadence of a rousing military band. A boy's dream I've never forgotten was marching proudly as a soldier in a parade before cheering crowds of civilians. Now, as the Fourth of July approaches, a youthful dream of mine is on the verge of being realized. We're told a number of companies from our division are to parade through downtown Columbia as part of the Independence Day celebration. Even the thought of participating in such a parade and being cheered by its residents from the sidewalks is bound to be exhilarating.

Near the end of June, drilling in platoon formation begins in earnest at the close of the training day. I grow hoarse counting cadence, trying to get and keep every man in the platoon in step. After a few days of this, we're trucked to the division's parade field. There, a lieutenant takes over to practice marching us in a company formation and then, joining with other companies, as a battalion led by a captain. This is hot, sweaty tiring work. The reward for me will be to march in a battalion with its companies' guidon flags flapping in the breeze on parade in Columbia's downtown streets. It's just this thought keeping up my spirits, while drenched in sweat and despite my aching feet.

We spend the night of July third telling each other stories of the picnicking and fireworks of past Independence Days at home. All the while we're cleaning our rifles, polishing boots and brass to get ready for the big day on the morrow.

Predictably, the morning of the Fourth dawns hot and muggy. Clean and dressed in freshly starched khakis and carrying our M-1 rifles, promptly at 0900 we load onto trucks and are carried to a high school football field. It's then I discover to my disappointment we're to march through Beaufort, a small town near Columbia, rather than through the capital city itself. But still, a parade is a parade, no matter where it takes place. And at least, we'll be marching to a live military band, and imagined being cheered on by enthusiastic patriotic crowds.

Arriving at the school turns out to be a classic example of the disheartening military exercise of "hurry up and wait." In the rising heat and with no shade in sight, we begin to wilt. Finally, just before noon, the band arrives; we're ordered into marching formation and then to shoulder our rifles. By the drums' cadence, we start out marching from the school's football field to the city's main street. Then, with the entire band playing at full volume, we step off, our backs straightened and heads lifted. The sound magically aligns our ranks. Ours is no victory parade, but with the war going on in Korea, patriotic citizens have turned out en masse and crowd the sidewalks along the route. As we march by, their cheering so enthusiastically, their miniature American flags waving so passionately, the experience could be no less thrilling than if we were marching through the center of Columbia. Marching at the head of our platoon, a small part of the massed troops, I still feel a sense of patriotism and the admiration of the actual cheering crowds. And during the process, whatever its significance, one long-held of my boyhood dreams has finally come true.

In mid-July, the sixteen weeks of hard days and short nights of infantry basic training finally have come to an end. In retrospect I wonder most at my audacity in elbowing Jimmy aside and taking over the platoon. Surprisingly it has worked out as well as it has, and eventually men have responded to my command and control. On the last night, a group of us sit around drinking the beer Sam has smuggled into the Fort in his Ford. Amidst the joking and telling tales on each other, there's a good feeling we've all made it through in fine shape.

Later, with my duffle bag in hand, just before leaving the barracks to check in at my new housing at the leadership school, one of the college guys calls me aside.

"Who will take care of us when you're gone?" he asks, seems nearly in tears. For a moment, I think he's putting me on, but I realize he's deadly serious. With my hand on his shoulder and looking him in the eye, I tell him, "Don't worry, in the Army there'll always be someone to tell you what to do, whether you like it or not. Just do your best and I know you'll be fine."

Chapter 9

PITFALLS

———•◆•———

LEADERSHIP SCHOOL MEANS CHANGES AND MOSTLY FOR the better. It also includes a promotion, but only once again to the grade of Private First Class. The barely higher rank at least comes with a little more pay, though still short of a hundred "Greenbacks" a month. Now, there's more classroom instruction focused on training leaders and turning civilians into soldiers. Here I'm being taught the same tactics and techniques used on us in the previous sixteen weeks of our basic training, but this time with more insight.

A less intensive schedule leaves our evenings free, and the freedom on weekends to explore Columbia. The eased pressure and our newfound liberty come with a warning: *a sense of independence can be deceiving.* Leadership asks us for higher personal standards with the trust we act responsibly, especially during our off liberty hours. Indeed, the increased free time is euphoric, but fraught with giving in to temptations could spoil chances for returning to Officers Candidate School in a month.

Besides Sam and me, three other guys in the class are prospective officer candidates: Rick Mender, a Californian, Bobby Melton a Texan and Jack Cault from Kentucky. Despite our diverse backgrounds our shared future as officer candidates, we have in common a new, higher degree of self-regard.

On the first Saturday, with excitement mounting, Sam drives our group into Columbia. It's the first city in America founded the year 1786, and as the first capital named for Christopher Columbus. And it sure does look like an old city with a long history; one of mostly one-story buildings in the tree shaded downtown business area. At first glance, with its population of barely more than 100,000, it doesn't appear to offer much to intrigue a bunch of lonely GIs with time on their hands. A walking tour of downtown and a late lunch are pleasant enough, but the best parts are the welcome change of scenery, and simply being free until the time to return to the Fort.

On the way back to the barracks in the late afternoon, Rick proposes renting a hotel room for the next weekend to take better advantage of our free time. It's a way, if we want to stay out later, we'll have a place to hole up in and stay off the city streets, and importantly avoid the risk of violating the Fort's 2300 hours curfew.

There's a unanimous enthusiastic agreement with Rick's suggestion. The next weekend we try out the rented-room idea, everybody kicking in his share of the expense. Its only drawback is two pairs of us will have to share the double beds and the guy who draws the shortest straw will have to sleep sitting up in the room's only armchair. The idea of asking the management for another bed or a cot gets voted down, since we're only paying for two people, and we know the price would certainly go up.

Except for so-called private clubs, the city pretends it's dry, but really one can buy any kind of booze at a state-run liquor store. Except for our tee-totaling Baptist Bobby, we agree on vodka, which we'll mix with grape juice, to make up a "Purple Passion," the palatable but infamous high school favorite.

The next weekend, we spend Saturday morning together exploring more of the downtown area, later splitting up. Jack and Bobby go off, one to get the vodka, the other the grape juice. Rick, Sam, and I leave to rent the room and find our own entertainment. We end up in a small café specializing in southern traditional deep-fried catfish, served with pickles and hush puppies, a delicious and filling combination.

While talking about our backgrounds over lunch, Rick produces a business card naming him as, T.J. Quent, a principal in a Los Angeles business of he's been part in civilian life. Like the rest of us, he had to decide whether to enlist or be drafted. But in his case, he agreed only to enlist specifically for Officers Candidate School. Brushing off the questions his card raises, he declines to tell why he uses an alias. I think he may just want to make himself appear mysterious and more interesting. But choosing an assumed name still suggests a shady background, and maybe it's what he has in mind. Yet it leaves me wondering if the Army Investigation Agency will uncover this in the routine background checks before we can be commissioned.

In the afternoon, before going out for the evening, we regroup at the hotel, not only to find out who'll have the sleeping pleasure of sitting up, but also to decide how to spend our first night out. Never at a loss for how to have a good time, Sam surprises us with the phone number of a girl he dated in his brief days in college. She now lives in a suburb well outside of Columbia. With our encouragement he phones her. And true to the tradition of Southern Hospitality, Constance not only remembers him, but also invites all of us to an evening party. She says it is starting later in afternoon at a house she shares with two other women, and gives directions to it. Bobby declines the invitation in favor of a movie, and Jack, somewhat shy, decides to go with him.

A short time later, Sam, Rick and I take off for the party. Constance's directions take us to a wealthy residential neighborhood somewhat about an hour and a half drive away. The party features a barbeque being held in the lantern-lit patio of a beautiful spacious Colonial-style home. Activities there are already well underway when we arrive. There's a group of about 20 people present enjoying food served up by a Negro chef. The couples are eating and drinking, talking and a few of them dancing to recorded music. There's also an ample supply of liquor at a self-service bar.

Constance greets Sam warmly and perfunctorily introduces to the group the three of us as soldiers. It isn't long before she and Sam, acting like they can't wait to take up where they left off, disappear into the house. Looking around, I see Rick, with a drink in hand, chatting with one of the couples. I feel a little out of place; most of the gathering appears older than college age. As I start for the food table, a tall attractive buxom woman, whom I guess to be in her late 20s, intercepts me. She puts an arm through one of mine, and says she's claiming me for herself.

"Hi, soldier," she says, smiling, "I'm Bertie, one of the housemates. You probably want a drink, right?" As she leads me to the bar, Rick giving me a knowing wink as we pass by. I'm flattered to have someone so glamorous be interested in me. But my usual reaction to being approached by a woman at first is wariness, rather than being receptive. While I'm assuming, she's just being hospitable, it soon becomes clear Bertie wants attention. She's already pretty high and a little unsteady.

"Come dance with me, soldier," she says, rather than using my surname, since having been unsuccessful trying pronouncing it the first time.

"Oh sure, I'd love to," I answer, feeling like I can't refuse, and lead her to the section of the patio serving as the dance floor. We move well enough together to the music, though she seems mostly interested in being held and pressing her ample body into me, which I don't mind at all.

"Bertie, let's sit the next one out, while I get something to eat," I suggest.

"Oh, I'll bet you are hungry," she says, leading me to the buffet.

"Would you like me to get you something, too?" I ask.

"Nah, you go ahead. I'll refresh my drink and join you right over there," she says, pointing to a cushioned ornate iron bench. In a few minutes she's sitting with me while I eat. Seemingly curious, she asks questions about being a soldier and continues sipping her drink. A short while later after finished eating, we return to the dance floor, a slow number playing. As the piece ends, we remain holding pressed together for a few more moments.

"Honey, let's go for a ride," she says, "I need to clear my head," she adds. "My car's just over there," she points.

"That sounds like a good idea, Bertie, but only if I do the driving," I hasten to add. "Is it OK with you?"

A clear, warm beautiful night, a drive in her new Buick convertible with the top down seems ideal. Following her directions, I drive slowly around for a while, which take us into another residential neighborhood.

"Honey," she says, "See the streetlamp over there? Pull over and park under it, so, I can see you while we talk." No sooner I've parked and turned off the engine, she's suddenly all over me: Kissing, pawing, fingers brushing through my crew cut hair, even feeling my crotch. Wow! Is this the real famed Southern Hospitality I've been hearing about? It's more than surprising, though not at all unpleasant. But if she's thinking we'll end up making love here she's mistaken. It's not going to happen, at least not in her condition, nor especially in this location.

"Come on, handsome, I really want you. Let's fuck, honey," she says, her speech slightly slurred. Her surprising request leaves no question what she wants. One I've never been asked for by a woman before, it startles me, and I'm momentarily speechless. While it's exciting, but even more it's alarming as I look up at the houses surrounding us and we're under the streetlamp.

More frightened than aroused, I tell her, "Bertie, listen to me, we can't do it here. Let's put up the top and drive to somewhere else where it's dark."

"Oh, come on, now, honey," she insists.

"Bertie," I repeat, "we just can't do it here," I say, more forcefully.

"Sure, we can, honey," she mumbles, "everybody's asleep," lazily waving an arm toward the houses. She pauses, seems to focus on me, and then abruptly blurts, "Now, just get out of the car!"

Immediately, I'm more surprised than understanding, wondering what's going to happen next. Thinking she's angry, I get out as she demands. But once I'm on the street, she quickly pushes the front seat back. She lies down and pulls up the skirt of her dress and starts to struggle out of her panties. I realize I have to stop her.

"Bertie, don't do that here," I say. "Please sit up. We're under a streetlamp with the top down. Anyone looking out of an upstairs window can see us. Come on, please cover yourself and sit up."

Her eyes half closed, she insists, "Aw, come on, honey," she murmurs. "Don't worry, they're all asleep," she repeats. Her thighs now splayed, arms reaching for me, her voice rising, she demands, "Come on, I want it, now!"

From out of nowhere, the line from a book pops into my head: *When a woman calls a man to her bed and he refuses, God is angry.* Well, I decide, whatever, or whoever it is, it'll have to live with its anger on this night, because it's not going happen here or now!

The exposed sight of her is anything but arousing; my fear instead is rising to near panic. Though it's well after 10 o'clock, I take a quick look around for lights could might be turned on in the nearby houses. If anyone sees us, they won't hesitate to call the police. And I have no doubt I'll be arrested--not only for indecent exposure, but also for taking advantage of an inebriated woman. When I look back at her, to my great relief, I see she has either passed out, or has fallen asleep.

Quickly, I move into action. Covering her, I struggle to raise her to a sitting position in the passenger side, hold her in place while I close and lock the door, leaning her against it. I get back into the driver's seat, move it forward and start the engine. I have no idea where we are, much less how to get her back home. I don't even try to raise the convertible's top, since I don't know how, and just start driving. All I want is to get us away from under the damning streetlamps, and hoping I can find our way back to the party.

It's a surprise and a great relief at how easily I do find the way back to her house. Once again at the party, I get one of her housemates and Sam to help me get Bertie up to her room. Once she's there and we're back on the patio, I confide to Sam, "Man, I'm thinking this night is over."

Chapter 10

HITTING BOTTOM

WITH RICK ASLEEP IN THE BACK SEAT, IT'S EARLY MORNING by the time we get back to our hotel in Columbia. On the way back, Sam tells me how the reunion with his former girlfriend nearly ended in disaster. She fails to mention she's engaged, and her fiancé shows up unexpectedly. When he does arrive, thanks for being in a hurry, Sam and Constance have already consummated their get-together and are innocently once again in the patio among the group.

"Constance must have wanted one last fling before getting married," Sam says, "and I was happy to provide it," he continues. "Anyway, the experience has been wonderful," he adds, "but a repeat performance is now out of the question."

When I tell him, what happened to me with Bertie, he has a good laugh. He agrees I'd have had a real problem trying to explain the scene, not only to the police, but also especially to the MPs and the Commandant of the Leadership School.

After dropping Rick off back at the hotel, Sam and I go in search of breakfast and then return to the room to sack out 'till the early afternoon. By the time we're up, Rick has joined Jack and Bobby for a walk tour in the city. During the Sunday afternoon, while driving around the town, Sam and I discover a private girls' high school on the north side of town. The campus isn't gated, but it does have an unmanned guard shack at the entrance to its grounds. The shack, though even empty, should be a warning enough for anyone. But Sam, his libido apparently not-yet-satiated, won't be put off. He insists at least on driving through. When sighting a few of the girls, he's like a hound on scent, eager to stop and talk to them, even when I remind him, they're underage and we're trespassing. It's all I can do to tell him to get us off of the school's grounds.

After picking up the other guys at the hotel, we return to the Fort in time for evening chow. On the way back, we recount our respective adventures. Sam tells about the party, but omits his conquest. I tell about meeting Bertie, dancing and our short drive, but leaving out parking and the actions have followed. Neither of us mentions the girls' school, but I'm wrong to think Sam has forgotten it.

Failing to show up for Monday's morning breakfast, Sam is still later absent from the class, and a rumor is going around the Columbia police have picked him up during the night. Unfortunately, the story is true. Last evening, after driving us back to Fort Jackson, Sam returns to the girls' school and fails to leave immediately when a guard orders him off the campus grounds. The Columbia police are called; they arrest and keep Sam in jail overnight, and tow his car to a city impound yard. Then early the next day, they return him to the Post's military police. His status is now in jeopardy for being in police custody and also being out after curfew. Then, having missed the morning classes also makes him AWOL.

During the day, I'm having trouble concentrating on the instruction. After the day's classes, I visit him in a cell in the Post incarceration center. He brightens when he sees me. It's good for me to see him, too, but I'm exasperated with him.

"Man, I can't believe you returned to the girls' school," I tell him.

"Well, I just thought it would be fun if we arranged dates for the next weekend," he says. "I wasn't trying to pick up one of the girls just then. It's all I had in mind." His head bowed, staring at his hands, while talking.

"But, Sam," I say, "you knew they were high school girls, all of them underage. The guard shack was there to keep out people like us," I say, annoyed at his foolishness.

"Like I told you," he says, "I only stopped to see if I could talk them into a date for next weekend."

"I know, I heard you," I say, knowing his missing my point.

"The ones I called to really looked interested," he says. He's still trying to justify himself, and I'm not amused as I stare at him, shaking my head.

"That's all you did? Only talked to them?" I ask, doubtfully.

"Yeah, that's it," he says, "Really, nothing else."

Unfortunately as it turns out, the only date he gets is the one set for his courts martial.

The military police notify Sam's parents, who arrive in Columbia a few days in advance of Sam's hearing. Released into their custody on the eve of his court appearance, Sam is allowed to go out to dinner with them. When he tells them I'm his best friend, they invite me to go along, too. His mother in particular tells me how much they appreciate my befriending their son. But as our first meeting continues, I can tell his father is more than a little curious about me, his sidelong glances making me nervous. After dinner, as we walk together to his car, he asks, "Where are you from, Bob?"

"I grew up in the Los Angeles area, Sir," I say.

"So, what are you?"

I know exactly what he's getting at, but instead I answer, "Like Sam, I'm a Private First Class, Sir."

In a low voice, he says, "That's not what I mean. What kind of name is Sanabria?"

"It's a Spanish name, Sir," I say.

"Oh, so you're Spanish?" he says, sounding relieved.

"No Sir, I'm an American of Mexican descent, born in El Paso, Texas."

He is silent for a few moments, and then he surprises me asking, "But couldn't you say you're Spanish? It's what you look like, anyway. Wouldn't it be better for you to say you're Spanish?" Apparently, he can't bear the thought of his son being soiled by having befriended someone like me. I flush from the affront.

"No, Sir," I reply, firmly. "It would not be better to claim to be something I'm not. I am Mexican American."

There it is again. When I left California, I thought I'd left the kind of prejudice behind. But I can see it's here, too, and maybe something I'll encounter and have to endure no matter where I go in our country. Starting in high school, being light complexioned, I did try to hide who and what I was by claiming to be Italian, Portuguese, or Spanish. But it made me ashamed of myself. My family owns and operates a Mexican restaurant, and the only person I'm deceiving is myself. Later in high school I come clean and resolve never again to deny my heritage. Now standing up for myself with Sam's father is a small victory. And it really feels good.

Mr. Calder hires a civilian lawyer, who gets Sam's punishment limited to a demotion and disqualified from going on to Officer's Candidate School. He's back in the replacement pool for reassignment to an infantry unit. Gone in a flash, I never see or hear from him again. I send a letter to him at his Little Rock home address, but it goes unanswered. For all I know he's been shipped off to Korea. In spite of his behavior, his departure is a real loss to me. Among hundreds of men I've met in little more than a year, he's one of the few seemingly real friends I enjoyed I've managed to meet.

Sam is only the first of our quintet to be dropped from OCS. Rick is next. His FBI background check has uncovered his T.J. Quent alias, and his past role in the business. Whatever it was, it disqualifies him. I never learn if he's actually a criminal, or what's the cause, but for whatever reason, he's gone. Then there's Jack. Repeatedly showing up late for class and scoring low on a few of the tests, he, too, fails to return. It leaves only Bobby, the reserved one, and me going on to the Infantry School.

The goal of our little group returning to OCS made us feel cohesive. It's one of the few times I've felt the camaraderie I've so often heard exists among soldiers. But it's short-lived and, when it ends as it does, I feel a sense of loss and the weight of solitude settling on me again. It brings back the realization I really am alone and maybe always will be.

In mid-August, I'm granted 15 days of leave before reporting back to the Infantry School in September. But California is a long way off and, with only two weeks to get home and return, flying seems the only sensible way to travel. I phone my parents to explain this, and after promising I'll repay, they wire me money for the airfare. For the moment, I'm more excited about flying for the first time, than about making it through Leadership School and celebrating my 21st birthday at home.

Chapter II

IN THE PRESSURE COOKER

———•◆•———

BEING BACK AT THE INFANTRY SCHOOL MAY BE DÉJÀ VU. But my anxiety is every bit as high among this new batch of candidates as it was in my aborted first attempt. Having been through a few weeks of it before, I know what a lot to expect and have the confidence of experience. Though Bobby Melton and I are both in the same 160-man class, the alphabetical order of the platoons puts us well apart, he's in the third and I'm in the fourth. After greeting each other on the first day, later we only speak to each other occasionally. We'd been fairly close at Ft. Jackson's Leadership School, and now being among a crowd of strangers again I miss his friendship. In this high-pressure organization it's clear we're all in our own boats, each man pulling his own oars with the best effort doing for himself.

TAC officers controlling the platoons demand more of us than we can accomplish in the allotted time, which I suspect it's by design. Unlike my classmates, who're most scrambling to keep up, I move ahead more calmly anticipating what needs to be done and what comes next. I have to confess to a little smugness watching other candidates rushing around in near panic, some swearing, others threatening to leave and a few actually doing so. The requirements for organizing and maintaining our clothing and equipment are many and maddeningly specific. So are the rules for keeping our low-walled cubicle space spotless, shining and neat. None of it is a problem for me. On the contrary, I relish the order and the efficiency with which I meet the requirements. In daily inspections I rarely get demerits. The walls separating each space give a semblance of privacy, but not enough to hide the late-night sounds some of us seeking needed release.

Physical training seems non-stop, and I manage it. The formal physical training periods are not only designed to test our endurance, but also to understand how to lead the exercises ourselves, when we'll be leading troops. Soon, we're called out to demonstrate and conduct the day's drills. Even when passing through stations set up along the mess hall line, at least two pull-ups are also required. Ten pushups are demanded on the spot as penalties for minor infractions. We're marched in double time, another name for short-stride running, whenever possible and for increasingly longer distances. Improving in all forms of exercises is mandatory; failing to pass periodic physical training tests can be grounds for dismissal.

Intermixed with these activities are classes in military subjects, all bound in the training manuals issued to each candidate. Our studying must be done amidst all the other requirements. The most anxiety provoking tasks are taking our turns before the group acting as an instructor. While few if any of us have public speaking experience, much less leading a class with demonstrators, now we all face this fearsome prospect. Even though I've led a platoon in Fort Jackson basic training, this is different, with all eyes on me making the experience more daunting.

After evening chow, each man rehearses leading an instruction drill against the chance of being called to lead one the next day. He'll have to explain and demonstrate before two or more platoons arranged in a large circle. The experience can be frightening, in varying degrees the effects showing up in faces. The most extreme example is a candidate from New York. When called, he strides bravely to the center of the circle. But once there, he begins to fall apart. First, forgetting to call for his demonstrators, and then forgetting the sequence of moves he means to explain. Completely flustered, he stammers, and his body starts to shake. The longer he stands there, the worse his fright becomes feeding on itself, as does his shaking. Finally, he is left speechless and reduced to sobbing. The rest of us stand staring in silence, while he's being led away by a TAC Officer and never to be seen among us again. Watching this unlucky man breaking down has an unnerving effect on the rest of us in the platoons, as imagining ourselves in the same predicament.

The spectacle recalls awful school memories of my stammering when in the ninth grade. Interrogatory sentences began with who, what, when, where, why and how, could set me off. Sometimes, even the word, "is," could start it. For a while, whenever I needed to ask a question, the use of one of these words could leave me tortured and nearly speechless. Now, faced with performing before my fellow candidates, I fear a relapse. But working hard committing the assignment to memory seems enough to avoid it.

The assignment of leading the platoon and later commanding the entire the 160-man company rotates among us every few days. Learning to move a body of men of this size efficiently from one place to another, on time, even in traffic, is imperative. Moving a 40-man platoon is difficult enough, particularly with a TAC Officer carping at your heels. But the real trial is taking the turn as student company commander. We often march on the roadways going to, from, and between classes, the student company commander usually positioned at the midpoint of the body of troops. Four platoons take up a lot of road space, about half the length of a football field, which means the commander must know just when to call a turn. If it's too soon, he could march the company into the side of a building, or, if too late, into a roadside gully, usually deep. In advance of the company's arrival, failing to order road guards out to stop vehicle traffic at intersections can be dangerous. Forgetting to call them back once the company has passed brings demerits and major embarrassment. To ensure that all of the platoons can hear and understand his commands means learning to use the so-called "command voice," which essentially is shouting.

A joke going around has it the most dangerous weapon in the Army is a 2d Lieutenant with a map. Issued a compass and told to navigate on unknown terrain, we soon discover it isn't funny. Open country navigation isn't too difficult. Once you've located your position in relation to a physical terrain feature, such as a hill or a cross roads, you find it on your map. It's then possible to move from one feature to the next, if visible, or if aided by compass to get to your destination. One can also learn to move from one place to another solely with the compass. But navigating at night, or in woods, I find especially frustrating, if not next too impossible. It's bad enough losing your way, but there's nothing funny about getting your platoon or company lost, which could be dangerous. I'm hoping it'll never happen to me.

The Author is on the right, at the Officer's Candidate School, with Candidate Bob West, at Fort Benning, Georgia in 1953.

Instruction covers a variety of lethal hardware. Though we'll be firing most of the weapons ourselves, we'll also have to know how to use and deploy all the armaments available to an infantry company-size unit. Qualifying with the pistol and the M1 Rifle come first. Crew-served weapons, like the .30 and .50 caliber machine guns, follow, then on to firing the 62mm, 81mm and 4.2-inch mortars. Somehow, my hearing survives the blasts of the 3.5-inch rocket launcher and the earsplitting explosions of the 72mm and 105mm recoilless rifles. Familiarity with the weapons is fundamental, but is ineffective without knowing when and how to deploy them. Integrated in our training are platoon tactics, wire and radio communications, the use of artillery, and how to call in close air support.

Testing in all of these and other subjects occur weekly, another major source of pressure. The margin for error is narrow and class standings are posted regularly. Finding time to study is a problem. The hours between evening chow and 'lights out' at 2200 hours are often filled with demerit-earned extra drills, caring for one's clothing and equipment and preparing for the next day's classes. At 'lights out' on most nights, candidates rush to claim lighted space in the latrines and shower rooms to study, shine brass, or spit-shine boots until chased out by those of us assigned to clean them. These sessions often last well into the early morning hours. The nearby laundry keeps us in clean, starched and pressed fatigues and khakis. It also guarantees I'll nearly always be broke.

Near the end of the year, halfway through the course, I'm confident I'll be among those to get the coveted gold bar in March. Up to then, I've managed to max nearly every test, until early December, when to my chagrin, I'm called before a panel of TAC officers.

"Candidate, you failed the communications exam," I'm told, something I already know. "Was there a reason you only answered half of the questions on it?" he asks.

"Sir, the reason is simply I didn't turn the test book over to see the questions on the back page," I reply.

"That's obvious," he says, "and why didn't you?"

"I know it's not an excuse. But before each test," I explain, "instructors usually inform us if there are questions continued on the back of the last page. In this case, he didn't do so."

"Is that all?" he asks.

"Yes sir, uh, it was also because the tests are always timed, and we're under pressure to finish. Probably another reason is I failed to check the backside of the test booklet. But, as you can see on the test booklet, all the questions I did answer were correct. If I'd known there were more questions, I could and would have answered correctly all the rest of them, too." I was then dismissed without further comment.

Had my standing not already been near the top of the class, I might have been discharged from the company, without further delay, or recourse. Though my record saves me, I'll miss being first in the class at graduation and being commissioned in the Regular Army, rather than the reserves. I later learn my standing is seventh in the class of the 97 graduating men. Still, it's not bad at all.

In mid-December, the OC Company closes down to give us a two-week leave, a welcome relief. I haven't paid off the loan for the flight I took in August, but this time my parents spring for the airfare. Business at the restaurant must be good, I'm guessing.

A few months earlier, to be closer to the restaurant, my parents have decided to move from Los Angeles and rent a house in Hermosa Beach. Though I'm staying with them there, this time they don't ask me to work with them. I spend much of my time at the beach trying to unwind. Walking along the boardwalk one day, I run into one of the boys I grew up with at the orphanage. My initial reaction to Mario is a pleased surprise. He's four years older than I am, but we'd been very friendly during our years at the Home, mainly I believe, because he had a thing for my older sister. Now, instead of greeting me with a smile, his focus is on my uniform, especially the OCS insignia patch on each sleeve.

"Oh, so you wanna' be a shave-tail looie, huh?" he sneers. His obvious jealousy is a disappointment; it puts me on the defensive. He's been a soldier during the war and I recall he may have reached the rank of corporal. Now instead of seeing me as an old friend, I somehow demean him.

Despite his disparaging question, I greet him anyway with, "Hey, how are you, Mario, long time no see. What brings you to the beach?"

"What do you care," he says, and walks away. I learn later he has become a California Highway Patrolman. Maybe then he might have been friendlier and not so obviously jealous.

Back at Ft. Benning the weeding out of the less qualified candidates has been thorough. With barely more than two months left to go, upon our return in the New Year, the attrition in the company is obvious. Rolled-up mattresses on empty metal cots in vacant cubicles tell the story of our diminishing platoon strengths. With the declining numbers of candidates, the platoons are reduced to three. Attesting to our senior status, our olive-drab colored helmet liners are exchanged for ones painted in Infantry Robin's Egg Blue. They identify us as near-graduates, and give us the authority to visit other Officer Candidate companies, where we will be saluted and have the right to descend upon and chew out "delinquent" candidates. It's heady stuff and I enjoy it, as do my classmates.

In early March, we're excited to learn a dance is arranged at the school's officer's club. We're also informed debutantes from an Atlanta private school will be bused in for us to dance with. But for reasons the promised women never show up is never confirmed. Still, this being Georgia, we guess it's the presence of the Negro candidates in our class. It puts a damper on the party, and who ever organized it should have known better and could have avoided the embarrassment. Nonetheless, we celebrate as best we can. During our party, I discover I have a taste for whiskeys of scotch and rye. Despite my past bout with Canadian Club whiskey, I now discover I haven't become a teetotaler after all.

Graduation day finally arrives for which we've all been yearning. Candidates' parents from all over the country attend and proudly pin gold bars on their son's shoulders. But the absence of mine neither surprises nor disappointments me.

Throughout OCS, I've been in touch with Hal Naud, a high school friend, who's in the Naval Aviator School in Pensacola, Florida. Hal has arranged dates for us with a couple of girls he knows in the town. I look forward to busing there after graduation for a night of partying with the three of them. Instead, at a stop near the southern North Carolina border, while using the men's room, I manage to miss my bus and spend a long lonely day in the small desolate bus station waiting hours for the next bus to come along. When it does, I still won't arrive in Pensacola until early the next morning. And meanwhile, there's no way to contact Hal to let him know about my screw up.

I'm furious about missing the bus, but there's no one to blame but myself. Nonetheless, hours of waiting for the next bus give me time to reflect on my decision to go to OCS. Even if I'm sent off to Korea, and even should I die there, I'm satisfied I've made the right choice. On the other hand, if I live, my length of service will be shortened. By my calculation, I have only a year left before returning to civilian life. Still, in retrospect these speculations I know are naive.

But even more importantly, I realize I've now been seized with the feeling of a metamorphosis. I've arrived at this new status entirely through my own efforts, rather than circumstances. I've been allowed to do so by the flat playing field, which is the equal opportunity provided by the U.S. Army. It cares nothing about my impoverished background, or the second-class status I'd been made to feel as a Mexican American. I have no illusions about what motivates the Army in commissioning me. I know what it cares about is having a sufficient number of trained platoon leaders to lead its infantrymen in combat. I'm convinced it's the sole motivation in creating this opportunity of which I've taken advantage. And it's reassuring to know I've competed in a mixed sample of one hundred and sixty American men and have come out near the top. It's a terrific boost to my self-image and dignity. And it has all happened in less than two years. I've purged the persistent feelings of inferiority plagued me for so long. I not only now see myself differently, but detect others seeing me doing as well. Instead of weighing them down, the hard-earned gold bars lift a weight from my shoulders, and I now feel the cloud of second-class status rising and blowing away. I'm feeling genuinely liberated with new energy and a tremendous self-discovery.

I'm back at home once again with thirty days of leave before reporting to my new station at Fort Ord. To complete the grown-up image I have of myself, I buy a pack of Camel Cigarettes, the same brand, Felipe, my stepfather smokes. I imagine it's a simple matter to smoke a cigarette. But my first inhale brings on a coughing fit lasts for some time and leaves me very dizzy. I can see why Felipe is smiling, for him it's amusing. He also assures me, if I keep smoking one or two cigarettes a day, I'll soon get used to it. But being a responsible man he is, he also tries to talk me out of becoming a smoker at all. Even so, I ignore his advice and press on. And sure enough, in the following days, the coughing stops, but the dizzy feeling, if somewhat lessened, it continues.

Two weeks later, finished with the pack of Camels and taking Felipe's suggestion, I switch to Kent, a filter cigarette brand then becoming popular. As the first trendy filtered cigarette, it's introduced around the same time as a series of articles identifying smoking as "cancer by the carton." Nonetheless, Kent promotes its "famous micronite filter" and promises consumers it's the "Greatest health protection in history." Sure enough, the cigarette's filter reduces irritation in my throat, and its longer length makes it look more sophisticated. By the time I leave home for Fort Ord, I don't realize how addicted I've become, nor giving any thought to what the nicotine is doing to my lungs.

Chapter 12

INTO THE FRAY

THE INFANTRY SCHOOL'S FOCUS AND ITS RIGOROUS demands has tended obscuring why I'm there. But now, with graduation just behind me, it brings the reality back to the fore. And all at once, I'm very aware of the clock's ticking toward my time to deploying for the battle zone on the Korean peninsula.

When it began, the sudden invasion by North Koreans set off a scramble of our forces to deploy and reinforce on the south with men, arms and materiel. Caught up in the rush were many inexperienced newly commissioned second lieutenants, ordered to replace those wounded or lost during the North Korean early overwhelming assaults. It's many of these untried young officers who consist partly of the high number of battlefield casualties. In protest of the extreme losses, both parents and field commanders together force a change in the policy. The result of the new rules now give "Greenhorns" at least six months of stateside experience with troops before being shipped out. And it's why we're now at Fort Ord, normally the home of the 40th Infantry Division, California's National Guard. In the emergency, the 40th and other nationalized state guard divisions are formed as a fire brigade. It has been rushed into the Korean peninsula to stay the flood of North Koreans, and later the Chinese hordes pouring into the south.

Now, with its usual division gone, Fort Ord shifts its focus to basic training turning draftees into infantrymen. Before shipping us overseas, five of my OCS classmates and me are ordered to report there for six months of the newly required training with troops. But, in typical Army fashion, the execution gets ahead of the planning, and upon our arrival we find there are too many of us to train the few available troops left behind. In inglorious fashion, this how my career as an Army officer begins.

Killing time for a week, the six of us are finally ordered to move on to the Presidio of San Francisco. Though the post is entirely new to all of us, we're now delighted upon hearing the place is something close to paradise, located in the northwest area of the fabled City of San Francisco. It simply seems too good to be true. In addition to the post, I look forward to exploring the legendary city with my classmates.

With orders in hand, I try to learn what I can about our new post's history. In the spare literature available, I find in the same year the United States declared its independence from England. Meanwhile, Spain has established and fortified this outpost on the northern tip of the San Francisco Peninsula. The king of Spain named it the Royal Fortress of Saint Francis, the English translation of *El Presidio de San Francisco*. Later in 1821, Mexico gained and held the fort after winning its independence from Spain. But then, it's lost to the United States at the end of the U.S.-Mexico War in 1848. I brief Bob West, my OCS classmate, about all this during our ride in his Ford convertible driving north along the 120 miles of the beautiful Pacific Coast Highway. And, of course, with the car's convertible top down moving through the warm pleasant air and sunshine.

More than its history, we're interested in what our assignments will be there. The installation, as beautiful as advertised, is literally situated within San Francisco's City limits. But this Fort, too, has no troops to command. In his welcoming speech, the commanding lieutenant colonel informs us, though we're part of his command, we'll actually be assigned to Fort Baker, a base established during WWII to defend San Francisco Bay. Our stay there will also include a turn serving as duty Officer of the Day on the Presidio's grounds.

Located on the bay's coast near the north end of the Golden Gate Bridge, Fort Baker is now the home of the 505th Military Police Battalion with a mission to train military policemen. A cozy isolated place, the small base and its surroundings are really quite pretty. It has a private beach with a gorgeous view of the bay, and across from it is a panoramic skyline view of the City of San Francisco.

I'm assigned as the weapons instructor and share an office with another lieutenant, a big friendly Military Police officer from New Jersey. Joe Papp teaches MP tactics for crowd control, riots and traffic. With so few officers on the base, I have a room to myself in the Bachelor Officers Quarters, which house all of us who don't live off post. Joe, a neighbor in the room next to mine, makes it his mission to show Bob West and me the delights of San Francisco's City itself.

A captain is nominally my new boss, whom I rarely see, and I'm surprised and pleased to learn he's also a Mexican American. Meanwhile, the man I have the most to do with each day is a grandfatherly master sergeant, whose job is to make up the training schedules. I find it slightly embarrassing to be addressed as "sir" by this senior, silver-haired NCO, but having served in the Army's pecking order for more than 30 years, it doesn't bother him in the least. At first, his inordinate friendly interest in me is puzzling; that is, until I learn he's on the husband hunt for his 19-year-old daughter. I'm flattered when I realize that he's singled me out as a match for her. But I turn down a second invitation to his home off base, ostensibly for dinner, but which I actually believe is to meet her. But still, he won't be denied, and instead he brings her to the office to meet me. Because he's a widower soon to retire, the sergeant wants to put his daughter in another pair of capable hands. She's pretty enough, but I know those hands won't be mine. Though I appreciate the Master Sergeant's concern for his daughter's future, I manage to avoid further involvement without alienating him.

My job is to teach military police trainees how to shoot and qualify in firing the .45 caliber pistol, the 12-gauge shotgun, the .30 caliber carbine and the .45 caliber submachine gun. Weapons training, in the classroom and on the firing range, are interesting and put little pressure on me, or my time. The troops are draftees and, while a class above of the average intelligence level of soldiers, they quickly catch on to the instruction. While I get up to speed refreshing my skill in disassembly and reassembly of the various weapons, my staff sergeant assistant carries the classes. But any live firing duty on the various ranges is entirely mine, a commissioned officer being responsible and required to control.

Extra weekend duty is rare, but when it does come, it can be demanding. It includes a turn as Officer of the Day at across the bay on the Presidio's grounds, and for me, it comes around sooner than I expect. Patrolling the park-like area in an olive drab, Military Police marked sedan gives me a chance to discover the broad extent of the Fort's sections. Citizens are allowed to drive through and enjoy its grounds of beautifully maintained lawns and garden areas from one end to the other. Even so, it's my duty to see visitors respect the facility, and, people being people, it's not all surprising there are some who'll abuse the privilege.

Once on duty, it isn't long before I find myself turning on my sedan's siren to pull over a vehicle from which a passenger has thrown debris out of the car's window. With my sedan's red light flashing, I stand next to the driver's window and offer him the option of picking up the trash, receiving a ticket, or, if he refuses, more serious consequences. The driver mutters something, but then steps from the car, walks back and picks up the rubbish. As he drives away, I hear him chewing out his child, apparently the guilty passenger.

As part of my duty, I'm also expected to be available on call all during the night. The task appears easy enough, until later, when I'm called out to investigate a Saturday-night domestic quarrel at one of the post's enlisted quarters. The situation is well beyond the scope of my training, and I feel ill equipped to intervene. But, ready or not, I go ahead and soon learn just showing up in uniform with an MP marked helmet and an armband, a holstered .45 caliber pistol hanging on my belt. The also implied threat of more MPs available has an immediate calming effect. The encounter is enough excitement for the night, but there's still more to come.

Shortly after midnight, I receive a call from the office of the City Police. I'm directed to take custody of the body of a man found floating face down in the Presidio's section of the San Francisco bay. Once again, in over my head, I relay the requirement through to the post commander at home, who walks me through the procedure with the City Police. With his calm directions, I quickly realize this has happened a number of times before. The night's events are my first exposure to the serious responsibility comes with a commission, even for a 21-year-old. As it turns out, I've comported myself well enough to earn my first letter of commendation.

With most of our evenings and weekends free, Bob and I turn to exploring the nearby town of Sausalito. Junior officers at Fort Baker previously have adopted one of its bars as our Officers' Club, or OC. Delighted with the idea, the proprietor has made sure the beer flows freely and at a discount. But what he can't provide are young women with whom to share our conviviality. Drinking to stupor, even with friends, is not my idea of fun, and the novelty of evenings at the bar quickly wears off. Joe always declines to go to the OC, preferring to save himself for the Friday-night dances held at the elegant Fairmont Hotel in downtown San Francisco. Fancying myself as a good dancer, of course I want to go there, too.

Revived for the Korean Conflict, the United Service Organization, or the USO of World War II fame, sponsors the dances for young officers like us, now destined for uncertain futures in Korea. Besides non-alcoholic drinks, the organization arranges for a live orchestra and gathers San Francisco young women and from its surrounding towns, to provide dancing partners and companionship. The USO requires women, who are mainly secretaries, receptionists, nurses and some college girls, all must be over eighteen years of age and single. Arriving for the first time at the hotel ballroom, the sight of its dance floor occupied wall-to-wall with beautiful, enthusiastic young women is breathtaking and immediately elevates my pulse.

The dances start at six in the evening and continue to nine-thirty. If a man wishes, he can find a partner for every dance. Because there are more women than men, we're encouraged to change partners for each dance, and to avoid spending the entire evening with the same one or two. But there are some who let me know they'd like to spend the entire evening with me. While a mutual sexuality atmosphere permeates the ballroom, the women are not allowed to leave with a serviceman. Of course, dates for the rest of the weekend, arranged on the dance floor, can't be prevented. The overnight interval presumably provides a cooling off time for any previously aroused passion. Once discovered, for a while, Bob and I rarely miss the Friday night dances with Joe at the Fairmont.

After a Mid-June dance, there are so many receptive young women, I suggest to Joe, who has a car, and we follow up with dates. Though hesitant, he agrees. I ask Shirley, a receptionist with whom I've danced once or twice before, if she'd like to go to dinner the next evening with Joe and me. That is, as we'll be going in Joe's car, if she can find him a date, too. She assures me she can arrange a date for him and does so right away. The following evening, in time to watch the sunset, we drive into the city, pick up the girls and set out for the Land's End, a restaurant on a beautiful spot overlooking the Pacific.

More than the beauty of the sea's sunset vista, I'm stunned the moment I set eyes on Joe's date, Marion Becker, a nurse, nicknamed, Becky. Only once before have I been so stricken by a woman. I can't keep my eyes off of her. In my state, she seems even surrounded by an aura. I can't get over her and her attraction to me also seems very evident. I'm thinking this must be love at first sight. Needless to say, my distraction does not please my date, Shirley, while Joe doesn't appear to care, probably because he's married. Before the evening ends, Becky passes me her phone number, confirming our mutual interest. During the following week, we talk on the phone every evening. Meanwhile, she's all I can think about.

A green-eyed, dark-haired beauty of German heritage, Becky is vivacious, of medium height with a nice figure. As a nurse she works at a local hospital and lives alone. Our meeting the following Saturday night at her apartment begins with a feverish few minutes of kissing and groping. She's passionate, but after a few minutes she slows down and holds me off. Though it doesn't happen, I allow myself a fantasy of sleeping with her before the night ends. My obvious ardor, I guess, may be the reason she drinks so little of the wine I've brought for dinner she has prepared. After having eaten, we're finally alone together with time. Between intermittent fondling and kissing, we exchange our life stories, or at least as much as we feel comfortable revealing. Though my sexual fantasy fails to materialize, the evening is still satisfying. I leave her at the last possible minute to get back to Fort Baker using Bob West's borrowed car by curfew.

After two more weekends together, my infatuation has waned. I discover she's three years older than I am, and this is part of the reason. She's pleased I've been baptized a Catholic and lets me know she considers herself very devout. When intimations of possible marriage creep into her conversation, I try to ignore them. But she makes frequent references to her faith and her desire to have a large family. Very soon, the prospect of having sex with her before marriage is obviously out of the question, and it's also clear once again, I'm being measured and tutored for a husband.

We don't dwell on it, but we're both aware I'll soon be leaving for Korea. So, when I receive my orders to ship "out" they're not surprising. Among other instructions, they include thirty days of pre-embarkation leave. And now I'll have to decide how to divide my time between my parents, the rest of the family and Becky, who wants me to stay the entire time with her in San Francisco. A few days with her are appealing, but having no wheels, I don't want to be staying alone in her apartment all day, while she's at work. She finally concedes I have an obligation to spend some time with my folks and siblings before shipping out. Since I'll be flying out of nearby Travis Air Force Base, we agree my time with her should come near the end of the thirty days. It will give us time together and she'll be able to see me off.

Near the end of August, on our last evening together the sweet sorrow of my departure for Southern California is soured by a misunderstanding. As a practicing Catholic, she has let me know that we aren't to be any more intimate than kissing and touching. But on this night after dinner as we lie spooned together on her sofa, she suddenly turns to face me and begins to hump! Startled, I freeze, which she interprets to mean that I don't want what her actions imply.

Misinterpreting me, she sits up and covers her face in her hands. "Oh, I'm so sorry. I've embarrassed you." she says. "I shouldn't have done that."

Collecting my wits, I, too, sit up, put an arm around her. "Becky," I say, "there's no reason to apologize. Making love is exactly what I've been hoping for all along."

"Oh, you're just saying to ease my embarrassment," she insists.

"That's not true," I insist. "I don't know how else I can put it. Not sleeping together was your idea, not mine. Just now, I didn't respond because you've so often let me know sex outside of marriage would be a sin." Reminding of her oft-stated virginal preference only seems to reinforce her vow to remain appearing chaste, and also it has killed any possibility of making love. In any case, now it's too late, the passion of the moment spent and the opportunity now gone by. Since my teenage, I've somehow absorbed the idea having sex with a girl implies a commitment. And as I leave Becky that night, I'm glad we haven't made love. If we had, I'd probably have been left feeling I'd made a promise I wasn't ready to make, much less keep. We part with fervent assurances to stay in touch and look forward to a wonderful reunion when I return.

Later, while rehashing in mind our last evening together, I suspect with her act on the sofa wasn't honest and belies her implied chastity. And I can hardly believe I turned down the chance to make love with her. Still, my moment of anger surprises me; how I was insulted and might have been used for her whim.

Though they don't say as much, my parents are really worried about my going into the war zone. My mother, in particular, whenever she looks at me, telegraphs her silent concern with a pained expression. Having experienced the revolution in Mexico with its random horror, they can both foresee my injury or death. And they have a good reason. By now, in this summer of '53, everyone knows our forces have been decimated the previous year by the Chinese People's Army entry into the war. None of us now have any illusions about what I might be facing.

As a send-off for me, my parents have planned a ten-day trip to Mexico. They don't explain it, but I guess if I'm killed, they'll at least have shown me where they'd been born and spent years when they were young. They've often spoken about growing up in their respective hometowns, so now I guess they think those birthplaces must matter to me, too. I'm thinking perhaps they do, and I'm ready to visit them. I've heard stories about their early lives and look forward to seeing

Chihuahua, Mother's hometown, and Saltillo, my Stepfather's. The timing is right. We'll be in Chihuahua on September 16, in time to celebrate Mexico's Independence Day.

Chapter 13

LOVE'S WHERE YOU FIND IT

———— •◆• ————

FOR A WHILE, I'M ONCE AGAIN WITH MY FOLKS IN HERMOSA Beach, where thoughts of Becky and San Francisco soon begin to fade. Probably intended as I want to put behind me, it's the misunderstanding during our last evening together and with its confused implications. Now, faced with the Labor Day weekend and time to spare before our trip to Mexico, I pass up the idea of calling her. Instead, I decide to see if any of my old high school buddies are still around. Out of touch for nearly three years, my phone calls to some of them have so far failed to turn up any one of them. I suspect their ranks have been thinned by the draft, or enlistments. Others may have married and moved away. Some, perish the thought, one may has even died.

Finally, one phone call connects with Charlie Rivas, who's in town for a few days, before returning to UCLA for his senior year.

"How's life treating you?" Charlie wants to know.

"Can't complain. Could be worse," I say, trying to sound casual. "I was commissioned an Army second lieutenant in March."

"Hey, congratulations. Where are you stationed?"

"Well, I was at the Presidio of San Francisco and Fort Baker for the past six months. Now, I'm on a pre-embarkation leave."

"How long will you be in town?"

"A little less than a month. I'll be spending some of it in Mexico with my folks."

"And where will you go next"

"Can you believe it's to Korea?"

"No Shit. I thought we were working on an armistice to end all that mess."

"I wish. Even so, an armistice only stops the fighting temporarily. Technically, we're still at war. The shooting could start up again at any time."

Charlie waits a few beats, maybe wondering how the war will affect him when he leaves college, and says as much.

"Well, I'm hoping it gets done before I graduate next year," he says. "My draft call has only been deferred." Then he asks, "You busy this weekend?"

"Charlie, that's exactly why I've called. Have you got something in mind?"

"Yes, I do. You remember my brother, Ray? He's in the Navy stationed in Long Beach. We've booked a room on Catalina for the weekend."

"Hey, really sounds good. What's the number? I'll call for a room."

"Don't bother. With Labor Day just around the corner, the place is already booked solid. But you can bunk with us."

"That'll be great, and I'll reimburse you with my share."

"OK, but I should warn you, we'll be drawing straws to see who sleeps on the floor."

"I'll take my chances. I've slept in worse places before. When do we leave?"

"Let's see, it's ten o'clock now. Where're you staying?

"Hermosa Beach with my folks."

"Good, that's on the way. Give me your address and I can pick you up, say at one, and then we'll get Ray. The launch for the island leaves San Pedro at three."

"Anything I should bring besides beach wear, change of clothes, a towel or money?"

"That should do it. Before we board, we can chip in for wine, or something stronger."

"I'm surprised you didn't invite a couple of girls to go along."

"Don't think I didn't try. I've been away so long all the ones I knew have married or moved away."

"You know, calling around I've just had the same sad experience. My address book is so out of date, I've just tossed it."

Charlie's offer is a huge relief. I love being with my folks, but the thought of two weeks at home with nothing to do until the trip to Mexico is hard to take. At least they haven't suggested I work in the restaurant, like they would've before I was commissioned. Looks like I've moved up in their eyes, and I'm no longer a boy to be put to work at their whim. My little gold bar changes everything. I've gone away a boy and come back a man, at least I like to think so.

It's a clear sunny afternoon, when the three of us arrive at the crowded dock at San Pedro. It means seating on the 30-foot launch, rocking gently in its berth, will be crowded. The seats are nothing more than long benches on either side of the cabin facing each other.

When the signal sounds for boarding, there's a rush scrambling for space. Not by chance we've seated ourselves across from three attractive young women. They're looking us over, too. I elbow Charlie to get his attention, but he and Ray are already staring and smiling at them across the deck. The potential in the weekend has suddenly become exciting, even pregnant with possibilities.

I make a move before the others have a chance, leaning forward. Shouting my question to the girls over the thrum of the idling engine, and say, "This your first time?"

They all nod.

"Will it get rough out there?" The one asking points her thumb at the water over her shoulder, maybe worried about getting seasick. The dark clouds starting to crowd the sky have given me pause, too.

"Hey Ray," I say, "You're our Navy guy, what do you think?"

"Hard to tell," he says. "Inside the breakwater it looks pretty calm right now. But if it turns stormy, in open water it could change fast." Awaiting us is a 22-mile trip, and Ray's assessment sobers all within earshot.

As if he knows what he's talking about, Charlie tries to be reassuring. "Don't sweat it," he says, "If you keep an eye out along the way, you might even see some flying fish. Besides, if it does get a little rough, we'll be there before you know it."

The brothers are both partly right. The threatening storm appears to be holding off, and once beyond the breakwater in the open channel, the waves are only a little choppier, nothing enough yet to worry us. For the next few minutes, all aboard settle down. But the calm doesn't last long. The skipper fails to head the launch across the wake of a passing freighter and, when its bow wave hits, our little boat lurches violently. With nothing to hold onto, many of those sitting across from us are propelled to our side of the boat. So, talk about luck; the girls literally end up on our laps, which solves the question of how to meet each other.

One of them, Marilyn, is now actually sitting on Charlie's lap. She's all smiles, and is delighted to be there as much as he is to have her. Ray and I are similarly introduced to her companions as abruptly, Shirley to Ray and Helen to me.

The launch rights itself, the heaving from the passing freighter is almost as quickly forgotten as it happened, everyone again talking and laughing at once.

After an easy introduction, relations between the six of us warm more quickly than we could've hoped for. By the time the launch docks in Avalon Bay nearly an hour later, we've rearranged our seats. While we're now paired off, we exchange basic information, make sketchy plans for spending at least the evening together, and I hope for the next two days, as well.

If we have thoughts of later intimacy, they're spoiled by the room arrangements. Like ours, the room the girls are in is so cramped one of them will also be sleeping in a chair, or on the floor. It doesn't seem appropriate to suggest visiting them there, or vice versa. But we make plans for dinner and dancing later at the island's Casino Ballroom.

Marilyn, the tallest and most gregarious of the girls, makes a good match for Charlie, an inveterate joker, always ready for a good time. Buxom and a little plump, Marilyn is as pretty as she is talkative. We soon discover it was she whose idea for the three of them to spend the weekend on the island. They're all from Chicago and all three, glad, they say, to get away from The Windy City's frigid winters. Now they feel liberated in their company's newly opened L.A. offices.

Shirley, Ray's new companion is outgoing, delightful, and curious. She's slight and vibrates with nervous energy. Once the ice is broken, she's full of questions about life in California, which gives us natives the chance to show off and create some laughter. It really makes conversation easier.

Unlike her companions, Helen, petite, is attractive if not pretty. She's quiet, even serious. Her pensiveness inspires my protective instinct, while her gorgeous figure isn't lost on me, either. It arouses outright lust. With these mixed feelings I wonder how to approach her. When I first saw the three of them on the launch, I favored Marilyn. But destiny's pairings pushed Helen toward me. For the moment, I'm disappointed that we might be stuck with each other. Worse, I sense she might be feeling the same way about me.

Helen doesn't smile much, either. I learn later, it's because she's embarrassed about her teeth. But as far as I can see they're all there and apparently normal. Indeed, her smile, when she flashes it, is actually very white and quite pretty. After all, I think, no one is entirely satisfied with his or her appearance. It always seems like there's always some feature they'd change if they could. Actually, I'm quite happy with her appearance and look forward to the next day on the beach, where I'll see more of the voluptuous rest of her.

In the evening, the crowds overwhelming every café and restaurant make dinner a noisy cramped affair. It leaves little chance to linger over coffee and make conversation. Afterwards, there's another disappointment; dancing will have to wait until the following night, when the ballroom opens. In the gathering twilight, we opt for a walking exploration of the island.

We all start out together, but soon each couple goes off in a different direction, or lags behind. Helen and I choose a trail surprisingly leads to a lookout point. There, on a shrub-surrounded bench we have a lovely view of the harbor. The remaining daylight fades to dark as we sit and talk, watching the harbor lights turn on. At first, without the company of our companions, we're a little awkward. But when she starts talking about her family, she also seems to warm to me in doing so. Being of Irish extraction, it's not surprising that she's from a large family. She's the only girl and has six older brothers. She's given up a modeling career in favor of a steady salary as a secretary.

In turn, she first wants to know about the meaning of my rank and asks about the surname printed on the small suitcase she's seen me carry off the launch. Learning I'm headed to Korea in a few weeks, seems to change her attitude to real concern. When we're more relaxed, I put an arm around her shoulders and press her against me to hold off the cooling breeze. The opportunity is too good to pass up.

My first attempt to kiss her is a little awkward, but not spurned. I don't want to risk spoiling the evening, especially even the whole weekend, by rushing things. But, encouraged by her acceptance, I follow with more kissing and tentative fondling. If anything, she's encouraging, and I realize she wants affection as much as I do. Still, this kind of petting can't go on for long before it becomes problematical. Going further at this stage I decide would be premature.

It's late when I return to my room. Ray, having drawn the longest straw, snores softly in his bed. Charlie, who hasn't been as lucky, is waiting up for me, maybe so I don't stumble over him. We chat for a while about our luck meeting the girls. If Charlie's experience with Marilyn has been similar to mine, he doesn't mention it, for which I'm glad. I don't want to talk about Helen, either.

I'm only awake for a few minutes before joining my mates into a deep sleep.

Chapter 14

INTO THE DEPTHS

AS WE MEET THE GIRLS FOR A LATE HURRIED BREAKFAST, the morning brings a clear blue sky and rapidly rising temperatures. Then, we're off to a beach on the less-crowded south side of the harbor, where we stake out an area with our towels. We rub on sun tan lotion and arrange our beach supplies before Charlie and Ray lead their dates into the gentle surf. I'm following them alone, checking the water and getting my feet wet, then return to and lie next to Helen on my towel.

"I've just checked the water and think it's still a bit too chilly for comfort," I tell her.

"OK, I'll take your word," she answers, smiling. The look on her face tells me she's still remembering our intimacies of the previous evening.

"While we're waiting, would you like me to rub suntan lotion on your back?" I ask her.

"Yes, and I'll do the favor for you, too," she says. After done her back, though I'm already pretty much covered myself with it, I still accept her offer. Like her companions, she's in a one-piece bathing suit that does nice things for her figure. Or is it the other way around? It's clear enough our previous evening together has had a transforming effect on her. Noticing the change, Marilyn and Shirley are having fun teasing about her sudden conversion to cheerfulness.

Around noon, though still somewhat reticent, Helen agrees to go into the water with me, but also says she isn't much of a swimmer.

"And how about you?" she asks.

"Oh, I can swim," I say, "but I'll never look for a job as a life guard."

"Well, you don't have to worry about saving me," she says, cheerfully.

"There's very little surf and the water looks fairly shallow for quite a way out," I tell her, suspecting she really may be afraid. "And, in any case, we'll stay close together." Hand in hand, we run into the lapping wavelets and are soon splashing each other and carrying on like a couple of kids.

While I'm looking around for our friends, Helen ventures farther out into deeper water alone. But suddenly, it's her screams I hear next.

"Bob, help me!" I whirl around to see her go down in over her head. Almost immediately, she comes up again sputtering and struggling, her arms flailing and barely able to keep her head out of the water.

For a moment, I'm still unaware of the depth she's in; I also can't tell if she's really in trouble, or playacting. Deciding it's not a time to wonder, I immediately decide it's better find out without delay. Diving and swimming to her in two strokes, I intend to pull her back to shallower water. But just as I arrive, she starts to go under again.

Damn! It's when I discover I also find myself on a sandy slope making the water much also deeper for me, too. Just right then I feel how the bottom inclines steeply to still deeper water. The realization, my sudden surprise quickly changes to fear.

My high body density means I don't float easily, and has always make swimming a major effort for me. If I have to, I can swim just well enough to save myself, but I realize now somehow, I also have to save Helen, too. My thinking flashes the only way possible I can help her is to dive under, grab her ankles, lift her up, and walk both of us up the sandy slope to where she can stand with her head above water.

Gulping a lungful of air, I dive under. Forcing myself down into the colder water, I fight to keep water from entering my lungs, while resisting the natural impulse to come up for another fresh breath. Forcing my eyes open, I see and grip her ankles lifting her up as high as I can, hoping it'll be enough for her head to break the surface to be breathing.

My lungs are already craving air, my heart hammering, while I'm trying to walk and looking up to see if her head has cleared the surface. Now, traction for our doubled weight is even more difficult with sand giving way under each step of my feet. In a flash I can imagine myself drowning, which I've heard can happen fairly quickly, maybe not painless but only briefly uncomfortable. True or not, but damned if I want to find it out for myself.

With each step the sand is giving way under my feet and find I'm making very slow progress up the incline. As seconds tick by, I see bubbles of my escaping breath rising in front of my eyes, and I'm aware my lungs are on the verge of giving out. Then, just when I'm certain I can't hold out any longer, I see her feet touching sand, I let go as she begins to walk on her own. Hoping she's safe, in the last seconds I kick to break the surface, gasping for a breath and then with a few strokes swim to her. Still gulping for air, I take her hand and we take slow steps together to the shallower water.

Now, knee deep, I bend over with my hands on my thighs. Still panting a few more times before I'm able to breathe enough to talk, I finally ask, between gasps.

"Are you OK, Helen?"

"Yes," she whispers, nodding. Both of us exhausted and panting, I take her hand and walk us back to our towels. While I flop down and stretch out, Helen sits and, for the next few minutes, her face in her hands, she's softly crying. Hearing her sobs, I sit up and moving to her to stroke her back to calm her. At my touch she looks to me with tearful eyes.

"You could've drowned," she whispers, "couldn't you?"

"Yes, and I was afraid we both might," I say, nodding.

"I really thought I was going to die out there," she says. "And you, you saved my life."

Without a word, I reach for and touch her cheek, lean in, and kiss her forehead. She reaches for my chin, kisses me and as we sit with our lips touching, she moves in closer, while her tongue explores mine and her hands hold my face. Our contacts feeling electrifying.

In a few minutes later, it strikes me, my short military career, not to mention my only 22 years of life, could easily have ended out there in the surf and right then. I'm also amazed our little drama apparently has gone unnoticed by any others. Though while for us it seemed to last for many minutes, in reality it was likely only a few. Since I was being under the water's surface, no one, neither the lifeguard, nor anyone else, including our companions, if they'd witnessed any part of it, might have thought it unusual, much less an emergency.

If I'd thought to check, as I do later, I learn this particular beach really consists of only a narrow strip of sand then suddenly falls steeply into a deep ocean gorge. Had I paid more attention to the other nearby bathers their sparse number might have indicated a warning. But we had to find out for ourselves the hard way.

Later in the evening, in the open and active music filled ballroom, Helen and I hold each other closely for a number of slow dances. Then we leave the dance floor early and return to our previous night's trysting spot, finding it unoccupied again. This time she's more than encouraging. Passion, yearning and sharing the exhilaration of being alive, making it a night to remember. But being in the open on this narrow bench couldn't give our passion its full rein.

A few days later, back once again in my parent's home in Hermosa Beach, the planned trip to Mexico, as part of my pre-embarkation leave, starts in our family's new 1953 Chevrolet sedan. I'm pleased to be given the wheel and do most of the driving through Arizona and New Mexico during the day and night to the Texas border with Mexico. Arriving in El Paso in the morning at a very new-looking Hilton Hotel, we check-in and decide to rest. My younger sister, Connie, shares a room with my parents, leaving me in a room by myself. In the afternoon, we cross over the border and drive on to Ciudad Juarez, Mexico. There my mother has arranged for us to meet Aurora, the youngest of her two sisters and three brothers, whom she now hasn't seen in many years. During the Great Depression, when their mother died in El Paso, Aurora was the only one of the children who decided to return to Mexico with their father. My married mother was remaining in Texas, while her other siblings went on to California.

When I see Aurora's resemblance to my mother, I know I'm seeing someone whose blood I share. Though she's nine or ten years younger than my mother, her heavily lined face speaks of a hard-challenging life.

My mother introduces Felipe, Connie and me to her, who seems very excited to see us. While looking at me, Aurora tells my mother,

"*El se parece mucho como tu, Fina.*" Understanding what she's saying, I feel a small thrill creep up my back, and surprise her by answering, but unfortunately, I can only do so in English.

"You're right, Tia, many people say I do look a lot like my mother." Hearing me address her as Aunt, she smiles and comes over and embraces me. She then turns to Connie and asks,

"*Tu entiendes español, Conchita?*" Connie, not understanding a word in Spanish, looks at her blankly and turns to our Mother, who translates and tells Connie to give her aunt a hug.

We sit sipping drinks and snacking in Aurora's living room for the next two hours, while the sisters try to catch up on their respective lives in the gone-bye decades. It's clear the parting is sad for my mother, as both tearing women promise to stay in touch. As we drive back to El Paso, I feel strangely disturbed being exposed to family history I've never known; a history I was a part of as a very young child.

The next morning, we check out of the hotel and drive back into Mexico. Beyond the Ciudad Juarez metro area, we're soon driving through the desert landscape on the highway to the city of Chihuahua, the capitol sharing its name with the State. The roadway is well maintained, but crowded with heavy truck and passenger vehicles, even a few horse-drawn carts. By late afternoon, we pull into the city and check into another Hilton Hotel there. We're excited to see the colorful green, white and red Mexican flags fluttering along the main thoroughfare in anticipation of the next day's celebration of Mexico's Independence Day.

My mother had lived and grown up to age fifteen in what passed for a suburb of the city, and she has many memories of shopping and dining in it with her family. Some of the places she recalls are still in existence, but many of her memories of the place are mostly unhappy, due to her recollections of living through Mexico's revolution. Yet, at least she's still willing to talk about them.

After re-settling in our hotel rooms, we walk to La Casona, one of the famous old restaurants Mother recalls in which her father especially liked its cuisine. After the meal, unfortunately, Connie comes down with a fever, and seems seriously sick to her stomach. Our parents hurry her off to a local dispensary, where they spend the rest of the evening. Though I'm sympathetic, I see no reason why I shouldn't explore the main drag and absorb some of the energy of the place.

The next morning Connie is better but still not feeling well. Now, we are trying to decide whether to stay a while longer in Mexico, go on to Saltillo, Felipe's home town, or start back to Texas and then to continue returning home. Though Connie's illness is uncomfortable it's not an emergency. So, we delay our departure long enough to watch the Mexican Army of Chihuahua's garrison soldiers make a holiday morning parade marching through the city. Its troops in general don't appear being as tall as American soldiers. I recognize the rifles they're carrying are US Army M-1's, their helmets also of US Army origin, but the dark green uniforms, unit patches and other markings are distinctly of Mexican Army. The unique band music is rousing accompanied by ranks of enthusiastic drummers and trumpeters, with the drums marking the cadence. The cheering crowds lining the thoroughfare are every bit as enthusiastic as Americans would be watching our army parading.

Because of Connie's condition, my parents decide they should cancel our planned visit to Saltillo, located deeper into Mexico's interior. So, we start the drive home. I'm thinking my mother and stepfather have waited too long to make this excursion. It should have been done many years before and included everyone, my older sister, my younger brother, stepbrother, as well as us. Realizing I might not return from Korea, I wonder if this is to be my last taste of Mexico, or of any other place else.

After we return from the trip, for the remainder of September, Helen and I see each other as often as possible. Becky, the pretty nurse I've left in San Francisco, and whom I've promised to return to before shipping out, is all but forgotten. Shucking off a nagging feeling of guilt, when we've returned home, I'd managed to send her a postcard from Mexico, but nothing else, not even a phone call. My strong feelings for Helen have driven any thoughts of Becky from my mind. Still, I have to admit I'm not proud of making her a casualty of the Catalina Island adventure, which recalls the paraphrased words of a musical's song: *"When I can't be near girl I love, I'll have to find another one to love nearer."* It sure applies to me.

I can only justify my treatment of Becky with the fact I'm now infatuated with Helen. Though we never say as much, our actions seem to express it. On our last night together, we promise to write each other faithfully while I'm in Korea. And before parting, we consummate our love in the back seat of my stepfather's '53 Chevrolet sedan.

Chapter 15

CHANGING VENUES

———•◆•———

BEFORE RETURNING TO SAN FRANCISCO, FEELING GUILTY
and in a futile attempt to apologize, I finally call Marion Becker.

"Becky, it's me," I say. "How are you?"

"So, you've finally decided call me?" she's sounding huffy. "Well, if
you really want to know, I'm furious. This is the first I've heard from
you, since you left almost a month ago." Now she sounds bitter, and of
course with reason.

"Didn't you get the postcard I sent you from Mexico?"

"Oh, I got it all right, but only yesterday, and it hardly counts instead
of a call." She's silent for a moment waiting for me to explain myself. My
excuse I know will be pathetic, but I make it anyway.

"Well, I can't control the mails," I say, ignoring reference to my failure to phone her, and still trying not to sound sheepish.

"That's not what I mean," she says. "What you wrote on the card
could've been written to anyone." At once it's clear no explanation nor
my apology will appease her.

"Becky, I'm really sorry, things just didn't turn out as I planned," I
say.

"Well, I find it hard to believe. As far as I know, you not only had plenty of time on your hands, but also plenty of opportunities to write or call," she says.

Ignoring the accusation, I continue, "I was distracted because my younger sister was very sick while we were in Mexico, and we had to return to the U.S."

"I still don't see why you couldn't have sent a card sooner off to me."

"Well look, Becky, I'd really like to see you before I have to report to Camp Stoneman."

"Isn't that nice of you. But I'm not sure I want to see you again," she says. "Actually, it won't even be possible, anyway."

I don't need to ask why. In the background, I can hear a man's voice asking what I'm saying and whispering his suggesting for her replies. He's either a new man in her life, acquired while I was away, or she's giving an old one another try. Still, his presence helps to dispel the guilt I'm feeling, and brings a sense of relief and closure, though I do regret being so thoughtless. I still have feelings for her, so much so I would like to see her again, even if just to apologize in person. But obviously it's not going happen, either.

Now, with no reason to return to San Francisco, I report directly to Camp Stoneman, a processing and replacement center near Pittsburg, California. To demonstrate its welcome, the city has erected a huge billboard at the entrance of its main highway with the message: "Soldier, We're Proud of You." Though intended to be sincere, somehow, it leaves me feeling more suspicious than welcome. Located forty miles to the northeast of San Francisco, the camp served as a major Army staging area in WWII. Now it's serving again for the Korean War. Named after George Stoneman, a Civil War cavalry commander, it was activated following the Japanese attack on Pearl Harbor in December of 1941.

During my month's leave, with the Korean Armistice continuing, the Defense Department has decided a partial reduction in force, or RIF, can start right away. But when I sign in on September 24th and learn about it, I'm crestfallen. Damn it! If I'd known of the policy and requested my discharge by September 15, the Army would have let me go, there and then.

Later in the transit BOQ, I'm upset, actually furious and still mentally wringing my hands. It's when a familiar voice calls out.

"Hey Bob, so you missed it, too, huh?" The voice is Harry Spalding's, one of the lieutenants from Fort Ord who'd been transferred to the Presidio with me. At least, when he enters the room it's good to see a familiar face.

"I'll be damned if it isn't *Captain Spalding the fabulous explorer!*" I voice back in a paraphrased line from Groucho Marx. "Harry, how the hell did you end up here, too?"

"I was also on leave, just like you, when the word came out about the RIF, you know, the reduction in force," he says, shaking his head.

"Man, that's really dirty pool. The CO at Fort Baker could at least have tried to contact us to let us know what was happening," I say.

"Yeah, but you know how it is, once you're off their books, they couldn't give a damn about you."

"Even so, I've just been up the admin chain of command here to request a reconsideration," I tell him, "but it got me nowhere, because I still have more than nine months of service left. If I'd had just one day less there might have been an exception. But no luck," I say. "Looks like we're on our way to Korea, Harry, whether we like it or not."

"Well, at least the fighting there has stopped, so how bad can it be?" he replies. "I'm trying to console myself by thinking this isn't all that bad. Going to Korea is a chance to see something of the world. And we'll be stopping for a while in Japan on the way. How about that?"

"You mean if the fighting doesn't resume, right?" I remind him.

"Well, even if it does, we'll get to see some of Japan, anyway," Harry says. Double deep-dimpled Harry, always smiling, seems to get through life as a Pollyanna. He might have a point, but I still have a crushing sense of disappointment at just having missed an early discharge. Now, I face more than another year before returning to civilian life.

The processing center swarms with others who missed the early out like Harry and me, or who otherwise don't qualify for it. Meanwhile, mostly paperwork and required immunization shots, pre-embarkation lectures and preparations are moving along at a snail's pace. The waiting between processing and actual departure at nearby Travis Air Force Base is yet another typical Army hurry-up-and-wait event. To fill the time, there are around-the-clock poker, craps, penny pitching and other gambling games. I consider joining a poker game, but notice one lieutenant is winning most of the pots. When he loses, the pots are small and he's playing against only one remaining player. But in the next round, when two or more players are staying in and a large pot has been built, he moves in with heavy raises. Even when the other players show high hands, his is still the winner. After watching the game for an hour or so, I'm convinced he's reading the other players' cards! They must be marked, somehow! Suspecting other cardsharps at work in other games, Harry also thinks as much and encourages me to avoid all of them.

The town might provide a diversion and we decide to go to check it out. Despite Pittsburg's entrance highway welcome sign, a better name for the city would be, "Pitfall-burg." When the so-called Police Action started in Korea, the town's economy suddenly boomed for a number of reasons, not the least of which was the opportunity to hustle the bored servicemen passing through it. At our pre-departure orientation, we were warned the town teems with prostitutes and many fixed poker and crap games. After the city protested it being designated off limits to servicemen, we learn we still aren't prohibited from going there, but told we'll be doing so at our own risk. Our curiosity and despite the warning, Harry and I both have to see at first hand this den of iniquity.

At the two poker games we visit, the players are mostly older men and no doubt residents. I'm certain their cards are also marked. The barrooms also teem with women, both young, even to older in age, yet many of them quite attractive. Their enthusiastic welcomes are warnings enough not to get snared. One pretty young woman, unusually aggressive, follows me around trying to attach herself to me. Finally, I have to turn to her, place both hands on her shoulders, look into her eyes and tell her, "I'm not interested. Find someone else!" Feigning disappointment with me, she finally detaches and is soon on the hunt for another soldier.

Finally, on October 2, our Boeing, four-engine, propeller-driven flight takes off from Travis Air Force Base for Japan. After refueling stops in Honolulu and Midway, the twenty-seven-hour trip finally ends at an airbase outside of Tokyo. From there, we're trucked to Camp Drake, the Army's replacement depot set up to handle troops bound for in and out of Korea. Besides Harry, at Camp Stoneman I've met some friendly Puerto Rican lieutenants, who, because of my surname, thought I might be a *paisano*. Now, Harry and I catch up with them again at Camp Drake. As soon as we can, the five of us make the 30-minute train trip into Tokyo to discover it.

Wandering up and down the Ginza, Tokyo's main thoroughfare is a marvelous new experience. The massive crowds fill the sidewalks and spill onto the roadway along the main avenue almost devoid of motor vehicles. It's a unique feeling to be walking among them and seeing over the heads of nearly everyone else around me. The heads popping up above the mass of people inevitably belong to GIs enroute to Korea, on R&R, or waiting for transport home. The surprising opulence of goods in the stores belies the devastation the city had suffered only eight years earlier. Absent, too, is any visible hatred or resentment I think the

Japanese must harbor seeing us in uniform moving head and shoulders so freely above and among them. I see the reason why Asians are called being inscrutable: they hide whatever feelings they might harbor of hatred and anger.

In our eagerness to get into and experience Tokyo, we've skipped chow at Camp Drake in favor of eating something authentically Japanese. I suggest we look for a small restaurant away from the main avenue where dining might have a truer taste of Japanese life and its food. What we find is a small cave-like café only a block off the main drag, its floor, walls and ceiling all appear to have been hewn out of grey granite. A short, older waitress brings us menus on which none of the listed dishes we can understand or translate. Though no one here speaks English, we still refuse to give up on the adventure.

Harry takes the matter in hand, looking around to see what other patrons are eating. Though it's somewhat rude, he points to something that looks appetizing other patrons are eating and nods to the waitress and orders the same thing. Meanwhile, I try to get the waitress to understand the word "rice." Just then, one of the Puerto Ricans remembers customers usually are likely to eat with more gusto than care. Acting on his thought unhesitatingly, he digs between the seat cushions on our bench and finds a grain of rice, which he now holds up in his palm to the waitress. Upon seeing it, she smiles broadly and shouts triumphantly, "Ah, Gohan!" Taking and showing the grain to the other patrons, who've been watching us, they, too, take up the cry, repeating, "Rice," though instead what we're hearing is, "Lice." Now armed with the name of the country's staple food, we won't go hungry.

As darkness falls, crowds on the main streets are thinning, until mostly leaving behind are numbers of young women. Besides being pretty to a Westerner's eye, they stand out also for being nicely dressed in western-style clothes, in high-heels, neatly coiffed and attractively made up. In broken English, they advertise their availability for "a short time" with them for surprisingly low prices. Takers can be led to a nearby hotel or apartment building for consummation. Transactions are hampered because all US military on arrival have had to exchange their few U.S. dollars and yen for military script, which are unusable by the Japanese. Nonetheless, deals are still managed, though the women risk the loss in the event of an unannounced script series exchange. Military currency control is a tactic done purposely and changing its issue can happen at any time.

My companions and I, daring each other to get laid, have little difficulty finding a nearby "pleasure house." But once on the scene, the sordid reality of the place, and the pathetic looks of some of the women, mostly young but others much older, put a damper on our presumed intentions. In the chilly semi-darkness of the passing night, we see clusters of the girls huddled around *hibachis,* small charcoal-burning stoves. We wonder if they're homeless and maybe desperate for a GI customer to pay for the warmth and comfort of a hotel room during a chilly late October night. By now, we're all ready to return to camp, having had enough for one day and a night in Tokyo.

Once the initial attraction of Tokyo diminishes as so does our cash, we grow bored waiting in Camp Drake for the next leg of our journey on to Korea. It's a relief when our departure orders are issued ten days later. Our time at Camp Drake has drained both our interest in Tokyo and most of our money.

Our next destination is the southern and main port city of Sasebo on the most South Island of Kyushu. The uncomfortable daylong train trip, smoky and cold, carries us through vast expanses of countryside, spared much of WWII's bombing destruction. What has been a critical operation here was a coal mining area. It was one of two major targets for our B-29 bombers and still shows the war's scarring. The other, harboring a naval base during WWII, the City of Sasebo has also been heavily bombed. But it, too, now shows little of the earlier wartime devastation. Our stay in the port city will be another week of a hurry-up-and-wait experience before boarding our troop ship to Korea.

In balmy weather of the early morning on November third, we're ordered to board our assigned troop ship. It's when we learn the 400 of us lieutenants are likely to be the last of such boatloads bound for Korea. The news brings an optimism the armistice will hold. It also occurs to me our hundreds in number imply the expectant great losses of young officers we'll be replacing.

Finally, underway by late morning, our ship starts to thread its way through the calm harbor and into the open ocean's choppy waters. By late afternoon, we've reached the Yellow Sea heading for western Korea's Inchon harbor. Evening chow is a welcome change from the fare we've been served so far in the Army's mess halls. Rumor has it the Navy always serves the best food in the armed forces. True or not, the ship's mess is crowded with hungry soldiers. After the meal, Harry and I join others on deck to watch the sun sinking below the horizon. Even as we're standing there, the skies begin to cloud up bringing with them the winds of a sudden storm. At first, we're told the change in the weather is nothing to worry about. But, the farther we move northwestward the blowing wind steadily increases, and the ship begins to mimic the heaving waves; rising on a crest then plunging into the trough on the other side. Despite the growing wind, ranks of men stick to the ship's railings staring in awe at the ocean's ferocity. But it isn't long before even more men arrive on deck, not to marvel at the sea's spectacular performance, but to give up all the good chow to the ocean's creatures below.

I'm grateful I'm not getting seasick. Instead, I'm actually enjoying the ship's rolling plunging and plowing its way through the heaving seas. The only thing missing, at full volume, would be the accompaniment of Wagner's, *Ride of the Valkyries,* which it is now playing in my head. Gripping the railing, I remain watching the ocean's drama until the rain drives me and everyone else to cover inside.

The next morning, breakfast in the mess is sparsely attended. Once again, I enjoy the Navy's chow to start the day. Facing my upcoming life in the field, I suspect this will be the last good meal I may have for some time. Though the storm has blown itself out during the night, the skies remain grey and threatening. While the rest of the voyage is expected to be uneventful, still the anticipation of landing in Korea is full of portent.

Chapter 16

THUNDERBIRDS

ON THE WET, CHILLY EARLY NOVEMBER MORNING, WE
debark under South Korea's Inchon harbor's troubled sky. At high
tension, our mass of 400 young officers is ordered to begin sorting into
numbered groups, each bound for an American fighting unit deployed
somewhere inland east and south. Heading into the country's interior a
short while later, anxious and wide-eyed, two-dozen of us find ourselves
rumbling east in a bone-jarring truck convoy through the devastated
countryside.

While on the way, we seem to be passing endless lines of desolated
Koreans: men and women, many families and seemingly abandoned
children moving in both directions. With their wooden, peasant back-
rack trussed possessions, they snake along the sides of the road clogged
with our trucks heading in the eastern direction. The lines of people
along the roadsides are all trudging through the remaining destruction, going nowhere to discernable destinations I can imagine. I'm left
wondering how and if they'll survive, especially the children, who look
so dirty and ragged, frightened and surely must be hungry.

Leaving all of it behind, we finally arrive at our destination, a place called Chun Chon. Remnants of what was once a thriving village, it is left now in so many piles of destruction. It lies thirty miles south of the recently established Demilitarized Zone, or DMZ, nestled in a valley in the embrace of war-scarred mountains. The remnants of this once humbled settlement now hosts the headquarters of the 45th Infantry Division, my small group's new assignment.

A few dusty hours later, on arrival we park at what passes for the division's headquarters. Next, ordered to file into an enormous olive-green tent, we all scramble onto a bank of bleachers. Before us, on a makeshift stage, there's a huge map board displaying the division's logo: A golden American-Indian Thunderbird symbol on a diamond-shaped crimson background. Standing to one side, a master sergeant, with deadpan expression and in dark-green starched fatigues, faces us at "parade rest," his hands crossed rigidly pressed against the small of his back. At some unseen signal he comes to attention, pushes aside the facing map board exposing another behind it. This one displays a giant mailed fist clutching a hand grenade. Overarching the war icon is the word, "POWER," all superimposed on a map of the entire Korean Peninsula.

Suddenly whirling to face us, the sergeant bellows, "A-Ten-SHUN!" Scrambling to our feet, we watch mesmerized as a bantam rooster of a man leads a gaggle of senior officers tramp across the stage. The hardware of paired silver stars, gleaming on the leader's collar and his billed cap, leaves little doubt that he's our division commander, Major General, by name, P.D. Ginder.

While his staff officers move off to one side, all eyes are now riveted center stage on this resplendent figure. Also uniformed in impeccable dark-green starched fatigues and spit-shined black combat boots, he wears a chrome-plated, .45 caliber pistol on his right hip, its ivory handle stark against the polished leather of its ebony-colored holster. With his right hand, he toys impatiently with a shiny black, silver-tipped swagger stick, slapping it repeatedly against his thigh. Though while another six inches of height would make him more impressive, he still easily fits a casting director's idea of a modern major general.

In the throaty bass-baritone of a man used to his authority, he orders, "Take seats, gentleman." Haloed by the arc of "POWER" above the mailed fist on the map board behind him, he struts back and forth across the stage, the swagger stick still slapping. He finally stops to face us with arms akimbo, feet planted wide, then he looks us over for a long moment. Suddenly, waving the swagger stick in our direction, he booms:

"Men, this is the most unfuckin'est war I've ever been in." There are murmurs of wonder and not a few nervous chuckles. While the meaning of the remark sinks in, the general resumes.

"Men," he says again with the same urgency, "this division will rotate stateside early in the New Year. In the meantime," here he pauses to nail down our already rapt attention, "the armistice signed in July could break down at any time, and we must be ready to resume combat at any moment." With his remark my anxiety it raises to a new level. I've already been thinking one way or another I'll probably die in this place. If not killed in battle, then maybe freezing to death in the upcoming bitter Korean winter. And it's the good reason this country's known as "Frozen Chosin."

This Division, the 45th Infantry, formed from Oklahoma's National Guard, has been federalized for the Korean Conflict. In World War II it was distinguished in combat in the North Africa Campaign; afterward slogging north and fighting its way through Italy, France and on into Germany. Major General P.D. Ginder, now its commander, is no less proud of the 45th's record in Korea, and, by his telling, is nothing short of heroic.

In the following staff briefing, we learn the Division's exploits are told in a song, a paean to soldiers and their commander. After committing it to memory, we'll be expected to sing it any time the General visits our units. As a newcomer, I take it on faith our starred leader is beloved of his men. And, given a majority of his citizen-soldier fighters are from his home state, he feels a special obligation to bring them home alive, undamaged and whole. He intends to ensure their care and well-being in or out of combat. And his concern, we're told, now also extends to us, his new soldiers. At the master sergeant's order, we again jump to attention as the general wheels on a boot sole and departs.

As the master sergeant bellows out unit assignments, we sort ourselves accordingly. The six in our cluster move outside, collect our duffle bags and climb into our three waiting jeeps, among others, their engines already idling.

The Author is on the left, a 2d Lieutenant with 1st Lieutenant Earl Owens, CO, of the HQ Company, 2d Battalion, 180th Regiment, 45th Infantry Division in South Korea in 1954.

It's an hour and one half dusty ride, pleasant enough in the fall, mild cloudless afternoon, to the division's 180th Regiment, 2d Battalion. Pulling into the concertina wire-enclosed compound, a coterie of the battalion's officers greets us. The CO, Lieutenant Colonel Disharoon, short, balding and the embodiment in speech and manner of a southern gentleman, makes introductions and then gets right to the matter of assignments. Three of us, he says, will be rifle platoon leaders, and are directed to their respective company commanders, who're also standing by. The rest of us will remain with battalion headquarters. As part of this latter group, for no good reason I can think of, I'll be the Communications Officer; Lt. Rogerson, a lanky New Englander, will be Assistant S1 (personnel); and Lt. Jenkins, a stocky southerner and our only Negro officer, Assistant to the S4 (supply). Though my immediate boss is nominally the First Lieutenant Owens, commanding the HQ Company, the Battalion Executive, Major Wingfield, immediately claims me for his own bidding.

Besides our primary tasks, we're informed we'll perform "other duties as assigned;" such chores being the bane of junior officers since "Christ was a corporal," then a popular expression. This means carrying out odd jobs at a senior officer's whim. For me, while the battalion is in reserve, includes keeping the movie projector and a makeshift generator to run it in operating condition. Then our troops and officers can watch movies when films are available. And because of my putative Catholic faith, I soon learn it will usually fall to me to get the chaplain to his tent any night he's too drunk to get there on his own. I imagine it will no doubt be a regular depressing happening event.

Besides supply-related duties, Lt. Jenkins will run what passes for our officers' club, including a couple of cooks in a Quonset hut. Under its curved ceiling is also outfitted with a plywood bar, a few handmade tables, benches and chairs, and at one end a makeshift movie screen.

In addition, set up in a separate Quonset, to his personnel duties, Lt. Rogerson will manage a minuscule PX. Available in it are cigarettes, toiletries, cameras and film, among other necessities for troop morale. And not the least of these is beer.

During in the ensuing weeks, we drill in live-fire exercises, make forced marches, and practice tactical maneuvers to maintain the battalion's readiness for the real possibility of returning to combat. The days settle into a routine. By well into November, I'm pretty much adjusted, though my California-acclimated blood continues to recoil from dropping temperatures and frequent snowfalls. I learn it's true about Korea's unforgiving winters whose temperatures regularly drop to well below zero. I especially dread trying to sleep through such nights on the ground in a pup tent.

To impress us newly assigned officers how well off we are, Major Wingfield, the battalion exec, one day leads and takes us to visit a Korean orphanage in a near-coast village. There, I'm stunned to see the children in what passes for an unheated schoolroom, which has windows without glass or even shutters to block the cold winds. It reminds me of my childhood years in the orphanage in California, but where it never got this cold and also always had plenty of warmth. Yet, here and now I'm shivering during through the entire visit. It makes me wonder how these poor Korean orphans without heat can manage to survive the seemingly endless cold. At least we have brought them c-rations, canned fruit and bread to help provide something to fill their empty little bellies. And in reply, they seem eager to sing for us, which nearly brings tears to my eyes, reminding me, when as a child of our orphanage singing for charitable church groups.

One night later in the month, at the end of a staff meeting, our colonel wants to know if anyone has anything else to bring up.

"Yes, sir," Lt. Jenkins offers. "Striking dockworkers in Japan and the Philippines have cut off the supply of beer to U.S. Forces in Korea. Division wants to know how many days' supply we have on hand." Because each man here is allowed a daily beer ration of one can or bottle, which he can buy from our makeshift PX, the cutoff is a serious matter. Suddenly, now Lt. Rogerson's operation has new importance.

"Lieutenant, how much have we got?" The Colonel wants to know.

"We're low, sir," Rogerson says, "two or three day's supply at most."

The 45th having just come off the line, General Ginder considers the beer cut-off is a morale catastrophe; there's no telling how long the strikes will last. Typically, considerate of his men and with Thanksgiving Day in sight, the General arranges to have a two-week supply of beer--thousands of cases--flown in. Though he expects to fully recoup the expense, the gesture again demonstrates his caring regard for the troops.

But, by the time the General's order is delivered, the dockworkers' strike has suddenly ended and the delivery of Japanese and Philippine beer resumes. Now, probably it wouldn't have mattered. Except, instead of a popular brand of American beer, the General's supplier has only been able, on such short notice and at a price the General's willing to pay, to ship a little-known brand of malt liquor named, "Getz." The General's kind gesture is now destined to produce a questionable military sideshow.

Though not well known, Malt liquor has higher alcohol content and claims the attributes of champagne. Grain rationing in World War II forced brewers to produce a reduced-alcohol beer. Then at war's end, they returned to producing prewar malt liquor, with potency about double of regular beer. Probably for this reason *Getz Malt Liquor* comes in a container half the size of a regular beer can. But to the troops, unaware of its doubled alcohol strength, it still seems an inferior buy. Now, with the preferred Japanese *Nippon* and Philippine *San Miguel* beers again available, the *Getz* can't compete, not even with its attractive Red Rooster label. And it tastes nothing at all like champagne, or beer.

As the cases of *Getz* remain unsold, the General faces a mounting financial problem. Reminders from division about selling the *Getz* become more insistent. Just before Thanksgiving, division calls a meeting of unit representatives to pass out the word on how the "*Getz* question," or more namely, the General's reimbursement, will be resolved. Club Officer Jenkins being unavailable, its Major Wingfield who orders me to get the latest "skinny" on the General's beer situation.

The crowded division war room tent buzzes with young officers like me, all standing with pencil and note pad at the ready. When the Chief of Staff enters, the room quiets as he takes a long look around. Without preamble, he wastes no words telling us how we'll "solve the *Getz* problem."

At the evening staff meeting, the colonel turns to me, and asks, "Lieutenant, what's division's word on the *Getz*?"

"Drink *Getz* and save your nuts, Sir," I say, straight-faced.

"What!" The response comes in unison.

"Drink *Getz* and save your nuts, Sir," I repeat.

"That's it?" The colonel looks at me, incredulously.

"That's all the Chief of Staff had to say about it, Sir, and we all wrote it down," I say, unable to keep a broad grin off my face. In civilian life, General Ginder was a businessman, as was our Colonel Disharoon, who understands the General's hard-nosed terms.

"OK," the colonel says, "We can't force the men to buy *Getz* when they know their preferred beer is available. Though not strictly legal, we'll use unit morale funds to buy the *Getz*, and serve it with the Thanksgiving and Christmas dinners." To Lt. Rogerson, he adds, "Be sure the daily one-ration-per-man is observed on those holidays. Malt liquor is a lot stronger than regular beer, and I don't want any trouble."

"Right, Sir." Rogerson replies, solemnly.

As the year is drawing to a close, the colonel's solution has only reduced our remaining supply of *Getz* by half. Serving it again at the New Year's Day dinner, it still fails to use up our allotment. Worse still, and hard to believe, we hear the battalion officers might be required to cough up what the General still owes on the remaining malt liquor's bill.

A few days into the New Year, we learn the 45th Infantry Division's return to stateside is at hand. Those of us newly arrived are to be reassigned to units remaining in Korea, the rest are to go home with the 45th. Forgotten for the moment is the matter *of Getz Malt Liquor*.

On our last night as a cohesive unit, I have the bad luck to draw duty as Officer of the Day. During the hours of darkness, it's my job to mount the guard protecting the battalion's perimeter. In the late afternoon, I inspect the platoon-sized force and instruct the Corporal of the Guard to "post" the first shift immediately after chow.

The evening movie is a western, an action film with lots of yelling, shooting, and the pounding of horses' hooves. After running it earlier for the troops, my commo sergeant sets up the projector in our improvised officers' Quonset club and starts the film. We all settle back to watch it and be entertained. Midway through the screening, while the sergeant changes reels, I duck out to inspect the guard. I've only just stepped outside when I hear the sound of automatic gunfire echoing from the hillside area between two of our rifle companies. Transfixed for a moment, I'm unsure what I've heard. Seconds later, the staccato of an answering burst leaves no doubt.

My adrenalin already pumping, I rush back into the club. "Colonel, there appears to be a fire-fight going on in the area between Easy and Fox Companies!"

As one, the room erupts, bodies rushing to empty the Quonset. No one has heard the actual gunfire over the shooting and hoof pounding going on in the Western movie! While we wait outside the club, at first there's only silence. The colonel and everyone else turn to look skeptically at me. And just as I'm beginning to doubt myself, the firing suddenly resumes.

"Lieutenant," the Colonel commands, "get the rest of your guard out and lead a patrol up there! Find out what the hell's going on!"

"Yes, Sir." I toss him a brave salute, wondering if this is to be my first--and possibly last--real combat action. I run to the guard tent.

"Corporal of the Guard," I shout, "fall out the guard with weapons and equipment, on the double!"

Silence! There's no movement!

Dumbfounded, I enter the semi-darkness of the half-empty tent to find men lying passed out on cots. The Corporal of the Guard nowhere in sight, I try to move around inside, kicking empty *Getz* cans strewn everywhere on the ground. Then quickly, I move from man to man shaking each in a vain attempt to rouse enough of them to mount a patrol. Shamefaced, I rush back to the club and report to the waiting Colonel.

"Sir, the rest of the guard to a man is dead-to-the-world drunk!" I report. Disgusted, he turns and orders the company commanders to take charge and deploy their troops in a defensive posture.

By now, sporadic firing is erupting in other parts of the encampment. Meanwhile, I decide I can at least ensure the posted guards are in place--and, I hope, are also sober. Certain my sentries are rattled by the firing I approach each post with extreme care. Before allowing me to approach, more than one demands I raise my hands in the air and utter the password to his challenge. Then, with one step at a time, I move in closer until he recognizes me. Meanwhile, as the officers and NCOs gain control of their troops, the firing dies down and finally stops.

Later, an investigation reveals we aren't under attack at all; rather our unit is in the midst of a celebration by nearly a thousand men, many of them leaving to start the movement stateside the next morning. Drunk and exuberant, they are also getting rid of ammo using it for fireworks, which should've been collected when they came off the line. A night seemingly endless finally passes without further incident.

The next morning, save for some monumental hangovers among the troops, the company commanders report no casualties. Nor does it take long to figure out Lieutenant Rogerson is the puppeteer behind the night's live firing. Realizing an opportunity to get rid of the unsold *Getz*, he's opening the PX to all without restriction. In a flash the word spreads and he soon sells out. With best intentions he hasn't considered how our men, consumed with the thought of going home, would react to a sudden relaxing of the one-can-per-man rules. He foolishly presumes his reward will be the General's thanks, rather than courts martial. As it turns out, at the least he is spared. But had the spontaneous celebration turned out tragically, our erstwhile lieutenant, while saving our nuts, would surely have lost his own.

Chapter 17

IN LOVE COMPANY

THE REPLACEMENT DEPOT, WHERE I'M PARKED FOR THE next two months, leaves me feeling like a castoff. Due to the reduction in force following the announced armistice, remaining units are being re-shuffled all over Korea south of the Demilitarized Zone, or the DMZ. In early March, I'm informed the 3rd Infantry Division's 15th Infantry Regiment is to be my new assignment. I have no knowledge of the 3d, except for rumors it might have many Puerto Ricans in the division who've been described as reluctant fighters. If true, I guess I'll have to find it out for myself. Meanwhile, unlike my arrival at the 45th Infantry Division, this time there's no welcome by Major General Charles Canham the division commander. Rather than greet me as a new member of his unit, by letter he reminds me as an officer I should have a college degree. Well, I certainly agree with him, but I don't see how I can do anything about it as long as I'm parked here in Korea.

This time, instead of being introduced to the division commander, a number of us meet the 15th Regiment's Commanding Officer. Its colonel speaks briefly to our few just assigned to the regiment before sending us on to our respective battalions, mine being the 3rd. A sergeant soon arrives in a jeep to pick me up and drives me to Company L, popularly referred to as the Love Company, located a half-hour ride away. Finally, entering a squad tent there, I meet its Company Commander, Captain Angel Irizarry.

"Lt. Sanabria, reporting, sir," I say, saluting him.

"Hey, I'm very glad to see you," he says, and really sounds like it, while returning my salute and rising to shake my hand. "Between combat losses and stateside rotations, we're shorthanded, especially lacking officers," he says. "So, we can really use you. When I saw your last name, I thought you might be Puerto Rican. Sanabria is a well-known surname on the island from my home."

Despite the warmth of his greeting, I detect his disappointment I'm not a Puerto Rican *paisano*, after all. I imagine he's been looking forward to reminiscing about his island homeland.

"Come on, I'll take you on a tour of our area," he says, as he leads the way out of the tent.

"Have you decided on my assignment yet, sir?" I ask, as we're starting our walk around.

"Well, the fact is I could use you in more ways than one," he tells me. "The exec has been my only other officer, so all of my platoons are commanded by sergeants, some who led them in combat. I've finally decided I want you to take over the 1st platoon, the one most in need of discipline. And don't be surprised if you get some resentment and resistance from the sergeant who's been leading it."

"I look forward to it, Sir," I say, my feelings show in the flexing of my jaw. "Finally, this'll be my first experience doing what I was trained for," I tell him.

Captain Irizarry smiles and goes on. "If you haven't already been told, our 15th Infantry Regiment is manning a portion of the Demilitarized Zone, or the DMZ, and the responsibility is being rotated among its three battalions," he explains. "For the moment, ours is serving as the regimental reserve, with our Love Company acting as the regiment's so-called "palace guard," he says.

"That sounds a lot like a good bit of guard duty," I say.

"Well, you're right, that's exactly what it is. But, at least it's light duty, so far," he tells me, and continues. "The regiment, down to company level, has been augmented with South Korean Army troops. They're called the KATUSA, otherwise known as Korean Augmentation to the US Army. A number of these Korean soldiers make up an eight-man squad in each platoon."

"Do any of them speak English?" I ask.

"There's just one, your interpreter, and the only way you'll be able to talk to the rest of them."

"Anything else about them I should know?"

Captain Irizarry stops our movement and looks at me for a moment. Then he says, "Yeah, there is," as our walking resumes, "we have about thirty of them attached to Love. But I have to say they aren't much help," he says. "I've learned they never joined in a firefight, and many disappeared as soon as we made contact with the Chinese. Now I've never actually had the experience, but I've heard, when attacked, many of them abandon their positions, even leaving their weapons behind. But others some of them just hunkering down in foxholes and covering their heads with their arms wrapping around them. There they remain until the fight's over."

"Hell, that must be disappointing," I tell him.

"Yes, that's true enough, but it's understandable when you consider they were forcibly, mind you, forcibly hauled off the street and just given a weapon. Then, with little or no training at all, they're being shoved out here and expecting them to fight alongside with us. Their mingling with our troops so far has done nothing for their morale, or ours either."

"Do you have any suggestions how I'll make them feel more like a part of the platoon?"

"Well, right there, is exactly your challenge. You'll have about a month to get to know all of your men, before we'll be rotating duty with the other battalions," the Captain tells me, as we complete the tour.

"Any idea when our company's turn is next to patrol in the DMZ?"

"No, I don't know exactly when it'll happen, but I do know, sure enough, it'll eventually be our turn to re-deploy to near the DMZ itself. Meanwhile, like I said, Love Company is providing security for regimental headquarters."

"I'll get started right away, Sir, getting my platoon in shape," I tell him.

"Hey, look, let's get together this evening and have a beer. My other lieutenant should be back by then and I'll want you to meet him. One other thing, you and the exec will be sharing a tent. It's the one next to the HQ tent, where you checked in. You can haul your bag in there and I'll have the first sergeant round up a man to set up your cot."

Before meeting the staff sergeant now commanding the platoon, I'm thinking of the challenge its sergeant could give me for control of the men, wondering if he might even try to undermine my authority. But as it turns out I needn't worry. As instead, I find it just the opposite. He's obviously relieved to have the burden of the responsibility lifted from his shoulders and appears just as glad to be as my second-in-command. Asserting my authority right away, I conduct weapons inspections, call for daily PT I lead and practice squad tactical drills. Except for a couple of recalcitrant, the men respond well to the new discipline. Though pleased with the progress, I'm still wary about any unobserved behavior might be going on among them I might need to uncover. There are only a few men with Spanish surnames, who could be Puerto Ricans, but they don't seem much unlike the rest of the platoon's men and aren't clinging together.

The Author with a stray dog is the 2d Lieutenant a platoon leader assigned to Company L, 3d Battalion, I5th Infantry Regiment, 3d Infantry Division in South Korea in 1954

At the outset and despite my best efforts, which seem to be achieving good results, it's the unexpected and unrelated event shakes my improvements and control of the platoon.

Two of my men, good friends are from the same mid-west hometown, one engaged to the other's sister and they always seek duty together. There's no harm in it, I'm thinking. In fact, their relationship could be a boost to their mutual morale, something is usually often absent. But one afternoon, as they're preparing their gear for guard duty, one of them, while cleaning and oiling his .45 caliber automatic pistol, he shows it off to his friend. He must have forgotten he's already chambered a round following inserting the fully loaded magazine. Because he believes the weapon's chamber is empty, he playfully points the pistol inches away from his friend's head, and pulls the trigger. When the pistol fires, the bullet hits his brother-in-law-to-be squarely in the forehead.

A sudden invading the camp are a series of screaming coming from his tent. By the time the squad leader and I arrive there a few minutes later, the wounded soldier is already in the throes of death. There's nothing we can do to help him. But we are at least able to save his friend's life; the anguished shooter who's still screaming, while two other soldiers are also restraining him from wanting to commit suicide. Like the squad leader and me, Captain Irizarry is also aghast, when he soon learns of it, and feels as much responsibility for it as I do.

Within the next couple of hours, the dead soldier's body is taken to graves registration. His friend, the shooter, is arrested, taken away by MPs and placed in confinement and kept from trying to hurt himself. Meanwhile, Captain Irizarry calls a hasty meeting together with the casualty's squad leader, the first sergeant, the company exec, and me to thrash out every aspect leading up to the shooting. Knowing division will conduct a detailed investigation, the captain wants to find out if one of us has failed in our duty to prevent such an accident. After an hour's discussion, he decides blame rests with the shooter himself alone. But the death still leaves all of us shaken. Captain Irizarry will have to write the sad news to his family, and for another one we agree to the shooter's relatives, as well. Now, he debates with himself out loud if he or I should visit the shooter first, who is now in confinement?

The next day, the battalion commander visits our company, ostensibly for a routine inspection. But we know it's more for the deadly event has just happened. The Military Police Criminal Investigation Detachment has already investigated the shooting and sent its report up the chain of command. And to satisfy himself, the colonel questions Captain Irizarry and me further in detail. In the Army, fault is always fixed somewhere, or and on someone. For a while I'm thinking every-body in the chain of command, beginning with me, could and would be held responsible for the soldier's death.

Thanks to my weapons inspections and safety lectures, I'm not at fault for failing to ensure proper safe weapons handling. The shooter was trained and qualified to use the pistol. I never learn if anyone is reprimanded, but the event brings to an end the company's stint as the regimental guard and the light duty accompanies with it. The loss also leaves my already depleted platoon by fewer two men.

Leaving us feeling as if we're being punished, within a few days later, the company is ordered to re-deploy to the DMZ in a time sooner than we've been expecting. The zone, a heavily land-mined swath of territory, snakes across the rolling terrain from the peninsula's east coast to its west. Parallel lines of concertina and barbed wire run the whole swath, and a third double line of barbed wire bisects it. As the company's only commissioned officer-led platoon, mine is selected to man a position along what is known as the general outpost line. It puts us at least two thousand yards, a little more than a mile beyond the company and the rest of the regiment as a warning unit alarming in the event of a North Korean attack.

My platoon's location of operations is dug in around the base of a sharply vertical hill, not surprisingly called the *Ice Cream Cone*, and not far south from the DMZ itself. We occupy bunkers and foxholes around the base of this stark landmark, the highest terrain feature all around the battlefield. Prominent on the plain it makes a perfect lookout, but at the same time an ideal registration target for North Korean artillery. Because of its isolation, it has to be defended on all sides. The landscape surrounding it is flat and only marked by the debris of destroyed mili-tary vehicles, general detritus, artillery and bomb craters.

During daylight, our mission is to observe our sector of the DMZ and report on any enemy activity north of the zone. At night, we patrol inside the concertina wire within our south side of the DMZ, looking for any North Korean penetrations, or preparations for an attack. US Army units preceding us have cleared mines from a narrow path running along the twisting patrol route parallel to the center barrier wire. The trail is just wide enough for one man, thus forcing patrols to move through in a single file. I'm warned how men have been seriously injured, even killed, by stepping on mines buried just inches off the path. From time to time, there have also been shooting incidents incited by the North Koreans aimed at provoking a reaction from our patrols.

The dangerous nightly excursions are exhausting and emotionally draining. To spread the load, I rotate the patrol duty, and every third night I lead a squad. With four eight-man squads, the one coming off patrol duty can sleep the following day. Patrols are conducted in silence and blackout, except for the leader's red-lensed flashlight. Starlight and moonlight provide our only illumination. But seeing in the dark is still possible, mainly with peripheral vision, and it improves remarkably with practice. The rest of the platoon, during hours of darkness, in two-hour shifts mans the defensive perimeter around our position.

There's little rest for any of us, every man serving either on a DMZ patrol, on guard in foxholes and bunkers and or working on their improvements. The Ice Cream Cone hill, jutting so visibly from the terrain plain, in past battles has been battered repeatedly. Weather has eroded the road to and around it, caving in foxholes and rendering some of the bunkers unsafe. During daylight, squads haven't been on night patrol I put their men to work repairing bunkers and the roads around our site. At night, they also guard critical entry points around the position. After the first week, we settle into this routine, carrying out one duty or another, day and night, living in holes in the ground and subsisting on C-rations. Drinking water is delivered to us daily. This is demoralizing duty, leaving everyone anxious and tired. Consequently, fighting low morale becomes my major concern, but there's little I can do to lift the men's spirits.

I share a bunker with my interpreter, a young Korean soldier. His limited English is garbled and heavily accented. Even so, added with sign language we manage to get along and through him I'm able to establish a reasonable relationship with my squad of Korean troops. I soon discover they are not the supposed cowards, and prove in fact to be willing workers. Unfortunately, they no doubt feel isolated in the platoon by their language and an obvious lack of training. They seem a little lost and perhaps too much in awe of me. I'm assuming they're uneducated, but as workers, they perk up when given a mission they can handle. They excel in reconstructing the road and our defensive positions and are the mainstay in those efforts.

By early July, the demanding duty is taking its toll on all of us. The heavy work schedule leaves little time for rest. When I begin to have night sweats and losing weight, I start to worry something more is wrong with me than overwork and a lack of sleep. Now I'm having coughing spells and chest pains, and I decide I'd better find out what's going on happening inside me. One morning, leaving my platoon sergeant in charge, I inform Captain Irizarry I'm checking in at the battalion aid station. There, with little hesitation, the doctor diagnoses tuberculosis and won't let me return to my platoon. Instead, now required to wear a facemask, I'm sent off by ambulance to the MASH hospital farther south in the rear area. There, I'm x-rayed and quarantined. Next, the doctor notifies Captain Irizarry my evacuation is imminent to stateside.

In the following week, while I await evacuation, Captain Irizarry and the battalion commander come to the field hospital to see me off. I learn then my Korean interpreter has also been diagnosed with TB, and is probably the source of my infection. Our sleeping in the close quarters of the bunker may have guaranteed I would acquire his Tuberculosis. While being examined, I'm told TB is rampant among the general Korean population. During a weeklong stopover at the Army general hospital in Pusan, lab tests and more X-ray's confirm my diagnosis and the extent of the disease in the upper apex of my right lung.

My evacuation by a series of Air Force hospital flights brings to an end my nine-month tour of overseas duty. I travel on to Tokyo in another hospital flight, and then spend two days in Honolulu. Though I can't see much of the place, I can certainly smell its sweetish odors from flowers and other vegetation. Then, because I'm from California, there's some discussion the Letterman Army Hospital at the San Francisco Presidio could be my final destination.

In isolation at Letterman, with time on my hands and lying in a hospital bed, I'm thinking about how I just missed the earlier discharge. This quirk of fate has changed my life in such an extraordinary way.

During the second evening at Letterman, I decide to call Becky. Fortunately, I still have her number in my wallet and call her at work to avoid any interference from her new man. When she answers, she's more pleasant this time and is sincerely sorry learning about what has happened, my illness and my condition. But then she hastens to let me know how happy she is about her engagement. Though I'm expecting to hear her say something about the breakup between us, but neither of us mentions it. In the end, she declines my suggestion she visit me in the hospital. Though she does wish me well, and, in turn, I congratulate her on her engagement.

The next day, instead of staying in California, I learn my journey is to continue. This time, it will go on to Denver, Colorado, where the nearby hospital will be my final destination and to an uncertain future.

Chapter 18

UNSETTLED MOVES

———•◆•———

INSTEAD OF WAGING AGAINST THE STILL THREATENING war in Korea, now I have to fight a real personal battle with Tuberculosis at Fitzsimons Army Hospital. In Colorado's Mile-High-City suburbs, the medical center originally was built by the Army to treat the large numbers of returning casualties from Europe in the First World War's chemical warfare. It's named for Lieutenant William T. Fitzsimons, the first American medical officer killed in the so-called Great War. I'm reassured this medical center is the world's best place to fight my battle by treating the lung's infection with tuberculosis.

Knowing the disease can kill me is a major worry, but I've also been reassured an array of new drugs now available can arrest its progress, restore me to health and allow me resume a normal life. This is why I've been transferred to this medical center from San Francisco's Letterman Hospital. The high mountain air here supposedly is also purer, and makes Denver a prime place for treating patients with lung diseases.

My new home is the officer's ward in a two-story brick build-ing devoted to treating tuberculosis patients from all of our military branches. A vacant patient room becoming available on the ward has triggered my transfer to it. Otherwise, I'm told, I might have stayed at the Letterman Army Hospital in California. At least there would have been easier for my parents to visit me. But this ward, because of its specialty, supposedly offers superior treatment for TB patients.

When I arrive, the patient floor ranges in officer grade from my second lieutenant rank to full colonel, and are mainly Army men. A few Air Force, Navy and Marine Corps officers are also here. Our ward's second floor is divided lengthwise with the north side having sixteen private rooms. The opposite half of the building's south side is a wide aisle with an array of chairs facing large expansive windows allowing the sun's restorative rays to flood the space. A common social area at midpoint of the floor has a dumbwaiter, a pool table, sofas, armchairs and a large color TV set. On the ground floor below us are the doctor and nurses' offices, treatment rooms, kitchen facilities and an elevator to bring up the daily food carts.

Having a room of my own, like the other patients, it has to do with isolating the disease. For the entire first month, I'm confined to bed for complete rest, though allowed to get up to use the bathroom. My physical activity is so restricted I'm even to be bathed in bed by a corpsman wearing a protective mask. The first goal, the doctor tells me, he wants me to regain the ten pounds I've lost to the disease while in Korea. And it should likely to do so with the well-prepared food, milk shakes, juices and other between meals snacks arriving for us three times every day. Supposedly, the non-stop eating and with little if any physical activity are to put back the lost weight, and then some. But I'm determined to maintain at least a minimum of physical conditioning. So, despite the ban on physical activity, in the privacy of my room I do a daily routine three sets of stretches, pushups and sit-ups. The effect of the no-exercise policy is on display in the overweight of my mates.

Besides bed rest, the infection in my right lung calls for treatment with three drugs I'm to take in daily. Two come in pill form, the third a yellowish liquid, it's so foul flavored not even a cold grape juice chaser can right away erase the lingering aftertaste. But, beside their unpleasantness, the combination has proven its effectiveness.

Some of the other officers, whose TB disease is more advanced, are also having to undergo major surgery to remove the lung's diseased portion. Though I'm not needing it, I still want to know what's involved and asked to have it described. The operation begins, the doctor explains, with an incision starting from a point at the spine just below the shoulder blade. Then, cutting around to the sternum, exposing and forcing a space open between two ribs, even removing one, if necessary. The enlarged opening allows the surgeon to reach in and pull out enough of the lung to cut off the diseased portion. Suturing its incisions and replacing the remaining healthy lung completes the operation. Its description may seem simple, but it leaves me shuddering and more than glad to miss it.

The surgery patients are reassured their reduced lung capacity will regrow and expand to refill the vacated space within the ribcage. But they still dread the procedure and the very painful physical therapy that begins immediately after the surgery operation. It will also continuing for weeks afterward. I'm fortunate my lung's infection has been discovered early enough so surgery isn't necessary. Even so, it's still unnerving to learn I'll never be entirely free of the disease. The drugs I take at best will only help to encapsulate the TB bacilli within calcium cells and, providing I stay healthy, won't be released to re-infect my lung and kill me.

Once a week in the very early morning, to monitor the effects of the drugs on the TB bacilli, a nurse or corpsman wakes me to take a sputum sample from my stomach. The process, though uncomfortable and often gagging, it becomes routine. I sip and swallow ice water to ease the passage of a lubricated flexible tube pushed up through my nose. It's then directed through my throat and eased down my esophagus finally into my stomach. With the tube in place, the nurse, or corpsman with a large syringe, suctions a liquid sample. They are checked regularly in the process to record the declining presence of the bacilli in subsequent weeks.

Another routine operation, still more disagreeable and anxiety provoking, involves removing the fluid continues to collect in the bottom of my diseased right lung. This time, using a sizeable syringe, the doctor pushes a large needle through a Novocain-deadened section of my ribcage. And then, through the pleural lining near the lung's bottom, it aspirates the fluid pooling there. The extracted liquid is also analyzed for TB bacilli to track a patient's progress in recovering.

One morning, during her weeklong visit, my insistent mother is present while the doctor performs the fluid extraction routine. I suppose her presence, besides visiting in her mind, she's also there to ensure he doesn't hurt me. With a face mask on, she's watching with a worried expression I can see in her eyes. Even so, she remains composed while the doctor injects Novocain to deaden the area near the base of my right lung. But, when she sees the large needle and syringe next to be used to extract fluid from my lung, she suddenly appears shocked, inhales audibly and looks like about to faint. An assisting corpsman comes to her aid, and escorts her from the room.

While the drug treatment continues, after three weeks I'm declared no longer contagious. Then, if I have anyone who cares to visit me, my relatives and other visitors would be allowed, without masks, in my room. But besides my mother, who has already visited me, and has since departed, I don't expect anyone else to show up. Now, I'm noticing the other patients' wives, and other relatives and friends have brought books, games, small TV sets, and other homey things to make their rooms more comfortable. On our floor, when a room's doors closed and its windows are shuttered, it's likely for conjugal visits are also underway and being enjoyed.

Particularly in the room next to mine, occupied by a former telephone lineman, turned Army doctor, he has regular visits from both his wife and his lover. The muffled cries and other squealing pleasure noises coming from the room leave me no doubt about the nature of the visits. For a while, he manages his schedule to avoid a confrontation between his wife and his lover. Still, despite careful planning, he can't prevent an inevitable confrontation.

One evening, both his wife and lover mistakenly show up at the same time. An argument erupts behind his room's closed door and shuttered window. When the noise finally quiets down, it appears an agreement has been negotiated between the two women, so their separate visits can continue. A number of the other officers have conjugal visits as well. And for those without spouses or girlfriends, I think one of the women aides, who works here, is servicing some of them in one manner or another. She also sneaks in orders for liquor. Though always friendly towards me, she never offers me any of her other services. I assume it may be because of my relative youth's presumed innocence, or assumed I can't afford to pay whatever any charge might be, for whatever are provided.

For the next five months, though the treatments continue, I'm free to roam the ward, visit with other patients, shoot at the pool table, play cards and watch television. I spend most of my time reading, learning to play a silent piano keyboard under the tutelage of a volunteer music teacher, and do crafts. I buy and have delivered a portable typewriter, resurrecting the typing taught in high school to write home and to Helen, who has since returned to Chicago. At first, with no idea how long my treatment will take, or how long I'll be kept in the hospital, time drags on. Yet, life becomes more interesting as my variety of activities are permitted. In time, I'm allowed to leave the ward and to use the facilities on the grounds. To revive my first attempt at a college education, I enroll in Denver University's off-campus courses offered on the hospital grounds. I also take up oil painting and practice the piano daily at the recreation center. It's remarkable I can pursue all of these interesting activities and still receive my full military pay.

The young women who abound on the campus haven't escaped my notice, either. As soon as I can, I'm flirting with one of the occupational therapists and a couple of the younger Red Cross workers. Dating them is easier when I buy a new Ford convertible with back pay and money paid from my GI Insurance. Now, with wheels it's simpler to engage with the younger, single Gray Lady women, too. I focus on one in particular, Lisa, a beauty whom I find very approachable. After a couple of dates, she tells me about her background has been nearly as troubled mine. Though I want to have an affair with her, what she mainly wants is to tell me all about other men on the campus who're after her. And, instead of becoming her lover, I become her counselor, not the role I had in mind. It's obvious Lisa wants someone on whom she can unload her troubles. If we were to become a couple, the last thing I'd want to hear about would be her former lover history and woes. I realize everybody comes with baggage, even the most otherwise are desirable, though they might appear to be. Meanwhile, I set about to put an end to our relationship.

Within weeks of my arrival at Fitzsimmons, I'm promoted to First Lieutenant. I also receive the Army Commendation Medal for my command of the platoon at the *Ice Cream Cone* in the Korean DMZ.

This recognition and my TB recovery are altering my view of remaining in the Army. By leaving the U.S. Air Force for the Army's Officers Candidate School I mainly meant to reduce my time in the service. Then, I'd planned to return to civilian life and pick it up where I'd left it, especially with my education. But, by the end of September, this plan has been upset by reality, when my doctor advises me to remain in the Army for at least five more years. If discharged, he explains, my TB treatment will be taken over at the Veterans Administration, or VA, facility near my home. Having been previously employed by the VA, he assures me I'll receive much better care by remaining in the Army. Until this point, my dreams have been about returning to California and going back to college. But now, for my health, I'm convinced to remain in the Army for at least a three-year extension, before I decide on the next step in my life.

While in Korea and at Fitzsimmons, Helen and I had continued writing to each other. But with passing months, the intervals between her responses have grown longer. I realize our short time together after our Catalina experience hardly revealed us enough about each other. For some time, I've realized we don't have enough on which to build a relationship. Though it's disappointing, I know her interest in me must be waning. In an effort to find out and hopefully to renew our connection, I suggest we plan a reunion in Chicago as soon as I'm allowed to leave the hospital on convalescent leave. Though she agrees, yet it's obviously lacking in enthusiasm. I suspect she may not be looking forward to my visit.

A few weeks later, when I'm finally free to leave the hospital, I set out driving to Chicago to see Helen. I leave Denver with a passenger, an Air Force major, a patient I've befriended on the ward, who offers to pay for gas for as far as he goes with me. Of Italian descent and a devout Catholic, soon after we'd met on the ward, he's been trying to strengthen my faith, though I suspect it's really more about his own. Aware I've planned a visit with a friend, as our trip launches, he discovers my meeting is more a reunion with a girlfriend, than just a visit. Now he wants to know all about Helen. At first, he seems encouraging enough, asking details about how we met, her education, her employment, religion and where she lives. But hearing more about her and assessing our relationship, he's not very subtle about discouraging my getting more involved with her. By the time we reach his destination, I can hardly disguise my anger with his presumptions, and I'm glad I can finally drop him off. Yet, as I drive on alone, his arguments begin to sink in, temper my lust, and raise my doubts. Though I've said nothing to Helen about it, I've had thoughts about our getting to know each other better and wondering if she might even become my wife. Seeing her again face-to-face could possibly make up my mind.

The visit is nothing as I've imagined at all it might be, neither happy nor exciting. For my short stay, she takes Friday off from work to give us a long weekend together. Otherwise she's made no other plans for us. Despite what she says to the contrary, her attitude upon seeing me again is at best obliging and tolerating, but obviously devoid of any joy. Only what she seems like to do is drink, ending each night being nearly drunk. Our lovemaking is also disappointing. Despite my patient efforts, she seeming has trouble becoming aroused, just goes through it nearly motionless and without any evident real enthusiasm or enjoyment. No matter how I try to please her, in or out of bed, we have little to say to each other, apart from reliving our brief Catalina Island experience, and the short dating time after.

Driving out of Chicago three days later, I'm disappointed with her drinking, the scant sexual pleasure and mainly the general lack of enthusiasm about our relationship. Still, the unhappy visit has still been very important. Now I know Helen will not be the woman I'll want to spend with the rest my life, much less have her be the mother of my children.

Once back at Fitzsimmons, my relationship with the occupational therapist I've been dating takes a more serious turn. Audrey Benner, a pretty Army First Lieutenant, is not only accepting me, but is genuinely enthusiastic. Unlike Helen, she's educated with two degrees, is qualified as an occupational therapist and comes from an established Ohio family of medical doctors. Though she's three years my senior, it somehow makes no difference this time, as it seemed had to be with Becky. She introduces me to a number of crafts to fill my time, while I'm confined, and lends me her record player and a collection of classical music. Once I'm sprung from the confines of the ward, we spend more time together and I'm surprised how well we get along. Before I buy the Ford convertible, we get around in her big Buick sedan, a gift from her grandmother given for her first college graduation. As soon as I'm allowed to leave the hospital's grounds, she drives us into Denver to share dinners, movies, and sightseeing. Before long we discover a favorite trysting spot--though one regularly raided by the local police--and are soon necking and petting to distraction.

Early in the New Year, the approval of my request to renew my service for another three years comes through, and soon followed by orders to report to Fort Lewis, Washington. Audrey, meanwhile, has received orders transferring her to Fort Bragg, North Carolina. The prospect of being separated will force us to decide about our future together. After a few serious discussions, we agree to marry. But this is easier said than done.

I make an appointment with the Catholic Chaplain to discuss Audrey's faith and mine. His first question:

"Are you both of Catholic faith?"

"No, Father," I tell him. "My wife-to-be is a Protestant."

"Well, in that case, unless she agrees to convert, I'll have to marry you in a side chapel," he informs me. "And I can only do so if you and she agree to bring up in Catholic faith any children you might have."

Hearing his requirement, it immediately raises my anger. I decide to end the meeting, telling the priest I'll have to discuss the issue with my wife-to-be.

When I tell her about the priest's conditions, she surprises me by saying, "Oh, it's OK, I'm still willing to convert."

"But I don't think that's very honest or fair to you," I tell her. "More importantly, I refuse to commit our unborn children's faith to Catholicism, or any other faith. Though I've told the priest I'm Catholic, I've mainly said so to please my mother. We both know we can't claim a belief in any faith simply to please someone else's desire. The truth is, I'm a non-believer," I add.

In the end, we agree to be married by the Protestant Chaplain, who agrees to preside without preconditions, except for our love and dedication to each other. And as if to differentiate himself from the priest, even more, he spends a few minutes discussing the use of a diaphragm, unless we want to have a baby right away.

My mother travels once again to Denver to be present at our wedding in December in the Fitzsimmons Hospital's Post Chapel. When I get around to telling her about Audrey's family and background, she makes the remark I'll never forget: "Don't you think she's too good for you?" I'm so angered I consider telling her to leave. Does she think so little of our family and me? I fume with anger for a while, but later, on reflection, I realize she simply means to protect me from being hurt.

In December, our wedding takes place in the Post's chapel attended by some of her former colleagues and some of my patient friends. Her mother and grandmother, whom I'd met during their earlier visit to Denver, are present and meet my mother, who invites them to visit her in California. Afterward, in Denver's foothills we take a weeklong honeymoon in a camp.

For the rest of my six-month convalescent leave, I accompany Audrey to Fort Bragg, where we live off post in a house rented near the military post. During the day, while she's at work, I spend my time practicing on a rented piano, taking care of the house and prepare our evening meals. She continues on duty, but applies for discharge and a transfer to the Army Reserves. The process takes a few more weeks.

Meanwhile, at the end of my leave, I drive on alone to Fort Lewis, Washington and to my new assignment there. Two months later, Audrey will join me following her discharge from the Army. Then, in nearby Tacoma we'll rent a house and begin our lives together as man and wife.

Chapter 19

A NEW LIFE

LIGHT DUTY IS PRESCRIBED IN MY NEW ASSIGNMENT AT Fort Lewis, Washington. As a consequence, I find myself in a disappointing housekeeping unit commanded by a major, a friendly officer who's counting his days to retirement. On any given day, the chores he assigns are whatever he decides I should do. Needless to say, I feel adrift with no idea what the future will bring. Now I wish I've asked for a discharge, instead of an extension for duty like this one. Still, despite the regret I have to remind myself I'm only in this assignment for my health, following my Fitzsimons Army Hospital doctor's recommendation.

My salvation from this holding unit is a temporary appointment as an aide to a brigadier general visiting the 71st Infantry Division, Fort Lewis' major combat unit. I have only a vague idea what an aide's duties are, but I do know my way around Fort Lewis' major units and its grounds. So at least I'm able to direct our sedan driver to the general's daily appointments.

Together during the week, the brigadier seems to have a keen observation and questions me. "Lieutenant, I notice you're really on the ball. Why are you assigned to this kind of job?" he asks.

"Sir, I've only recently been released from the hospital recovering from TB contracted in Korea," I tell him, "and I'm supposed to have fairly light duty for a while."

"Would you rather be assigned to a regular infantry unit?" he asks. "I'm sure there are assignments you could carry out and still be aware of your health's condition," he adds.

"Yes, sir, I sure would and believe I can," I say.

"Well, I'll see to it you're re-assigned to one of the division's units," he tells me. At his departure, I thank him and we're both hopeful he's successful with the transfer.

As a temporary bachelor I'm living in the Fort Lewis' BOQ. Among others housed there is a Red Cross worker whom I meet and befriend, a Jewish refugee from Mainz, Germany. Klaus Martin's story is interesting about escaping the Holocaust with his family in 1939, just in time, and then coming with his parents to the U.S. We strike up a friendship, and he explains he's only working for the Red Cross to give himself an income and time, while he develops a real estate business plan. He invites me to join his project, together with another lieutenant, Chas Patton, who's assigned to the post finance office. The three of us meet a few times to discuss plans, and each puts up his few hundred dollars for equal shares. Even though I can barely afford it, I find the project is exciting and I go ahead and sign the agreement.

Our pooled funds are for bidding on an old Army barracks building at Fort Lawton, a U.S. Army post located in the Magnolia neighborhood of Seattle. Of our interest is one of a number left over from WWII now being auctioned off by the US Government. If we're successful, Klaus will have the building floated down the coast and hauled to a small lot near Fort Lewis, on which he's made a down payment. Once moved, we'll renovate and convert the two-story building into a duplex apartment. The plan is to rent the apartments and eventually sell the building, hoping for a profit. If we're successful, then we'll try to do it again, as long as other similar old barrack buildings are still available. The exciting idea is entirely new to me, but it does seem pretty simple. Klaus assures us he knows what he's doing, and he has the whole project worked out in detail--at least on paper. It's only later I realize my naiveté in letting myself be involved in a project it could backfire. If we're not successful, the loss could be much greater than my investment and leave me owing a lot more.

So far, our bid for a barracks is successful, and Klaus, as planned, talks a transport company into floating the building on a barge down along the coast, then hauling it to the lot in Tacoma near the military base. The movement happens without a hitch and the structure is moved to the lot and set on a foundation of solid concrete blocks. I'm amazed and pleased at Klaus' ability to talk people into doing things without at least some payment in advance. In our off-duty hours, the three of us get to work renovating the building, both its inside and out.

For painting the interior, Klaus calculates the amount of paint needed and buys the estimated number in gallon cans. But soon, after we've applied some of the paint, it is so outdated it begins to blister and peel off the walls. Klaus immediately returns the paint cans, both those empty and still full, demanding a refund for all of them from the hardware store where he bought them. At first, the owner refuses, reminding Klaus he knew and agreed to the condition of the paint in the cans before he bought them. But when Klaus threatens to expose the store for selling a faulty product, one known outdated and probably worthless, the now frightened owner agrees to replace all the cans with new paint. Klaus is proud of his bargaining ability and leaves me amazed. I think he and the storeowner both knew the paint was faulty, and both took a chance with it, anyway. Though I say nothing about the transactions, I think Klaus should have accepted the loss or at least shared it. But instead, Klaus' threatening the storeowner leaves me wondering about his ethics and whether I want to continue working with him.

We repaint the building's interior, but it leaves me thinking, if a kind of dealing I've just seen is what it takes, then I'm no businessman.

Soon discharged from the Army, Audrey arrives and we set about to rent a house near Tacoma and Fort Lewis. The geographic area is usually kept damp with constant rainfall in all seasons. But in our luck, we're already enjoying warm and mostly dry weather and it turns out will even last through on into the fall. Washington State is lush with tall, beautiful evergreen trees, it's a new environment as new to her as it has also been for me. She also spends time getting acquainted with the area and especially the shops in Tacoma's town center.

Audrey's not used to being a housewife and left alone at home during the day. So, when I introduce her to Klaus, she's pleased to meet him and is excited about our project. In fact, she rolls up her sleeves and pitches in to help preparing the old building for rent. Like me, investing in real estate of any sort is also an entirely new idea for her. Caught up in the enthusiasm, she encourages me to continue in whatever Klaus' next project might be. Her eagerness continues until I tell her about the insinuations he's made about my ethnicity. After, we watch him more closely, we try to understand both his actions and commentary to develop an explanation for his conduct.

Our guess it's because he and his parents as Jews have been forced to flee Germany to survive, and Klaus counters those feelings of rejection by acting superior to the people he now lives among. He seems especially fixed on and makes belittling references to my Mexican heritage. At first, I take it as his way of joking, but eventually I bristle at things he says, like, "it's amazing you've become an officer." His actions and statements are classic reactions to the feelings of inferiority imposed on him and rejected as a Jew in Germany projected onto me as a Mexican American. Audrey's psychology schooling understands immediately

Klaus' behavior towards me is displacing his angry feelings of rejection. He boosts his ego with boasting about his business acumen, which he implies Chas Patten and I both lack. And meanwhile, he's having an ego contest with Chas, a Harvard Business School graduate. I can see Chas and I are both destined to be parting ways with Klaus.

When I get notified, I'm being reassigned to a US Army unit in Germany, I decide to withdraw from our ad hoc business group. Not surprising, Klaus isn't happy I'm leaving but assures me he'll refund my share and its investment, if and when he sells the building. Meanwhile, he offers to contact his former German friends in Mainz to introduce Audrey and me to them. We welcome the idea and think it will be an interesting aspect to the new assignment. Since I'm soon to be leaving Fort Lewis, I decide I don't need to face Klaus down about his behavior towards me. Having encountered discrimination for most of my own life, I think I can understand how he must feel as a Jew and especially now as a refugee. Apart from his attitude, I do find him interesting and want to avoid offending him and leaving an enemy behind. Our parting is friendly enough; though I now feel I may not want to continue associating with him.

In a few months after my departure, he does sell the building, refunds my share of the investment and profit. He then goes on alone to successful larger projects and the eventual wealth he's after.

In the meantime, the general I'd earlier escorted fulfills his promise. The order comes down reassigning me to the 5th Infantry Regiment's, First Battalion. Based on my experience in Korea, I'm assigned to the Headquarters Company as its Communications Officer. But with little need for field communications, once again I'm tasked with meaningless ad hoc assignments.

The new assignment in this headquarters company has not been much improved over my situation in the housekeeping unit. Commanding the company, Captain Peter Mantrey, in my judgment is incompetent and apparently angry he's been reassigned to command an infantry company. For most of his entire career he's been an aide to one general officer after another. Now, overage in grade, the Army has caught up with him and forced him into a regular infantry officer's command position. Unhappy in this assignment, he spends much of his time taking out his anger by finding fault with my performance.

Unlike a rifle company, its specific mission of training for combat, a headquarters company has more diverse support duties. I can't decide whether the captain doesn't understand the difference, or simply dislikes both his assignment and me. It's clear he has little interest in my background, so I conclude his behavior has nothing to do with me personally. The other lieutenant assigned to the company tells me he survives by always agreeing with the captain and otherwise steering clear of his attention. On a number of occasions, I bridle at orders for outside a headquarters company's responsibility, or the duties of the communications platoon I'm assigned to command. Of course, he's my commander and he knows I have to carry out his orders.

Events come to a head when he orders me to buy a semi-dress blue uniform, with an appropriate billed cap and ribbons. The sole purpose is for me to be formally dressed for an official dinner at the officers' club. He wants to show the battalion commander his company officers are in properly dressed and in full support of the dinner. He says he doesn't want to hear any excuses and refuses any discussion. Nonetheless, I still let him know I would follow his demands, if I could. But because I'm newly married and can't afford the necessary uniform, I won't buy it, nor will I attend the dinner, for which I would also have to pay extra for my wife and me. When he threatens me with an unsatisfactory performance report, I feel like I have to go over his head to the battalion commander, who, when I do, agrees with me. Unhesitatingly, he calls in the captain and gives him a dressing down. The colonel then excuses me from buying the dress uniform or attending the dinner. But, after this event, my life in the company only gets worse, though the captain now has to swallow any unjustified threats he might be contemplating.

Matters improve when I'm temporarily re-assigned in charge of live firing practice at the post rifle range. Since I've had successful experience in this type of operation, I'm now able to run the firing schedule smoothly. Whatever poor performance report Captain Mantrey planned to give me, he's thwarted when I receive a written commendation from the division commander for running the live firing exercises. Despite his grudging unwillingness, the Captain is obliged to endorse the commendation and adding his lauding remarks.

Thankfully, my troubled Fort Lewis assignment lasts only seven months. Relief comes with my re-assignment orders to the 10th Infantry Division in Germany. Audrey and I prepare for our immediate departure. Limited to ship only one automobile, we have to sell one of our two cars. Her Buick, a college graduation gift from her grandmother, upsets her about selling it. After a discussion, including tears, she agrees it's a few years older than my newer Ford and agrees to let the Buick go.

My feelings with great relief, on the first of November, we leave Tacoma in a driving snowstorm beginning what will be a long indirect journey to the east coast. We first head south along through Oregon and on to southern California to visit my parents. There we plan to spend a few days with them at Hermosa Beach before continuing to the east coast. Though I'm concerned about how they will accept Audrey, the visit turns out to be much better than I've anticipated. Whatever my mother might have been thinking about my wife before, Audrey charms her and my stepfather as well. They are especially pleased with her enthusiasm for the Mexican dishes they serve in their restaurant. Learning Audrey's trip to California is a new territory for her, on their day off they take us along on a driving tour of Los Angeles and Hollywood.

After the visit to Hermosa Beach, we continue on our drive across the country taking turns driving along the way without problems. The six-day trip includes a three-day visit with her mother and grandmother in Tiffin, Ohio. When leaving her hometown and continuing east, we almost immediately encounter storms of heavy snows, and continue driving on the now ice-coated Pennsylvania Turnpike. The drive includes a lot of dangerous skidding, including spinning wheels and one a heart-in-the-throat, 360-degree spin, before we can continue and finally check in at Fort Dix, New Jersey. There we learn, despite being married, we'll be traveling separately to Europe. I'm soon to fly across the Atlantic, while later, Audrey will travel by passenger ship with hundreds of other dependents. Sailing with her will be the car and our few household goods.

With little time to spare, she sees me off at the La Guardia Airport and turns in our Ford convertible for shipment. She and the car on the same ship will travel three months later to Bremerhaven, Germany. Meanwhile, waiting for her travel orders and departure, she bunks down in New York with a former college friend.

Within days, I'm notified and initially disappointed my assignment to the 10th Infantry Division has been changed to the Seventh Army headquarters near Stuttgart. I assume the change has been made according with my health recovery.

Within days, I take off as scheduled to fly cross the Atlantic for Frankfurt, Germany. And from there, I'll be heading south by train.

Chapter 20

DESK JOCKEY

ARRIVING LATE ON A SATURDAY EVENING IN STUTTGART/ Vaihingen, I check into the BOQ, located a short distance outside of the U.S. Seventh Army Headquarters. Fortunately, my arrival is just in time to get a meal at the Officers' Club, and finding it crowded with people dancing to a small band playing popular music. Everyone there looks like they're having a good time. I miss Audrey, who I know she would like the atmosphere in here, too, and I can easily imagine us enjoying it--when she joins me. Her absence reminds me it'll still be three months before she sails and arrives. My thoughts of her continue while I have a meal, then leaving the club to check in at the nearby BOQ, where I sign for a room, hoping for a good night's sleep.

Early the next day, as I'm eager to explore my new setting, I begin again with breakfast at the Club. It's not surprising to find the early Sunday morning dining room nearly empty, where a single man is having breakfast. After ordering from the chef, I help myself at the steam tables and approach where the man is sitting. He appears to be about my age, and when I introduce myself, he invites me to join him. In "civvies," Fred Stephens tells me he's also a first lieutenant assigned to the headquarters finance and accounting office. He has a welcoming and outgoing personality, and when he discovers I've just arrived from the States, he's quick to offer showing me around the nearby town of Vaihingen and later in the larger city of Stuttgart. During our breakfast conversation, to our mutual surprise we discover we've both been born on the same day and year, though in far different states. It's a happy coincidence and starts a friendship lasts for many years to come. I couldn't have asked for a better welcome to my new duty assignment. It begins the next morning, a sunny Monday.

"Jockeying," is called my new job, which means I'll be manning a desk in the G2 (Intelligence) Section at Seventh Army Headquarters. During WWII, the buildings and grounds headquarters now occupy, are known as Patch Barracks. In the past, it has housed a Wehrmacht, or a German army, garrison with apartment housing nearby for dependents. When my arrival in early 1958, the U.S. Army has long since moved in and established all the logistical supporting elements it needs for its forces and their families. Conveniences like hospitals, commissaries, Post Exchanges, even elementary schools, complete with American teachers are well established in the surrounding communities.

My initial reaction is one of feeling lost and left wondering what I can do here at such a high Army level. Still, the assignment is in keeping with the prescribed light duty following recovery from my TB. But the lost feeling doesn't last long after I meet my boss, Major Gandy, the G2 Section Administrative Officer, a fortyish bachelor from South Carolina. To my mind he's the stereotypical southern gentleman: courtly, impeccably uniformed, erect in carriage, and precise in his accented speech, or at least it once was. In the recent past, he'd suffered a stroke, leaving one side of his face distorted. But even so, he appears to remain very effective in his duties. His deep southern accent, and the effects of the stroke on his speech, detracts somewhat from the military image he's striving to present. In the early days of this assignment, my difficulty grasping his speech often leads to our mutual frustration. Repeating louder what he's trying to get across doesn't always improve my understanding. Though with a real effort and practice I eventually soon learn to comprehend the quirks of his locution.

The U.S. Seventh Army, the major American force in the North Atlantic Treaty Organization, or NATO, accommodates numerous member European military organizations. Their officers regularly visit our G2 Section. Major Gandy, charged with arranging meetings with our section officers, is usually the first to greet visitors. Despite the NATO officers all speak English, some are stumped understanding what Major Gandy's version is trying to say. Their response is sometimes a blank stare. It's in such instances when I'm pressed into service as Major Gandy's interpreter. This sometimes create comic situations, when the three of us, the foreign officer, Major Gandy and me are all speaking in English. But I'm still needing to "translate" what Major Gandy's version has to say for the foreign officer.

As I get to know him better, I learn, despite his disfigurement, bachelor Major Gandy actively seeks female companionship. Arriving each summer, he tells me there is a crop of young, single, female American schoolteachers, who are welcomed by the Seventh Army Chief of Staff. The event is one Major Gandy never fails to miss. His purpose ostensibly is to assist anyone who might need help settling in, but at the same time, he's surveying the newcomers to see which one he might approach. Though hardly a parent, he also shows up at PTA meetings to follow up his personal need. Despite these tireless efforts, I'm yet to see him with one of the teachers as a "date" at the Officers Club, or anywhere else. Though, he still might be squiring a new teacher around off post, as he always has suggestions about where to shop. He has my sympathy about the loneliness I guess he is probably experiencing.

Of his first demands of me are to handle his correspondence. Besides reviewing and correcting my writing efforts, he also lectures me on how to respond to other section officers, who are all senior to me. It's obvious he also feels free to tell me how to improve myself. I do find some of his critiques of my letter writing is helpful, but his advice on my self-improvement is unnecessary and not a little irritating. My tolerance fails to ease with his nagging, and I'm hoping for his reassignment, or if not mine. But it's about time I learn Major Gandy has another, more generous humane side.

In the second month of my new assignment, an impacted molar is causing a painful swollen jaw and I must have the tooth extracted. The Army dentist treating me in the nearby dental clinic is new on the job, and soon reveals his lack of experience, especially in the extraction operation. Try as he might, he fails to remove the tooth, and only succeeds in shredding my lower gum. His superior, a colonel, busy with other patients, finally becomes concerned; the usually short type of operation has run on for more than an hour. In the end, pushing his younger colleague aside, the colonel with a properly aimed chisel blow he cleanly splits the tooth and quickly extracts its pieces. But unfortunately, it's only the beginning of my suffering. I've already been in the dentist's chair far too long. During the whole time I've been bleeding profusely with my jaw stretched to its limit. Consequently, I've also swallowed a lot of my blood.

Later, alone in my BOQ room, with a swollen face and in extreme pain, I become sick from the ingested blood and start to vomit repeatedly. Failing to show up in the office the next morning brings Major Gandy to my room to check on me. Shocked at the sight of my swollen face, my sickly condition and the bloody mess of my bed, he takes over as my nurse. He checks my temperature, secures pain medication, brings me ice water, hot soup and arranges to get my bedding changed.

Over the course of the next two days, he returns every few hours to check on my recovery and sees to my needs. Throughout the fog of the ordeal, my appreciation grows for his caring humanity. I realize there are aspects of his character I will do well to emulate. Yet, once back on the job, I suspect there's been a looming administrative problem, which it may have motivated much of his concern for me.

One of Major Gandy's primary charges is the mass of highly classified documents secured in the section's caged repository. Though he's nominally responsible, the actual day-to-day managing of the storage daily falls to a captain or a lieutenant, who works inside the cage. From the present occupant I learn the two previous officers who'd held the job had been disciplined for losing one or more Secret and Top Secret documents. Yet somehow, despite their failings, Major Gandy has not been held responsible for their mistakes and his reputation remained unblemished. It's now suddenly clear my assignment to the G2 Section has been planned for me to replace the incumbent, a captain soon to rotate stateside.

My recovery and return to duty coincides with the completed background check for my Top Secret clearance. Then, it's when Major Gandy surprises by assigning me to understudy the captain managing the repository. After two weeks, he and I finish our inventory of what seem like an endless mass of classified paper. Relieved to find all documents are accounted for, the Captain warns me their sheer volume could be my serious undoing. On his departure, I take over with trepidation determined not to follow any careless habits of any predecessors. Assuming the job, I'm worried losing something classified could end my short career and a punishment besides. After a lot of thinking, I decide one of the best ways to keep track of the sensitive paper is to reduce its quantity. To quiet my apprehension with the job, I make the paper reduction is my immediate goal.

In normal practice, each document has to be signed out by the user, and on its return it's my job to log it back in. In short, the responsibility for the document at all times has to reside with someone authorized to have it. In the cage, meanwhile, I spend my time checking the date each document last been logged out. If hasn't happened for more than a year, it's probably outdated and I decide it's a candidate for destruction. Apparently, the idea has not occurred to my predecessors, or at least not often enough. When Major Gandy at first is reluctant to approve my plan, he finally comes around when I point out his refusal may leave both of us accountable for a loss. The possibility is one he doesn't care to test. So, in the end, he agrees to take my proposal to the G2 himself to whom I sell my idea as improved security. Impressed with my suggestion, the Colonel agrees it makes good sense and gives us the go-ahead. To get started, he sends a memo to office chiefs ordering any document, unused for a year and whose retention can't be justified, will be destroyed. I'm pleased when the document destruction begins right away.

In the absence of a shredder, the only other approved way to eliminate classified material is by burning. I have to do this in the presence of another section officer, both of us signing off on a destruction receipt. To determine whether a document should be destroyed, I first have to get the approval from the appropriate office. For each week's burning session, the duty to accompany me rotates among the section officers. Consequently, over time this puts me in touch with nearly all of the senior officers in the section. What I don't fully appreciate at the moment is those associations may be the ones to review my assignments when I return to the States.

As it happens, impressed with my initiative and enthusiasm, two of the senior officers learning I'm not a Regular Officer, suggest I become one, and offer to recommend me. They make it clear becoming a regular won't increase my pay or promote my grade. But more importantly, Regular Officer status could protect me from the reduction in force, or RIF, then underway throughout the Army. Thanks to them, well before my return to the States I'm not only promoted to captain but also receive a Regular Army Commission. My new status would now give me a measure of control over my future in the Army, rather than being left to the mercy of events.

As Major Gandy's reassignment approaches, he offers to get me out of the repository job to something more to my liking. Since I'm in the intelligence section, I tell him I'd like to learn more what intelligence is all about. When the new man arrives, Major Gandy arranges to have me reassigned to the 532d Military Intelligence Battalion. Its Order of Battle Unit is co-located in the building with the G-2 Section, and is only a few steps down the hall from the repository. The new assignment will also give me some sense of relief from the cloud of a document possible loss hovering over me.

Chapter 21

A BETTER INSIGHT

————————◆————————

MILITARY INTELLIGENCE ORDER OF BATTLE, AN INTRIGU-
ing new world for me, deals directly with enemy forces, their capabil-
ities and intentions. The work is interesting, and requires a lot of my
research on the enemy forces facing NATO, as well as something about
the history of their countries. My area of responsibility also includes
the Middle East and North Africa. Though the new assignment makes
me feel somewhat overwhelmed, the world it encompasses is suddenly
opening, and I take to it with enthusiastically.

At the time of my transfer, it happens that France is fighting in the
Algerian War of Independence. It's a complex conflict characterized by
guerrilla warfare, terrorism and the use of torture by both sides. The
conflict shakes the foundations of the French Fourth Republic. It leads
to a state of crisis, to various attempts to assassinate President de Gaulle
and follow with a number of military coup efforts. Because France is a
member of NATO and U.S. Army forces can be embroiled in the North
Africa area, the Seventh Army Commander needs to be briefed on
developments there at least weekly. The area falling within my responsibility, I soon find myself regularly briefing the commanding general.

As a Captain, I quickly have to learn to gain control of nervousness talking to a roomful of senior officers, including a four-star general. Fortunately, when I can't answer questions asked by someone in the audience, an older and more experienced captain backs me up with an answer, or the questions are recorded for a later response in writing. Between the regular briefings, I'm also called to bring the general up to date whenever events might imply Seventh Army's action.

Three months into my new assignment I'm notified the troop ship carrying dependents from the States, my wife among them, is to arrive at Bremerhaven with our household goods and our Ford convertible. Given a three-day pass, I take a train to the port to reclaim my wife and our car. I drive it off the ship to the dock and wave to Audrey as she descends the ship's gangplank. With a three-day pass hooked onto a weekend in my pocket, after gathering her baggage we have a leisurely drive back to Stuttgart, with overnight stops in picturesque villages along the way. The return to Stuttgart is like another wonderful honeymoon, especially after three months of separation.

Until military housing opens up for us, we have to live "on the economy." Prior to her arrival, in nearby Vaihingen, I've found a small, furnished top floor apartment in an old building just off the town's main roadway. Signing up and moving in, we set up housekeeping there and go exploring the town in what will be our temporary home. Adjusting to life off-post in the economy is at first an exciting and interesting experience. Among the arrival of our household items includes my spinet piano. Our hosts, who fortunately speak English, are very impressed with the instrument and tell me they'll be delighted to hear me playing.

A time later, when our spare households arrive, the two workmen delivering our belongings survey the narrow winding staircase to our apartment. Up through it they can see they'll have to maneuver the piano with care as they carry it up. Deciding it's possible, they don harnesses also surrounding the spinet and with little difficulty they start up the first stairway with the instrument. Fairly easy movement so far, they make it to the second floor. But they seem unaware the stairway narrows a bit more up to our top floor apartment. After starting upward, the final flight, within minutes with a lot of loud and encouraging German *Schwäbisch* swearing to each other, they make it up to the last turn. At this point they fail to notice one of the spinet's front legs is overhanging on the stair's railing. Instead of checking the cause of stopping them, they continue moving. With a final push, an awful splintering sound emits as one of the spinet's front legs is being nearly torn off. As the result, I'm without the piano for the next two months, while it is being repaired and paid for by the moving company. Our hosts, who could have warned the workmen about the staircase, but failed to, seem to disappear and have no more comments about the piano or asking about hearing my playing it.

At this time, the current German rate of exchange is four deutsche marks for one US dollar. At first, buying on the economy is misleading, as it seems like I've been received a big raise. Evenings and weekends, we're soon out and about in our neighborhood discovering stores and restaurants. One in particular, a second-floor cafe with a view of the town's main street, becomes a favorite. Rudi, the young friendly owner and chef, speaks English and is enthusiastic introducing us to his menu. In tradition, he prepares each dish on a portable stove at tableside. His wife, Trudi, who doesn't speak English, makes up for it with her smiling personality and efficient serving. To us, the menu prices seem wonderfully low and we try a different dish each time we visit. But we're soon to discover our visiting turns out a bit too often.

As wine lovers, the low prices turn us into becoming regular fruit-of-the-vine imbibers at our evening meals at home, as well. Audrey, meanwhile, is also learning how to cook various simple German dishes, and loves food shopping. But our privileged living on the German economy soon comes to an abrupt halt when we realize we have spent too carelessly and is leaving us nearly broke. The exchange rate being deceptive has also resulted emptying my wallet. I'm now forced to apply for an advance pay just to meet our necessary expenses through the rest of the month.

It's probably just as well there's no such thing as a credit card available at that time. Startled about our unleashed spending, we begin keeping a daily record of every *Pfennig* and *Mark* spent and making adjustments. This works wonders, not only controlling our spending, but our new habit also yields a month's small saving. We agree to continue the practice, even after leaving the apartment and moving to our military quarters.

After nearly four months, somewhat expectantly, we move to a new apartment assigned in a building once housed German Army Officers. It's located just outside the *Kaserne*, or headquarters buildings and barracks, and comes complete with furniture, linen, china and kitchenware. Though I have to give up my housing allowance for the residence, the ground floor apartment is far nicer, roomier and better furnished than anything else on the economy we could afford to rent. This is where we'll be living for the remainder of our four-year assignment.

One day shortly after having moved in a month, a woman with a young girl comes to the door and introduces herself and her daughter as refugees from Czechoslovakia. The mother is looking for a job for a means of survival as a housecleaner. By the time I return from my office in the evening, Audrey tells me about this woman and she'd like to help by hiring her to clean our apartment every two weeks. When I ask why she was taken with the woman, Audrey relates the woman's moving story the woman has told. Though with an accent, Gizela, the woman's name, relates her story in perfect English and wins Audrey's sympathy. What most impresses her is the woman's lack of an appearance of desperation, but instead maintaining a confident attitude and an upright posture. Gizela implies that she and her family were upper class Prague residents who've been forced out of their homes during the war and have become refugees. Her daughter, Adina, who appears to be about nine or ten years of age, also speaks English and maintains a confident poise, too. What the woman asks for a wage I calculate is possible for us to afford.

During the ensuing weeks, our admiring grows of her work and she's also very interesting to talk to. There are times when she is so fascinating, we forget she's with us for cleaning our apartment. One day when I have a day off from the office and staying at home, Gizela arrives for her job with her daughter. While her mother works, Adina approaches me with a box under her arm and asks, also in perfect English, if I would like to play chess. I have little interest, but also, I don't want to turn her away either. Still, I tell her I won't be much of a challenge, since I don't know the game. Without another word, she goes to the dining room table, opens the box and sets up the chessboard with the red and black pieces. She quickly explains how each piece can move and what consists winning of trapping the king and removing all of the remaining pieces of the other color. At first, I hesitate, feeling I'm about to be embarrassed, but go ahead anyway. By the time her mother has finished her two hours of cleaning, I'm being beaten soundly in every match. But rather than wanting to quit, I'm by now completely fascinated with the game and sorry Adina has to leave. There are few more times when we can match, but of course she always defeats my royals.

The end of our relationship with Gizela and Adina come when they arrive one off-day morning, not to work, but to say goodbye. She's now leaving to return to Czechoslovakia having regained her status and property lost during the war. We're really sorry to see them leave, as we'll now taking over the housecleaning ourselves, but glad they're returning to their home restored to them.

To take the advantage of living in Europe, in the New Year 1958, Audrey and I can't wait to begin discovering more of its adjacent countries. Our first goal is to visit the Brussels World Fair. Excited to learn it's about to open in the spring, I realize Brussels is only a day's drive away. We rent camping equipment and invite Fred Stephens to do the same and ride there with us. After touring the Fair, we want a fuller sense of Europe and decide to travel on to Paris. For three days, we stay there in campsites occupied by a variety of Europeans who give us a more immediate feeling of the European life-style. The trip is satisfying and we're already making plans for visits to Italy and Spain. Also, on our plans will include England, Scandinavia and even other parts of Germany.

Chapter 22

A TASTE OF CULTURE

——•◆•——

BEFORE WE LEFT FOR EUROPE, ONE OF THE FASCINATING events Klaus Martin has told us we'd enjoy is an annual celebration in Germany. We'd heard of the Mardi Gras in New Orleans, but didn't know the same type festivity happens in a number Catholic parts of Germany. Klaus, who grew up in Mainz, tells us the celebration there is known as Fasching, Germany's carnival season. He insisted we make sure we'd meet his good friends, Ernst and his wife, Gerda, living and working in Mainz. Ernst runs the family's meat store located adjacent to his house where his mother, his wife and their children live. They are the first of the German families Klaus suggests we should contact, which we do. Through Gerda we also later meet Helmut, her brother, who it turns out is a "Prince" in the group organizing the annual Fasching celebrations in Mainz. We're told Germany is undoubtedly the most enthusiastic Karneval center in Europe, and soon we find that it's probably true.

The celebration starts on the 11th day of November at exactly 11 minutes after eleven in the morning. The celebration lasts about three months until Ash Wednesday, seven weeks before Easter. There are many party activities going on, but we'll only be taking part in the happenings near the end at the stroke of midnight on Shroud Tuesday--also known as Fat Tuesday; it's the Tuesday before Ash Wednesday. Fasching is a festive time and merry making, and for some, it's a time to ignore rules if not breaking them. They make their own rules and make fun of others who do the same. Sometimes, we're told there are births nine months later out of wedlock.

Arranging on simple costumes, we soon find ourselves involved in a number of various parties, dancing and dining, though with little understanding about the many activities. While Germans may plan to involve us in the many Fasching stages, we are able to participate in only a few happening near the end of the period. It includes watching the fancy costumed parades with big street processions of elaborately decorated floats, and then later taking part in dining and dancing in costumes. While many others remain up all night for the arrival of Lent, we decide sleep is more necessary. The Fasching Carnival is celebrated in a number of ways according to different local traditions. But in Mainz, we're explained it's known as Fastnacht, or fasting night the eve of Lent.

The experience turns out to be a memorable one but not necessarily we'd want to repeat it. Even so, we're very appreciative for the generously fashion we are being hosted by Ernst and Gerda. Afterwards, impressed with the unusual opportunity offering us, we conclude Klaus had used his friends´ hospitality to correct his unfriendliness toward me during our Tacoma teamed duplex construction. But if so, this event doesn't necessarily erase it.

The friendship with Ernst and Gerda lead to other involvements. One, curious about the former military establishment in Stuttgart/Vaihingen, they ask to visit us there. Our visits to them also opens German life a bit more, and their visits to us in Vaihingen might do the same for them. I think curiosity is mainly motivating to visit, to see how we're living in former German Army officers' quarters. The other visits to each other's lead to an invitation to boating on the Rhine on their motorboat. Their hometown is near the banks of the large, long

Rhine River, which serves many purposes for the countries it's flowing through. The anticipation is exciting, including an invitation to waterski. It's a new experience for both of us, and though Audrey declines, I agree thinking it won't be all so difficult. It's until I watch the lunch dishes washed in the river and emptying over the side the contents of the boat's commode, my enthusiasm is curbed. Though I don't ask, right then it strikes me maybe it is a common practice using the river's waters for a large toilet. And if so, it's also happening upriver and down, too. Without further hesitation, I decline waterskiing, complaining a stomachache. It leaves me wondering if Americans do the same when using our waterways for entertainment, and if so, it really wouldn't be so surprising.

A month before a ten-day, NATO joint winter exercise, our G2 section is charged with providing two officers to give briefings on the daily status of the "aggressor" forces. Two of the section's majors, assigned to make up the intelligence briefing team, begin preparing right away for nightly presentations. As the start date of the exercise approaches, one of the team majors is suddenly faced with a serious condition at back home in the States. His request for an emergency leave is approved and he departs leaving his other team member behind to carry on. After requesting a replacement, the remaining major continues on preparing alone. But a few days later, while walking to work, he slips on a patch of ice, falls and breaks an arm.

Now, still faced providing with the briefing team responsibility, the G2 holds urgent auditions to select replacements. From among the section's and the nearby 532d Intelligence Battalion captains, three of us audition for the position, each presenting a mock briefing. Because the captain from Florida speaks with a deep Floridian southern accent, he is dropped. The other captain's speech also has a strong accent of the Boston's flavor. Neither of the typical regional accents will go over well with the Europeans, who may have difficulty understanding either of them. In the end, I'm chosen for my unaccented middle-America speech. It's ironic I should be chosen, as originally, I only spoke in Spanish. My selection is also reinforced by my experience regularly briefing the Seventh Army Commander.

At the outset, Captain Jon Murphy, from the military intelligence organization, seems pleased to be the other half of our briefing team. Already our preparations are behind in timing, we pack our gear and travel to the exercise location in northwestern Germany. Once there, we continue arrangements and get to work.

But, when Jon realizes we'll be presenting before a few hundred senior NATO officers and the international press, he has no briefing experience and soon gets cold feet. He complains he has no idea how to prepare a briefing, much less prepare the appropriate graphics needed and expected. Yet, even before our first practice presentation he's already stuttering with stage fright. Yet, when I tell him we'll be trading off in presentations to our unique audience, he suddenly wants out. Immediately, I ask for a replacement, but I'm told it's too late, and with Jon's state of shock, I'll have to carry on alone.

Following my former briefing practice, I write out my talks based on the incoming field reports up to date. For graphics to accompany the briefings, I make maps and symbols for the aggressor forces for projection on a large screen. On the first night, and for subsequent presentations, I come on stage wearing a beret and a scarf with a mock raised-fist salute of an enemy. In the firmest confident voice, I can muster, I go through the briefing without a hitch. The first night performance, and those following, makes me a minor celebrity. *Time Magazine,* quotes me for suggesting West German forces failing to take an objective.

Our four-year assignment is passing quickly, and we try to include some more travel to surrounding European countries, while we still have the opportunity and are mostly otherwise free. At about then, we've decided it's time to try to have our first child, even with the realization of how important that will be and how different our lives will be changed. Even so, we both agree we really want a family and the time has arrived for it.

By early August, though Audrey is showing she's well into her pregnancy for our child, we manage a visit to Barcelona for a few days. Then we continue driving on south along Spain's Mediterranean Sea coast to Valencia. From there we take a flight to the Mallorca Grande Island for a three-day vacation. While there, two events are most likely to be remembered. The first, each time when turning on the water in the small hotel bathroom's tub it delivers a couple of small, blind colorless fish swimming in the bathwater brought up from an underground well.

Later, in the second event, during the day while hiking around the island, we meet an Englishman about our age, also vacationing. He invites us to go into the main town of Palma for an evening of dinner and entertainment as his guests. He's in a celebrative happy mood for his day's earlier bid on a number of sealed crates he has won and discovers they're containing new electric motors. His luck continues when he's able to sell them immediately for more than a million dollars. It leaves us wondering how he knew he would have such success instead of considerable loss.

Our three days on the island pass quickly and soon come to an end. We're also very aware our living as a couple will be ending soon, when a new person is about to be entering our family.

Back in our Vaihingen apartment, we prepare a second bedroom as a nursery for the anticipated birth of our baby to be born in the nearby military hospital. Audrey, and already having contraction periods, as I drive her there early for the birth, we have the expectation the baby will join us in a completely healthy condition. I stay with her in her hospital room while she continues to have cramps and the associated pains her body preparing to deliver. I hope to remain there with her during the birth event, but, when it's at hand, the head nurse asks me to leave. She assures me while the birth may be exciting it is also expected to be normal.

As I'm in another room nearby waiting, a sudden commotion of activity sounds seems to burst within Audrey's room. The delivering doctor, a Spaniard, rushes from it to another nearby, his face frowning and his attention focused, and as quickly he returns. Without any words to me while passing, he also looks very anxious; leaving me immediately alarmed and very concerned the birth is anything but normal. But within a few minutes, he returns smiling and tells me in his accented English, "You are the father of a boy." He invites me to see him, and assures me the baby is normal and his birth successful. After a moment, when I ask about the sudden commotion, he also tells me the birth was a breach and the baby's breathing starting was delayed a few minutes while his air passages were being cleared. The sudden commotions were fearful about possible complications and even hearing it's been a normal birth; it still leaves me concerned.

When I enter Audrey's room, she is holding our son with a full head of hair, who is asleep in her arms. While she looks exhausted, she otherwise appears happy. She then says our son will be staying in the nursery and she will also remain there overnight, too. We also agree to give him a name the next day for his birth certificate, which will also showing his birthday as September 27, 1960.

When I arrive the next morning to pick them up, she still appears worn out, but seems happy to have become a mother. I'm also very happy having become a father, though I still have some doubts about the birth being trouble free, despite the doctor's assurance about his health and robust. Then we agree to name him Robert II, rather than Junior.

During the few weeks following Robbie's birth, I've enrolled in one of the night courses offered by the University of Maryland, its overseas program. Eagerly, I enroll in a basic German language course, as wanting to gain some ability as quickly as possible. To speed the process, I also engage an English-speaking, retired German schoolteacher in Stuttgart. Besides the income, she's delighted to have an enthusiastic student, and goes out of her way to enhance my study. As part of her German language instruction, with Audrey and me she attends a series of the Wagnerian Ring cycle operas then being performed in Stuttgart. She explains they are four very big operas, all linked together by the same story. But after attending the first two, we decide it's enough to provide the opera's essence. Despite Hitler's fascination with Wagner's operas and music, the experience leaves me as a fan of these operas thereafter.

After nearly four years of living in Germany it has become somewhat home-like. It has turned out more agreeable than we might have imagined. As my tour nears ending, I'm notified on my return stateside, I'll be attending the Infantry Officer's Advanced Course at Fort Benning, Georgia. Acknowledging their interest and help, I thank the two G2 Section officers, who are so important contributing in bringing about my regular commission. And now they have again come through with their promise to boost my career. Still, I'm faced with the decision whether to make the Army a full career, or leave it as I've originally planned.

Chapter 23

THE TINKER TOY

———•◆•———

EIGHT MONTHS LATER, FOLLOWING ROBBIE'S BIRTH, OUR small family flies back home to the states. During the flight, he becomes infamous on board when he develops a fever. After landing, the chief pilot holds all the passengers delayed until a doctor comes aboard and clears Robbie's fever and determines it isn't contagious. Meanwhile, Robbie shakes off the fever, suddenly restores himself to health and greets passengers with a big "Hi," as each passes our seats. The three of us only get a lot of unfriendly looks from our temporarily quarantined traveler mates.

Once we're back in Columbus, Georgia, for his first year's birthday in September we buy him an electric train. To promote his creativity, adding a Tinker Toy set also seems appropriate. With it he can build bridges and skyscrapers for his train to traverse and pass through; at least, I imagine he will do so eventually. Together on the living room floor of our rented house, we get his career underway learning to be an architectural engineer and well as a railroad baron. All this seems a bit complicated for him just now, but I'm pleased how eagerly he explores the possibilities of the Tinker Toys. Seeing the possible constructions pictured on the box's cover, he starts at once to familiarize himself with the parts and pieces, getting both their intimate feel--and their taste.

During the past year, this time with my family, I've been back at Fort Benning to attend the year-long Infantry Officers Advanced Course, and have passed through it successfully. Meanwhile, our President John Kennedy's inauguration has introduced the idea of the "New Frontier," bringing major changes to the armed forces. As Kennedy's message ripples down the chain of command, we're told all officers should be airborne qualified. So, on completing the Advanced Course and before moving on to a command assignment, I enroll in Fort Benning's "Jump School," though admittedly with some trepidation. Meanwhile, Robbie is expanding his own boundaries progressing in Tinker Toy construction by creating abstract art, he at least just now understands their recognizable structures.

While I've never given much thought to jumping out of airplanes, I've known a number of others who have done so and yet to tell me why. But now, because it has become a possibility for me, I've decided to learn more about the parachute idea. It's been around for a very long time and I've always found it fascinating. In 90 BC, for example, a Chinese emperor used the air-resistance of two extremely large bamboo hats. He attempts jumping from a variety of altitudes and while hanging under them, surprisingly he survives. And later, in the 15th Century, Leonardo da Vinci had sketched but never tried his parachute idea. It took adventurist Frenchman, Louis-Sebastien, in the 18th Century to land successfully from a high tower using a device he called a *para-chute*. Since then, both his idea and its name have remained with us.

But even his state of the art still has failing to convince me of its safety. Now, facing with airborne training about to begin, I have to give the idea some real serious consideration.

At age 30, I'm pretty sure I can meet the physical requirements, although, breaking an arm or a leg on landing could put me out of commission for quite some time. And I can imagine the embarrassment of my fear freezing at the airplane's door, and even dying. But given the high survival rate for the jump course, the latter seems unlikely. Still, there remains the question of my stamina and earning my parachutist's wings with all of me still intact.

As a new father I have to ask myself why do this at all? Would the lack of the parachutist's qualification hinder my advancement in the Army? I find it hard to believe my future could rest on this one capability. Nonetheless, my doubt lingers while waiting for the course to begin. Still, I have more second doubts about future assignments being constrained by this failure to qualify. I know airborne infantry operations have been almost entirely replaced by helicopter-borne assaults. Even so, I also know the Army brass has nostalgia for WWII airborne heroism, and can't seem to let it go, even though helicopter landings are decidedly more predictable and much safer.

In the end, I recognize my rationalizations are excuses founded in the fear of falling, typical of most humans and other wingless mammals. I admit to being afraid, and know I have to overcome it to succeed in the course, about to begin. Finally, in mind going through and exhausting arguments pro and con, I decide to place my trust in the equipment and the competence of the trainers.

Landing from a jump, despite the parachute's slowing the fall, one still hits the ground with a substantial impact. A team of physiologists and doctors has figured out the best way to minimize injury is to land so no part of the body's bone structure directly contacts the ground. In learning to be a paratrooper, I'm taught to fall so it's our muscular areas will absorb the impact in sequence. If done so correctly, the fall thus distributes the shock along the body's entire length. It means not landing directly on one's feet, which would transmit trauma up through the bony joint structure of the ankles, legs and torso. Rather, the feet are kept together in a glancing touch of the ground only long enough to turn the body so it falls along its muscle-padded length on one side or the other. Our trainers assure us this technique is a proven way to hit the ground safely, but of course with a parachute.

Army training of any kind proceeds in graduated steps. The first one in Airborne School is Ground Week, learning how to fall in a way so as to minimize, or better, to avoid injury. This is not only logical, but also reassuring. The physics of falling is startling. Within seconds, a body reaches a velocity of 32 feet per second. Once opened, with 260 pounds suspended beneath it, the parachute slows the fall to 23 feet per second. This total weight consists of a 200-pound jumper with 36 pounds of combat equipment and 15 pounds of a reserve parachute. Here's the question: would my 165 pounds fall at a slower rate with a lesser impact on hitting the ground? I'm soon to learn it won't.

Ground Week starts off with a daily run in formation followed with a rigorous session of physical training, or PT. As a captain, I run with the majors and lieutenant colonels. But in learning how to fall, gravity treats us all the same way. We spend a lot of time practicing and perfecting the Parachute Landing Fall, or PLF. Our instructors, known as Black Hats, have us continue until they're satisfied, that is, we've learned how to do it properly. Starting at a height of less than a foot, we move up to platforms of various greater heights, even as high as four feet. Then we jump into pits of sand or pebbles to simulate an actual landing.

Practicing the PLF over and over does take its toll on the body. After a day of this, there's hardly a part of me not sore. At the end of the day, I look like I've been beaten up, my fatigues sweat-stained, wrinkled and dirt-covered. Five days of this can't end soon enough. Before we're finished, we'll be making jumps in a harness from higher towers. I intend to meet each requirement of the course, though not without fear of injury. We're told, if we follow instructions we'll get through it all in one piece, make jumps and still be able to get up and fight. Well, it all remains to be seen.

In the second, or Tower Week, we jump from greater heights. First from a 34-foot high platform, an apparatus called a Lateral Drift Assembly. Despite the complicated name, it amounts being attached to a pulley on a cable simulates landing while moving above and across the ground as if being blown by the wind. Once buckled into my parachute harness, in turn it's hooked to a pulley on the cable above my head. Jumping and briefly free-falling from this platform gives a shock much like what I'll feel from having jumped from an airplane and feeling the jolt from the parachute's opening. The harness must fit properly on the upper inside of each thigh to avoid squeezing the critical groin, and especially to prevent pain and trauma. An improper fit could put an end to future fatherhood, not to mention the startling agony exploding an involuntary shriek.

Suspended in the harness and jumping from the 34-foot platform, we ride the cable to a dirt mound about 50 feet away. This is known as the swing-landing trainer. It's the same type of rig we'll later be using at the 250-foot tower. And lest we forget we'll be jumping from an airplane in flight, we must learn to get from our seats to the aircraft's door without stumbling and getting tangled. To simulate our serial, or one after another leaving from an aircraft in flight, to avoid stumbling we're also taught to shuffle on our way to the door, rather than walking. Once there, we stand for only a moment or two before jumping out into the void.

The next question: how do you get from your seat to the exit? It's the Jumpmaster who controls it, by ordering, "Stand up, hook up, shuffle to the door." Added to this mantra will be: "Jump and count to four." These last five words for the final order are also very significant.

The end of the second training week is marked by parachute jumps from the 250-foot-high tower, and the transition from ground training to actual parachuting. Further instructions are steps seeming to come rapidly one after the other. I make a special effort to assimilate those steps during the parachute flight: exiting the aircraft, the parachute's opening shock, and then the deployment of its risers. The risers are the numerous ropes connecting the jumper's body harness to the parachute's silk canopy. When the canopy is properly opened, while moving downward, its possible to steer the parachutist's flight direction by pulling on the risers in the direction wanted. Pulling makes it possible for some steering the parachute even into the wind, and aiming for the center of the Drop Zone.

By now, the critical procedure is etched into my memory. First, making sure the canopy has opened. If it hasn't, panic won't help. Instead, at the right moment, I must know when and how to deploy the reserve parachute I've been carrying on my chest. We're also taught how to control the swinging back and forth during the descent. There are also types of landing dictated by the terrain and how to act when the parachute is dragged by the wind. Now, this is a lot to learn, needing to assimilate and doing it so, quickly!

By the end of the second week, we've completed practice of individual skills, and our training now switches to coordinated team action. Finally, we're deemed ready for Jump Week, the third in which we're actually jumping from an aircraft!

During the weekend at home, my wife, recalling my earlier doubts, wants to know how I feel now about the parachute training? To begin with, my earlier thoughts about breaking something, or losing my life have all but vanished. I now look forward to putting into practice what we'd been training for during the past two weeks. She also confesses to worrying every day I might get hurt, or worse. Now, however, we're both eager for the first of five jumps will make me a qualified parachutist. Audrey and Robbie will promise to be there for me every day I jump.

After a restless night, Jump Day dawns clear and warm, and finally I'm to jump from a real aircraft in flight. In a short time later, awaiting us jumpers in front of the hanger at Lawson Army Airfield, there are two World War II, twin-engine, twin-tail U.S. Air Force transport airplanes. It will be a very short flight from there to another field known as Fryer, or also as the "Fryer Drop Zone." In fatigues, combat boots and a steel helmet, the main parachute harnessed on my back, and the reserve on my chest, are awkward, but still manageable. Some 50 of us mill around in the "ready room" waiting for the order to load the airplanes. The looks on the faces of my companions are all smiles, all also hiding the anxiety I'm sure we're all feeling but are reluctant to expose it, much less share.

The aircraft, we're briefed, will fly at 1,200 feet high and at an air speed of about 150 miles per hour. My heart already beating faster, we board our airplane and take seats along both insides of the fuselage. We now wait as the flight crew completes its "pre-drop" and "slow-down checklists." The lines of jumpers on both sides of the aircraft are known as "sticks." By now I'm deep in thought, hoping I'll remember all we've been taught, and especially review what to do if my main parachute doesn't open. Yikes! I have to make the effort to resist pushing away the alarming thought.

The Jumpmaster abruptly interrupts my train of thought with a barked order for the stick opposite ours to: "Stand up." As one, the men rise from their seats, turn and face in the direction of the jump doors. On the command, "Hook up," each man holds the hook on the end of the strap attached to his parachute and fastens it to an overhead cable running the length of the cabin. As he jumps from the aircraft, the other end of his strap will pull out the parachute and break free. By now, I'm only thinking about the Jumpmaster's next orders. At his command, the standing "stick" on its side of the aircraft on order will begin "shuffling to the door." A "green light" turns on. He orders the "stick" to begin its shuffle to the airplane's exit, and one after another, men begin jumping out, continuing until the last man has gone. But, if there's been an emergency reason to stop the "stick's" movement, a red light can halt the process before the last man has left.

My "stick" is still seated while the aircraft begins circling back to the start of the drop zone. I know I'm within seconds for my brief time at the door. The "green light" comes on again and, in a firm voice the Jumpmaster orders, "Stand up, hook up." He pauses, then orders, "Shuffle to the door." My fear suddenly vanishes and is replaced by the strange sense I'm being outside of myself, watching my own movements. The effectiveness of our training then kicks in. When my turn comes, I stand briefly with a hand on each side of the aircraft's door, and jump! I immediately cross my arms on my reserve parachute, one hand grasping the reserve parachute's handle, to pull if needed, my head facing down and eyes wide open, checking to make sure my feet are together. All those moves are done in a quick, deliberate set of motions. All the while I'm yelling at the top of my voice, "ONE THOUSAND ONE! ONE THOUSAND TWO! ONE THOUSAND THREE! ONE THOUSAND FOUR!" On the last count there's a sudden jolt--as there should be--and with it, exhilaration as I feel the shock of my parachute snapping open. Whew!

Suddenly, I'm left in silence as the roar of the aircraft's engines fade away. Floating down, I look to see if I'm headed to the drop zone. In the remaining few minutes of my descent, I grab two groups of risers and pull them to steer me toward the drop zone. The almost dreamy fall seems to last only seconds, my excitement so high I hardly feel the bump of my PLF landing. But when the slight wind begins to pull at my parachute, it brings me back to the present. Instinctively I run in the parachute's moving direction and around it to deflate the billowing canopy, and then begin gathering up its silk.

Once I have it under control, I reach for my canteen, unscrew the cap and raise it to my lips; at the same time, I look toward the guest bleachers hoping to see Audrey and Robbie there. But they're too far away to find them in the crowd.

So surprised, I throw back my head and roar with near hysterical laughter. It happens as I start to drink, when I feel a strange object bump against my lips and I know instantly it's a piece of Robbie's Tinker Toy. Through this small object, I feel like he's been with me on the entire way as if urging me. I laugh thinking of him putting the piece into the canteen. Tears fill my eyes and stream down my face. A sense of his presence lasts a few moments, as I feel his approval with a sense of relief. Then, wiping my face and shaking off the moment, my focus returns to the job at hand. Collecting my parachute and other gear, if any, I move on to the rally point at one side of the Drop Zone. A bus waiting there will return us to Lawson Army Airfield. The afterglow I'm feeling of the successful jump briefly seems to continue.

To qualify as parachutists and graduate from Airborne School, we have to complete four more jumps, one of them made at night. The jump schedule is based on the make up of the class, the weather and the availability of aircraft. The first jump has greatly diminished my anxiety. But the effect is well known at the school and we're warned accordingly not to let up in our caution and attention to detail. There are schedule changes and jumps made under different conditions. One is made without carrying a load, known as the "Hollywood" style. Another is with a full combat load. The rest of Jump Week is somewhat chaotic, with large groups of soldiers gathering in the ready-room waiting to be loaded onto aircraft, one stick at a time.

Immediately after our second drop, and collecting our parachutes and gear, we're bused back to the airfield to make the third jump. The fourth, executed on a moonlit night, fails to raise my anxiety. The reason must be the thoroughness of our training--or is it just a false sense of confidence? I'm not so sure. The fifth and final jump seems routine, even regarded as a formality.

Almost as an anti-climax, graduation takes place on Friday, the last morning of Jump Week. My wife and Robbie have watched all of the jumps at the Drop Zone, and are at the Graduation Day ceremony to pin on my parachutist's wings--it is, of course, after Robbie has had to handle the badge, which I'm thinking he's helped me to earn it.

Successful completion of airborne training is rewarded with two weeks of vacation before continuing on to a new assignment. For some time, we'd been thinking about traveling to Maine, a place neither of us has ever been to before, but close enough to drive to and return within our short furlough. So, I make reservations at an inn in Kennebunkport. Rob is excited about a promised fishing excursion.

My surname is not the easiest to pronounce. It's more often mispronounced and I'm used to having correcting it, if needed, for people I meet. Yet, arriving at the inn, it's a pleasant surprise to hear the desk clerk greet me with, "Welcome to Kennebunkport, Captain Sanabria," perfectly pronounced.

Smiling and pleased, I ask, "Excuse me, but how do you know the correct pronunciation of my surname?"

"Two reasons," the clerk replies. "First, I collect stamps, and the author of one of the famous books of international stamps was published by a man whose surname is, Sanabria. The second," he continues grinning, "is because I was one of the pilots flying one of the airplanes you jumped from at Fort Benning a short while ago." Now really grinning, I extend my hand to shake his, and tell him, "Well done for both!"

The fishing is also wonderful. On the water our last day, we rescue a man who's fallen overboard from his boat. Afterward, we catch enough mackerel to feed all the guests at our Inn. I couldn't imagine a vacation with a better memorable ending.

Chapter 24

COMPANY COMMANDER

FIVE YEARS EARLIER, BASED ON SOME STRATEGIST'S IDEA, the Army infantry division has been reorganized into what's now known as the Pentomic Division. The descriptive term refers to a restructuring of the Army infantry and airborne divisions to answer the threat of tactical nuclear weapons on the battlefield. It's a meaning way of referring to five subordinate battle groups prepared to operate as a division in an atomic or non-atomic environment. Similarly, each battle group is reorganized into five infantry companies.

In the fall of 1962, with graduation from the Airborne School behind me, I move on to the 2d (Indianhead) Infantry Division located in another part of Fort Benning's expansive acreage. After reporting to the First Battle Group's headquarters, I meet its commander, Colonel Edward Planer, who welcomes and informs me of my assignment as the commander of Company D, or as Delta. I'm very pleased since command is the most desirable assignment an officer, junior or senior, can achieve in the infantry at the appropriate level. I know again I owe this opportunity to a couple of the senior officers with whom I served at Seventh Army Headquarters in Germany. They've followed through with a recommendation for any command assignment for me.

Commanding a unit of some 180 men is a much greater challenge than I've met before or even imagined. I've been suggested to get a feel for the troops I've inherited by checking the Company Punishment Book, usually kept by the company's First Sergeant. To my chagrin, the review depicts a high percentage of Delta members who have punishment records. The significant number of AWOLs, is another basic measure of a unit's morale and its level is also not very high. Even so, I know at the beginning of a new command is the best time to effect changes in attitude. I want to start out right, and let the men know I intend the unit to be the best company in the battle group, as well as in the division. It's equally important they know I'll treat them fairly, while expecting in return will be their good conduct and discipline.

On my first day, I show up immediately after reveille at 0530 hours, something, according to the First Sergeant, known as the "Top," tells me their previous commander has rarely done. The men, including the Top, appear surprised I show up at all. After breakfast, I have the Top call a full company formation to which I introduce myself and announce new company policies.

The Top calls the company to attention, turns, salutes me and joins the ranks, signaling I have the command.

"At ease," I call, and carefully pronounce my surname, then carry on with, "I consider it an honor and a privilege to be your commander. Right here and right now," I continue, "I want you to know I'm starting out fresh with you. Whatever problems you've had in the company before me, I'm declaring the slate clean." My statement stops the murmuring in the ranks. "It'll be up to you," I tell them, "whether your record remains clean and you move ahead," I pause, and add, "or not." I take time to make eye contacts, with some of them. "You'll learn more of what I expect of you as time goes on. But know it will be designed to make Delta the best company in the battle group, if not in the 2d Infantry Division. One more thing," I add, "every Tuesday evening after chow, beginning at 1800 hours, when possible, I'll be in my office for two hours and available to talk with you individually about personal problems. It's the only time you'll have direct access to me without going through the chain of command of your squad and platoon leaders."

I call the company to "attention," order it to face right and to march forward. Then I order, "double time, MARCH!" keeping the pace up for the next twenty minutes. I continue the double time practice every morning possible, increasing the time to thirty minutes. I re-introduce the so-called "Jody Cadence," which I know they've also learned in basic training.

For the next few days, including in my requirements I tour the barracks, and note the Company Day Room is disorganized and dreary. Besides daily inspections and weekly grades, I also set up reward 3-day passes for the members of the winning platoon. I also have the Top review personal records to see if our company has any members who are artists. He identifies three who are willing and I have him conduct a contest to produce a scale drawing of a military themed large painting for filling one of the dayroom's walls. The winner suggests an image of an historic 1907 battle scene of our American 9th Infantry Regiment soldiers. In July of that year they were fighting off an attack by Chinese during the Battle of Tientsin. Once the mural gets underway it excites the whole company's interest. When it identifies them with our unit's history, there's a noticeable lift in morale. And soldiers from other companies also want to visit to see the mural.

I want the company to think of itself as a cohesive unit. To achieve it, I modify the training schedule, from time to time, so squads and platoons operate as coordinated elements of the company as a whole. To give a more realistic sense of how a company is supported in combat, I request, through the Battle Group Operations Officer, Division engineers assist when our digging in and laying mines for the defense of our positions. The Division Operations Officer, or G3, is delighted with my requests and goes on to support my orders for other division support units to coordinate and supply signals, transport, artillery and close air support. This kind of complete battlefield support training has only been imagined, not actually carried out. Our battle group commander, impressed with my initiative, orders the other companies to follow our example.

The training program is interrupted in early October by what becomes known as The Cuban Missile Crisis, the country alarmed over the confrontation between the US and the Soviet Union. The Russian deployment of ballistic missiles in Cuba, confirmed by U.S. Air Force U2 photography, is the closest the Cold War has come to escalating into a full-scale nuclear war. The U.S. Navy is ordered to blockade Cuba to prevent more missiles reaching the island from abroad. While tense negotiations with the Soviets are ongoing, our division is ordered to prepare to invade Cuba. In the next few days, the assistant division commander solemnly addresses division officers, one group after another, alerting us to the real possibility of a war. The threatening situation brings a dramatic change in the attitudes and attentions of our men.

New soldiers from other units around the country begin to arrive bringing our division units up to full strength. In a short time, my company reaches its authorized full-strength of 250 men. More weapons and equipment arrive to fill the table of organization and equipment requirements. Meanwhile, from other companies one platoon at a time is sent to North Carolina to practice boarding and disembarking troop ships could be taking our battle group to land in Cuba.

Meanwhile, my Company Delta is selected to begin training with armored personnel carriers. They would carry us ashore in an amphibious assault on Cuba's northern coast. In this atmosphere of impending war, company energy and morale is as high as it's ever been. Training in attack formations with attached tanks and in the personnel carriers is exciting, difficult and serious. My goal is to maintain command of my newly mechanized unit while landing under fire on a Cuban beach. Making the order more real is the issuance of maps for the planned assault on the Cuban northern coast. The exercises are sober and keep us focused on the task at hand.

The arrival of four 2d lieutenants to command my platoons emphasizes the dead seriousness of preparations. There's nothing like the possibility of being sent into combat could tend to increase anxiety, but it also raises morale and individual effort. While it lasts, I find this new atmosphere exhilarating, a feeling my wife doesn't share. I try not to think about leaving my family behind, or even my possible death. I'm sure the same feelings permeate the thoughts of all the married men and their families.

Near the end of November, before we have a chance to settle in to our new strength and training, the Cuban blockade suddenly ends. All offensive missiles and Russian light bombers are withdrawn from the island. As rapidly as it increased, our strength is reduced and special training abruptly ends, too. The company returns to its former size and resumes its normal schedule. What we're especially sorry to see is the departure of the chief cook, who came with the personnel buildup. Imported from some higher headquarters unit, he had marvelously improved our meals to near gourmet quality. If not missing going into combat, we feel we've taken a casualty in the mess hall. I can only hope our regular cooks have learned something from the excellent cook, temporarily with us, and take a new pride in their daily offerings.

Despite the improved condition of my company in many aspects, the battle group commander seems constantly displeased and with difficult to get along. Conferring from time to time with the other four company commanders I learn Colonel Planer's years of command have been of--a desk. He's concerned if his present command assignment isn't successful in every respect, he might not be considered for promotion to general officer grade. To assure the battle group shines in the division's eyes, he inserts himself into each company's routine operations. In addition, observing our training in the field, he holds Saturday morning inspections, issues demerits for the least fault. His aide takes notes of his findings, which the company commanders receive the next Monday morning with a requirement to reply by endorsement. On more than one occasion I stand at attention in the colonel's office explaining why a soldier's rifle has a trace of rust in its barrel. The fact the weapons are quite old, leftover from WWII and Korea is no excuse, he insists. He hovers over field training exercises, issuing letters about deficiencies he observes, and requires letters of explanation.

For all his meddling, the commander defeats himself during a battle group field training exercise in South Carolina. In the mock battle we face another battle group representing the "enemy." At one point during the ten-day exercise, we're to be carried in stages in three Sikorsky helicopters across a river obstacle. The colonel insists on using one of the three choppers to observe from the air the movements of his troops. Consequently, by nightfall the two choppers have only been able to transfer my troops and those of one other company across the river. Because the choppers aren't equipped to operate in the dark, they're forced to leave the colonel stranded and unable to get him across, too. Because he's not there, he won't be able to command our two companies in the planned night attack against the "enemy." As I'm the senior officer present on the ground, I assume command and organize our two companies into a task force for the night operation.

Before departing for South Carolina, I've put out the word I want a bugler who can play reveille and other calls, including the bugle call for the cavalry battle charge. One of my soldiers reports he played the bugle as a boy scout and knows the entire repertoire of Army's regular calls. Luckily, he has brought it with him to the field hoping he might be able to use it. Now here, I've been hoping for the bugle-playing soldier would have a chance to do his stuff. As it happens, our current circumstances leave me in command of the two-company taskforce night attack, and I decide this is the chance I've been hoping for. I'm sure if the colonel were present, he probably wouldn't allow a bugle sounding a charge, since we're hardly cavalry.

The other company commander and I plan the "surprise" attack to launch just after dusk. It's to be initiated by the sound of the bugle, launching troops firing rifles and flares bursting in the night sky. With both companies in position when the time for the assault arrives, I order the bugler to sound the attack. Its inspiring notes pierce the darkness sending both companies shouting and firing as they march to overrun the hill in front of us, and startling the "enemy" holding our objective. As our attack arrives on the hill, the defenders have already fled. Taking the now abandoned hill is still no less exciting, while we're digging in.

The next day, he says nothing, though I'm sure the colonel has heard about our night attack, complete with light and sound effects. I suspect he wishes he had been commanding to be afterward commended, as I am, by the mock battle's umpires. I never learn whether he has ever received his coveted promotion, either. But for me, our night attack was almost exciting as the wild night of firing I'd experienced years before in Korea.

Social unrest in Mississippi provides another chance for the company to operate as a cohesive unit. Alerted we might be sent to enforce the presidential order to integrate the public schools there, we begin training controlling crowds more like military police often do. We've barely begun the practice when we're suddenly ordered to Oxford, Mississippi. Traveling by truck convoy on the way through Alabama provides a realistic sense of being against the "Enemy" in our own country. Passing through small towns, our convoy is booed, stoned and picketed by local townspeople. Fortunately, by the time we arrive in Oxford the showdown has come to a peaceful resolution. But every bit as threatening, if not more so, is the return trip through Alabama, where nothing has been settled as far as the Alabamians are concerned. I have to wonder how my southerner soldiers feel. I can imagine if conditions were to worsen, they might want to desert us and fight with their Southern comrades.

During the past few months, I've been proud of the way the company has operated. Yet some individual soldiers can't seem to get my message: good behavior and performance pay off. One day, a squad leader brings to me one his soldiers for discipline. Roger, who, despite a few years of service, has never been promoted beyond Private First Class. Talking with him alone, I learn he's been given repeatedly the most menial of tasks, like latrine duty. I can see how he feels denigrated and acts accordingly. I reassign Roger to the company's headquarters platoon and direct its leader to give him more meaningful tasks. During our next field operation, he's given the job with laying phone lines between platoon defensive positions. He does it so well and quickly, on our return to the barracks I promote him to corporal, a grade he should have received long before. The new grade brings a profound change in his attitude and conduct. Observing the changes in him makes me feel I'd made the correct assessment and followed with the right action.

On another evening, a squad leader brings in a private of Nisei Japanese ancestry, who has repeatedly failed to obey orders. In my talk with the soldier, I dwell on the disgrace his poor behavior can reflect on his family. But I've apparently misread the problem correctly, and I'm troubled when a few days later the soldier goes AWOL. I'm left wondering if I've taken the wrong tack with him, pushing him on to more serious refusal of duty. If I've made a mistake with him, I know these personal problems are valuable lessons in leadership.

My assignment to command I've learned there's no substitute for experience in leadership with its inherent responsibilities.

Chapter 25

A RESHUFFLED DECK

———•◆•———

NOTHING SEEMS TO STAY FOR LONG BEFORE IT CHANGES again, and apparently the Pentomic formation is no exception, as the concept seems to have run its course. In the New Year, orders come down returning the infantry division to its previous triangular three-regiment organization. Each of the regiment's three battalions are also reorganizing to a complement of three rifle companies. Two of the former five Pentomic battle groups will be disbanded, mine being one of them. In the re-organization, the new, 9th Infantry Regiment's 2d Battalion will be commanded by the battle group's former operations officer, Lieutenant Colonel Jack Sampson. My little known of him at the time, he requests I'll be his battalion's operations officer. Colonel Sampson, about ten years my senior, knowing my reputation as a company commander, he later tells me he will "allow" me to learn my new job on my own. And as for the battalion's operations requirements, he prefers not to supervise my every move, as did my last boss.

During the first few weeks in my new position, I arrive early and stay late getting my head around the scope of the job's aspects. My main task is getting company training schedules organized and getting them underway. Besides doing regular infantry training, while now operating as a tracked mechanized unit, it has to make extra efforts to bring the battalion up to an operational level. Our battalion's major headache is keeping the old personnel carriers in operating condition.

Two months into my new assignment, a major arrives to replace me as the operations officer. Colonel Jack immediately assures me this new arrival has no reflection on my performance. The position simply calls for an O-4 grade, a major, who has been assigned by division to fill the position in our battalion. He might have the correct rank for the position, but I can see right away he is neither experienced, nor up to the job. Instead of asking me to help him get up to speed, he only chooses to avoid the job by shifting onto me every requirement he can. When I don't seem capable of keeping up with the many requirements and actions, they start to fall through the cracks. He also tries to convince the battalion commander to believe any lacks and all failures are my fault. But during after a few daily staff meetings, it doesn't take long for Colonel Jack to unmask the major's ineptitude and wastes no time to get him transferred. Then, once again I'm back in the saddle, so to speak. I take over as operations officer again and get the 1,000-man battalion ready for a six-month's temporary duty tour in Germany. Our battalion will go as part of the Planned Rotation of Tactical Organizations, or ROTO Plan as known, in the event of an enemy attack. The plan is designed to keep stateside units familiar with potential operations to reinforce the US Army units currently stationed in Germany.

Attached to the 8th Infantry Division, our battalion's six-month temporary duty has to become operational quickly. Stationed in Mannheim, Germany our mechanized unit is also subject to monthly alerts. Then, like all the other Division's units, when alerted we have to mount up in our tracked vehicles and move to a regrouping location within a certain time frame. More than once, our battalion reaches its destination ahead of the division's regular units. After the second time it happens, the division commander takes notice and visits our battalion to congratulate our success. I also shake up the division's general's staff by asking for a statement of our battalion's training and combat missions, as the other division's elements already have. Apparently, no one has thought of it before and now they must spell it out, especially should we are suddenly faced with combat operations.

The highlight of our battalion's six-month temporary assignment is a ten-day exercise at the cold, rain swept and muddy Grafenwöhr armored field training grounds. In the three-day peak of the exercise, our mechanized battalion, reinforced by a troop of tanks, practices deployment in response to a mock attack by the Soviet Union. Following our defensive early-warning operations, we're finally to stage a withdrawal. It's my job to organize and control each phase of our operations, especially the withdrawal. In its role each company takes a turn deploying to provide protective cover while the forward companies withdraw through them.

While managing each phase to Jack Samson's satisfaction, I remain in control for nearly 72 hours without rest, or sleep. The controlling umpire finally decides I'm overworked and declares me a casualty. Forced to retire, I sleep for the next sixteen hours. Though I receive an overall high-performance grade, I also get a demerit for failing to yield control of operations to my assistant, a lieutenant, within a reasonable time. It seems I've over-managed some of the operation. Nonetheless, the battalion's performance during the exercises receives a high grade and a commendation.

At the conclusion of the field exercises, and as the battalion is preparing to return to our Mannheim barracks, a promised hot meal the first in more than a week, fails to show up. Under control of the battalion's executive officer, a major, for a time the supply trains lose their way. But when they finally arrive, the food is cold and the troops are hungry and understandably highly disgruntled. Though it fails to help the immediate situation, Colonel Jack fires the responsible executive officer on the spot. He appoints me in his place for our return to the states and to remain in the position as long it takes to find another executive officer replacement.

In the fall, with the battalion's return to Fort Benning, I receive orders to attend the Command and General Staff College at Fort Leavenworth, Kansas. Though still a captain, this promising development suggests I'll continue moving up in the ranks. There are two levels of the study at the staff college, each differing in length and the detail of material content. I'm to attend the shorter, four-month session, indicating my chance is highly unlikely of ever attaining general officer status. This revelation is disappointing, though I've never really aspired to reach the grade. In fact, I've been somewhat amazed, starting with my success in OCS, that I've gone as far and fast as I have.

The course material at the Staff College is interesting and well within my grasp of understanding. As the end one of a week's session approaches, an Army pilot classmate, who shares my desk, offers me to fly with him to visit his family in Milwaukie for the weekend. It's not only a visit for him; he's also accruing required flying hours. He assures me we'll be back in time for class Monday morning. After our arrival on Saturday evening landing in Milwaukee we're unaware the city has suddenly plunged into a deep freeze. On Sunday afternoon, preparing for our return flight, we discover the airplane's frozen engine can't be started. As the pilot, he's required to remain with the aircraft, though he's able to help me catch a train for the return to Kansas. But unfortunately, the returning train won't get me back to Leavenworth until Monday's mid-morning. In effect, this makes me AWOL and I have to appear before the school's commandant, a brigadier general. Fortunately, he's lenient and my course grades are good. When told of the circumstances, my tardiness is forgiven and is not considered grounds for dismissal.

Graduating successfully encourages me I'm at least eligible for promotions to three more grades, to colonel.

Shortly after returning to Fort Benning, I'm promoted to major and re-assigned as the training officer at the division's G-3 (Operations) office. Based on my experiences as a company commander and a battalion operations officer, I'm tasked with rewriting and simplifying the division's thick training manual. I'm commended for going through the manual and rewriting sections, adding others, eliminating some are duplicates or also outdated.

It's during this period President Kennedy is assassinated. The shock of his death shuts down division operations for two days. Shortly after, I receive orders to enroll at the University of Maryland, for the next year and a half, where, finally, I'll finish my bachelor's degree. Following graduation in the spring, the same orders direct me on to Vietnam, which hardly comes as a surprise.

Maryland's academic environment is one I enjoy, but the campus is beset with anti-war sentiment, strong opposition to our fighting in Southeast Asia. When it's discovered I'm an Army major bound for Vietnam, a number of classmates try to talk me out of going, believing, I guess, as if they could. But in the meantime, at the time and place their arguments sound senseless and unconvincing.

I graduate on schedule in early May, taking a BA Political Science degree with honors. It leaves me feeling I've finally made up what I'd felt failing by dropping out of college years before. Now it's time to check in at Fort Holabird, Maryland to attend the Army Intelligence School. The course is designed to prepare officers for Vietnam assignments as intelligence advisors to units of Army of the Republic of Vietnam, or

ARVN. Meanwhile, I've applied for transfer from the Infantry Branch to the fairly new Military Intelligence Branch, a move approved while I'm still at the university.

As a New Year's Day resolution on January 1965, it includes my decision to stop smoking. The habit, or addiction, is so deeply entrenched I've been smoking three packs a day. In the past, I've been smoking the day's last cigarette in bed, before turning out the light; I light up again as soon as I rise in the morning. There's no doubt I'm a slave to nicotine. My teeth are nicotine-stained, as are my fingers. Some of my shirts and ties are dotted with small holes from burning ash. To help kick the habit, following a "cold turkey" determination, I try mouthing on a hard candy whenever I feel the need to light up. As days go by, the urge lessens to smoke, and by the end of January, I'm cigarette-free, though at the cost of gaining some weight.

While attending classes at Fort Holabird, I'm with a group of officers, almost all who smoke during the breaks between classes. I'm feeling so smug about finally breaking my habit, I can't seem to resist telling others of my success. And as if to prove I could smoke occasionally without being re-addicted, I then allow myself to be talked into accepting a mentholated cigarette. The first puff I inhale doesn't make me cough, but by the time I've smoked half of it, I'm vomiting. I'm so sick I have to leave class for home, where I'm ill for two more days. It's a harsh penalty to pay for showing off, but now I'm certain I'll never smoke again.

As the date for my departure for Vietnam approaches, tension at home is growing. Three-year old Robbie doesn't know what's happening between Audrey and me. But I can tell he senses I'm preparing to leave, without them accompanying me, especially when he starts telling me with his heartbreaking, "Don't forget mommy, Daddy." Audrey is putting on her stone face, and I'm feeling guilty as though I'm abandoning them, possibly going off to my death. The trip to the west coast is so long, it only prolongs the "good bye" of my departure. Having them traveling there with me would only be to watch me fly off to Vietnam. So, I'm not surprised when Audrey declines and spares Robbie and herself the discomfort of the trip, which I can't help but agree.

While in California, before continuing on to Saigon, I first visit my mother and stepfather at Hermosa Beach and then spend a few days in San Francisco with Major Richard Cape, an Army doctor friend, another who also shares the same birthdate and year with me. His wife has shared Audrey through occupational therapy school, and we've enjoyed our relationships at Fort Benning and visited them in Panama as guests.

During the weekend, I also visit Klaus Martin's mother, who remembers my brief involvement with her son years earlier in the Takoma's real estate project. His parents, Jewish refugees from Mainz, Germany, have resettled in San Francisco and also established a handbag business. While we were in Germany, his mother had asked Audrey and me to scout at handbag exhibitions in Frankfurt and buy a few samples for her; she didn't like what we chose and leaves us with both the cost and the handbags. At least I've learned another lesson from the experience.

Now widowed, Klaus' mother is certain I will die in Vietnam. She insists on seeing me off at the bus station on the morning I leave for the San Francisco airport. She makes it no secret she's going to be there to keep me from going. I'd hoped she wouldn't come, but true to her word, early the next morning she shows up at the bus station. While I wait to load the bus, other passengers stare as she loudly begs me not to go. Her pleading is so sincere I don't try to hush her, or even ask her to stop. Instead I take her in my arms, hug and thank her for her sincere concern. As I turn away to board the bus, she's still pleading repeatedly,

"Don't go, please, don't go there, it's war and you'll be killed!" As the bus departs, she remains anchored there waving to me. I feel it's her own experience in Germany facing the possibility of her and her family's being imprisoned in one of Europe's Holocaust death camps.

Strangely, as my bus departs, I flashback to the years before when my mother stood at the Los Angeles train station waving desperately as I left for the Air Force Base in San Antonio, Texas. Departures are rarely seemed if ever happy.

Chapter 26

THE HIGHLANDS

———•◆•———

WHEN THE BOEING 707 LANDS AT TAN SON NHUT AIR BASE
in mid-June and I step off, everything evaporates I've read or heard
about Vietnam's Saigon. Though we've landed outside the city, its first
impact is a nauseating smell of rot. The stench grows worse as we reach
the city's center by the bus carrying us new arrivals for processing in
the headquarters of the Military Assistance Command Vietnam, or
MACV. The source of sickly-sweet odor is garbage, lots of the rotting
remains of vegetables and fruit. With other waste, it's strewn all along
the roadway's median strip waiting to be picked up. A delayed collection, I'm told, is a leftover practice that goes back to the years of French
occupation. While it may be true, the Vietnamese haven't made any
more efforts to correct it.

In a few minutes later, on Saigon's crowded main drag I encounter
hundreds of belching motorbikes jousting with as many taxis and military vehicles. Their horns all seem to be blaring and engines roaring
making an endless ear-pounding cacophony. The sidewalks teem with
a human motley: peasants bent under heavy cargos threading their way
through others scurrying in the opposite direction. Uniformed soldiers,

some armed and most not, many couples of them surprisingly holding hands, seem to be everywhere. There are also women, and more often young girls carrying a baby brother or sister on a hip appearing unperturbed in the crowds. Noticeable in this mass of humanity, seemingly mindless of the swirling turmoil, other attractive young women sail along, aloof in tight-fitting, white silk tunics and loose leggings under split full-length skirts. Some let their long shiny black hair falling to their buttocks. Their unique *ao dái* costumes, with the long, flowing split-skirts give them the air of floating gracefully through the throngs.

My fascination with these young beauties distracts me momentarily from feeling little hands touching, even stroking my bare forearms. My first impulse is to bat or shove the boys away, thinking they may be angling to pick my pockets. But in the next moment I realize it's the dark hair covering my exposed forearms intrigues them gathering around me. Obviously, what fascinates them and about what they're pointing to and chattering among themselves is the hirsute man in their midst. I'm so unlike the hairless arms of their fathers and brothers. Finally, chuckling, I allow each of the four to touch and stroke my forearms before shooing them away.

A few hours later, assignment orders in hand as I leave the MACV processing center, I almost trip over my friend Major Ralph Kanton. I've known Ralph, a Finance Corps officer, years before in Germany. We'd been good friends there and, seeing him again in this place, makes it seem less exotic. While nearing the end of his tour in country, we've been in contact prior to my arrival. The reunion still comes as a welcome surprise. And so, does the invitation for dinner he's planned the evening at one of the city's best French restaurants. He has arranged another surprise: a young, attractive, English-speaking Vietnamese woman as a dinner companion for me, a friend of the mistress he has taken on for his stay in country. To my questioning look, the temporary wife practice, he tells me, was common during the pre-war years, when the small U.S. Military Assistance Advisory Group (MAAG) trained and provided logistical support to the Army of the Republic of Vietnam

(ARVN). Now, despite the spreading war, if possible, many of our soldiers, marines, airmen and even government civilians still resort to the practice. It leaves me wondering what they tell their wives, if anything, when they're reunited back home.

During lunch, Ralph recounts highlights of the years since we've last seen each other. I'd known and liked his former wife and ask if they'd ever gotten back together again.

He shakes his head and speaks as if looking into his glass of beer. "No, I'd tried everything to keep her, but failed," he says. "We'd married in college and soon after had the two children you knew later in Germany. Yet, while stationed there, she met a German ski instructor and decided she wanted to stay and ski with him. It meant leaving me and the kids when we returned to the States," he says. "It took them and me some time to get over it," he explains. He adds that he'd gotten past feeling sorry for himself, and come to realize he apparently hadn't been all the man she wanted and needed.

"That hasn't been easy for you and the kids," I say.

"You know," he adds, "I finally learned the truth about nice guys finishing last." But eventually, he says he learns to accept his freedom as a blessing, leaving him unfettered to know other women, something he'd missed by marrying so young. "And it may be why," he says, "my Vietnam experience has been such a revelation." And in regard, he says his Vietnamese lover has taught him more than he ever imagined. Now he struggles not to become so deeply attached to her, as they both know they'll soon be parting. Leaving her will be a repeat of unhappy separation, but this time he'll be the cause of the breakup. About it, he says, "She's desperate to accompany me to the States. And I have seriously considered it, but I can't justify it either to myself or to my children." I listen without comment.

Smiling as we part, he suggests pleasures of the flesh are available later, if I wish. As an afterthought, he warns, "Don't be caught out after the 2300 hours curfew."

It occurs to me he has assumed some responsibility for my welfare and enjoyment. But he really has changed! Not the same gentle, conventional Ralph I've known in past years.

During my orientation week in Saigon, I hope to be able to have more time with him. He seems eager to show me around and give me the inside story, as he sees it, of our rapidly expanding combat operations in the country. But because our schedules fail to coincide, it's not to be, nor will I ever see Ralph again.

On the early morning of my third day in country, I catch a taxi to Tan Son Nhut for an Army flight to Pleiku, the major central highlands settlement and headquarters of the II ARVN Corps. After the hour-long hop, I'm introduced to the advisory team staff led by Colonel Ted Mataxis. I've been assigned as the assistant intelligence advisor to the Corps G-2, ARVN Lieutenant Colonel Nho Tan Nghia. My immediate boss, American Lieutenant Colonel James Allred, seems genuinely delighted to see me. But mainly, I soon learn, it's to turn over the intelligence advisory tasks to me, so he can spend more time improving his tennis game. I'm just as happy to have him stepping aside so I can dig into the substance of the job. The formalities completed; I want to get right into the enemy situation.

My arrival in Pleiku coincides with the advent of the monsoon season. Expected is the Viet Cong (VC) summer campaign of regimental-size attacks by the North Vietnamese Army (NVA) in various parts of the highlands. I don't doubt it's true. I have a lot to learn and need to do so quickly.

Surprisingly, Col. Nghia and I rapidly reach mutual respect, as my enthusiasm to find the enemy seems to match his. I have no doubt he takes his G-2 assignment seriously. While his interest is genuine, there's another motivation: He's also wealthy and has business interests, which include supplying MACV with large quantities of rice from the Philippines. The rice is then also doled out to ARVN troops, whose combat operations have depleted or have since been denied the in-country supply. Together with his wife, Col. Nghia also owns other businesses, which include a drug store in Saigon and a hotel leased to the U.S. Air Force at Tan Son Nhut Air Base. Our presence in the war no doubt is helping to protect his investments.

Without immediate contact, our knowledge of enemy activity is based on where they've been, rather than knowing where they are, or likely to be. In other words, until made contacted the enemy situation at best is opaque. To get a grip on their whereabouts, we try to synthesize information from various sources to create a pattern of the enemy's presence and movements. The large map of the II ARVN Corps area in the Intelligence Advisor's Office is cluttered with a lot of outdated sightings of VC activity. It doesn't even serve as history; much less provide the enemy's recent positions. With Colonel Nghia's help, I acquire and use a few more transparent plastic sheets to overlay the map of the corps' area each showing reported activity by type, date, location, and source of the information. Looking at a display of up-dated reports may reveal a lot more about VC and NVA movements. Now we have a more rational approach to counteraction.

When the map and overlays are brought up to date and kept so, I ask for Col. Ngia's opinion.

"This is good," he says. "We should have done this before."

"Thanks, and you're right," I say, "but it's not good enough. The map only shows us what's happened before, in the past. We have to know more about what the VC and the NVA are planning to do next." As I talk, Col. Nghia's blank expression makes me wonder if this is his way of saying I'm just re-inventing the wheel.

Instead, he says, "Everybody would like to know the future," he nods.

"I know it's impossible, of course," I say, "but we can begin to make some educated guesses. You know this area and what's in it, and especially what the VC need." He looks at me again with that blank expression. I wait, hoping he won't just walk out of the office. But instead he's actually been listening.

"The VC need food for themselves and to feed the people to protect them and to recruit more fighters," he says.

"It's what I'm thinking, too," I agree, "They'll be going where they can get those things, right?" Nghia takes a step closer to the map nodding. Now we're soon making educated guesses we hope will produce results. Our daily reports to US forces and MACV are soon given high priority. More importantly, they're also producing some timely successful contacts with the enemy.

Chapter 27

EARLY ENCOUNTERS

TWO MONTHS BEFORE MY ARRIVAL, THE VIET CONG HAD attacked the team's compound leaving a few advisory members wounded. Since then, there've been other attacks on outlying settlements and Vietnamese Special Forces positioned to protect local rice farmers and villagers. Within a week of my arrival, the VC, reinforced with an NVA unit, attacks a settlement southeast of Pleiku. Meanwhile, a battalion of Vietnamese marines has been dispatched to drive off the attackers. In such situations, the II Corps headquarters team flies by helicopter into the settlement area, to set up air support and determine the need for reinforcements of men and supplies. This time, my boss, LTC Allred, assigns me to accompany the team to gain some first-hand combat experience. While flying in with the team in a HU-1 chopper to the battle area, I'm at once fearful and excited at the prospect meeting the enemy of VC/NVA face to face. But upon landing, we soon learn just before our arrival the attackers have been driven off by a Vietnamese Marine battalion.

My eagerness for actual combat experience evaporates when I see the corpse of the outpost's US Army advisor, a captain, who would normally have briefed our Corps team upon arrival. While airborne in a spotter aircraft and directing artillery fire during the attack, he has been shot down. Now, awaiting a body bag, his remains are laid out on the ground, the missing top of his skull exposes his brain. How could it happen? I'm wondering. Our advisory team chief will see to it that his remains are extracted and his family informed of his death. The advisor's assistant gives us its briefing. But, the results of the battle scene also gives its own kind. I'm now more aware what has happened to the captain how easily it could happen to me. On the return to Pleiku, I'm aware the experience has left me shaken.

A month later, another outpost in a jungle clearing near the Cambodia border comes under attack. Once again, I'm assigned to and take off with the hastily assembled II Corps team, this time in two helicopters. As we near the site we can hear the sounds of the battle still underway and getting louder as we close in. Two US Air Force fighter-bombers are strafing and bombing to suppress the firing of VC/NVA troops dug in the jungle at one end of a makeshift airstrip. Under cover of the fighter planes, our choppers swoop in, hover low above the runway just long enough for us to jump off and make a crouching dash for the nearest bunkers. While the choppers race off, enemy fire increases. Bullets are snapping all around us as we make our short, heart-thumping dash. I cringe, fully expecting to feel the impact of one or more bullets. Amazingly, none of us is hit. I'm only armed with a .30 caliber carbine and with one spare a 15- round magazine, presumably to protect myself. I know I've no business doing much besides getting out of the firing zone. I end up in a bunker manned by a few ARVN troops and locals with none of them I can talk to. It's clear I really have no role in the defense of the outpost and don't know how I can be of assistance otherwise. I manage to find my way to the other team members so at least I'll know what's happening and be ready when it's time to fly out of there.

Two British correspondents, who've hitched a ride with our team, seem wide-eye thrilled to be in the combat area at first hand. But, with all their questions, they're also a huge burden, and getting in way of the support efforts. Now, hunkering down and with our air cover gone, the volume of enemy fire increases even more, suggesting that the VC/NVA have dramatically reinforced and may try to overrun the outpost. But a short while later, two more US Air Force fighter-bombers arrive to cover our position. Under their firing shelter, a US Air Force, twin-engine, C-123 cargo plane swoops in, lands and unloads the outpost's ammunition resupply. With its engines still running at near full throttle, the crew shoves the last of the ammo crates off the plane, and it takes off again in a steep climb. At the same time, outpost defenders rush out to gather in the ammunition crates and haul them to cover.

The Author is the Major in the middle holding a carbine, assigned to the U.S. Military Assistance Command Vietnam (MACV), as intelligence advisor to the Army of the Republic of Vietnam, II ARVN Corps in 1965.

During the next two hours, firing continues and so does spotty air protection, until our coordinating activities in the outpost are finished.

With no English-speaking leaders present, my main job is staying out of the way and observing the self-reporting activity. Called to return, the choppers arrive and hover low over the airstrip. Once again, with bullets flying all around us, we make a run for them and pile in. But right away I can see there are more of us clamoring to get on board than with our team arrived. The choppers could now be dangerously overloaded, maybe even unable to take off at all. And if so, I'm thinking we could be stuck here for some time and possibly be badly shot up. While our chopper's engine is increasing, we're still sitting on the airstrip. It's when the second of the Brit correspondents finally makes a frantic dash from a bunker for our chopper, now waving and screaming not to be left behind. At the last minute, the crewman near the chopper's door hauls him in. The Brit plops his overweight rear end right on my lap. For seeming more endless breathtaking seconds the chopper shakes and shudders at full throttle struggling to get off the ground. Finally, able to lift enough to tilt its nose some downward and forward, it finally heads up, over and out of the firing area.

Still sitting on me, the trembling Brit blubbers, as if the pilots could hear him.

"Don't go that way, you'll be flying over them!" he shouts, as if he has insight. "Now we're flying over their enemy positions! We'll be killed! I'll be shot!" Any fear of my own is squelched in disgust with the terrified man on my lap.

By yelling, I tell him, "For Christ sake, I'll be the one hit before anything reaches your fat ass," I shout in his ear. "Now, shut up!" Pounding on his back is finally enough to stop his screaming, but not his continued shaking and softly crying.

Later in evening, back at our make-shift club in the Pleiku compound, the Brit is now in his cups and telling anyone who'll listen how he'd nearly been shot and barely made it out of the attacked outpost. I'm wondering what he'll write about the experience in his dispatch, and especially of his role in it.

After four months in country, my first R&R break comes around and I have to decide which of the southeast countries to visit. Of the nine destinations available, Bangkok, Hong Kong and Kuala Lampur seem to be the most popular. Seven days leaves are also permitted for R&R in destinations of Hawaii and Sydney, due to their greater distances. After canvassing a number of the other members on our team, some seem most interested in visiting Australia. But others really enthuse over Bangkok as a more exotic stimulating realm. After checking with two or three of our team members, who have been to either country, I decide Thailand might offer a more unusual land than an English-speaking Australia.

Finally, among of our Pleiku advisors I canvass one I've befriended, a civilian working on airborne propaganda broadcast missions. He not only praises Bangkok, but also has a wife and daughter living there and allows me to contact his family. He assures me she'll be happy to recommend where to dine and shop to buy tailor-made silk clothing, the latter I especially want an outfit made for my wife.

Landing at the Bangkok Suvarnabhumi Airport, I hire a cab and arrange for the driver's availability for my five days in the city. We agree his total payment will be a combination of 20 US dollars in cash and the bottle of Scotch I've brought with me for trading. The driver takes me to my first stop, the hotel also recommended by my friend.

Once I've registered and rented the room, I call my friend's wife who seems pleased not only direct where to shop, but also to show me the city if I'm interested. Accompanying her would sure beat being alone. How could I refuse? I invite her and her daughter to lunch. She turns out to be a petite and a very attractive woman, who recommends a well-known restaurant favored by the Thais. During lunch, she presents me with a list of tailor shops she says are honest and fair, both for the quality of their work and their reasonable prices. She also suggests I'll find interesting the Thai version of horse racing to which I invite her and her daughter to go the following day. Meanwhile, she also recommends the Thai's version of kickboxing for the following evening, to which she graciously declines to accompany me.

As our contact continues, I suspect it may be my imagination I'm beginning to pick up from her a seeming air of forlorn. If so, it would be understandable. But then my mind progresses to wondering if she may be looking for companionship. I admit to my own loneliness and suppress the temptation to suggest we spend more time together. I know any move on my part would not only be betraying her husband and friend, but I could also leave behind a disaster, especially if I were to act on a misreading. It's why I hesitate to accept her dinner invitation at her home for my last night in Bangkok. But in the end, I accept it anyway, determined whatever gentleman I am, I'll ensure playing the straight arrow and leave early.

By the time of my return to Pleiku, my friend has received a complete report of my time spent with his wife and daughter. Within days, I send her a copy of one of my favorites, The *Rubaiyat of Omar Khayyam*. I'd brought a copy with me, which I'd mentioned during dinner at her home and learned it was also a favorite of hers. The gift caps the short memorable R&R. It turns out, when I've returned, I'll be seeing her and her husband once again later in Washington, DC.

For seven months I've successfully stopped smoking, though at the expense of gaining weight to 185 pounds, 20 over normal and climbing. With the increased weight, comes the need to let out the waists of my fatigues to wear them comfortably. And now I know the truth of what I've heard about stopped smoking: it increases one's weight because nicotine curbs appetite. Once the habit stops, eating tends to replace the urge to smoke. Whatever the reason, I'm determined to get my weight down.

My first effort is just to try eating less, figuring reducing my food intake at all meals is all I need to do. But the result has little measurable weight loss. In addition, I also give up my daily evening beer, the only I imbibe, but again with no noticeable results. Determined, I really need to get my weight under control, I decide to reduce the food intake even more severely by eating only the day's evening meal. It takes a while to get used to the hunger growling in my stomach during the day. But at last, I see my weight start to fall, though still not significantly. What finally brings about the weight control I want is a workout combined with the reduced meals. When possible, I work out daily with weights, calisthenics and a morning run, increasing up to a total distance of three miles.

Once back in the States and for the next five years, I'll be sticking to the weight control program and even get used to eating only once a day and running five miles. I'm told what my eating practice is unhealthy, but it does work and I remain fit, in spite of the practice.

Chapter 28

COMPOUNDED LIFE

SINCE MY ARRIVAL IN PLEIKU, BECAUSE OF THE INCREASED number of advisors, some are required to share doubly the available BOQ quarters. Now, in our compound, in most there are two officers per room, each equipped with a set of bunk beds, a bathroom and two portable armoires. By chance, sharing with my room is another Army major, a former in my OCS class at Fort Benning, Georgia. Though I knew of him there, I didn't have any real association with him. Now, we're sharing the same room and I'm assigned to do so superficially. In the 12 years since we were in The Infantry School, he has also become an Army Aircraft pilot. Beside our mutual awareness of each other in Georgia, we haven't had any personal contact since then. Though we now both share the same room, we still don't have much in common, or any reason to be more than cordial and apparently are friendly.

Our shallow relationship holds for a couple of months, until one night he comes back drunk from our makeshift officer's club. He's tipsy and long faced as he enters the room. Recognizing his condition, I should have limited myself beyond greeting him briefly and continued silently getting ready for bed, as I usually do. But seeing he's obviously upset, I decide to engage him.

"Ron, are you OK?" I ask.

He looks up, angrily, and says, "No, I'm not OK."

"Well, that's too bad," I say, trying to show some concern. "Do you want to talk and get it off your chest?"

He waits a few moments and then answers, "I've just learned I've been passed over for command of the Army Aircraft Detachment here," he tells me, his speech slightly slurred.

"That's tough. I'm sorry," I say.

"Yeah?" he blurts, his face, twisted and now reddened with anger, "what the hell do you care?" He now is nearly shouting and glaring. "You think I don't know what you are? I'm from Texas. You don't fool me and I know your kind!"

Instantly, it's obvious he's referring to my Mexican heritage. Momentarily, his attack leaves me speechless. But within a few seconds, I tell him off.

"You don't know what you're talking about. First, you're nuts if you think I've had something to do with your being passed over. I didn't even know you were being considered, but how your acting right now really may explains why. If you think attacking me makes you feel better, you really are sick. I've had to put up with people filled with hate like you all my life, and I won't put up with it. Now, besides losing the promotion, you've also just lost any respect I may have had for you."

The next morning, sober, he attempts to apologize for his behavior.

"Look," he begins, "I'm really sorry. I was angry and a little drunk."

"Oh, I know all that, crap!" I tell him, "and I don't accept your poor excuses. You might be sorry for mouthing off at me as you did, but your sick prejudice is still there. It's what you need to work on," I say, and walk away. If there'd been some conversation between us in the past, now there's none, nor will there be. My next act is to get him or me moved.

Among the officers in our billets there a few who are older and have a room assigned singly. Even so, they don't occupy it and actually are living in the nearby village. One of these majors shows up once in a while in the compound with a Vietnamese woman and two children of preschool age. Though I never question it, the children look somewhat like they're the officer's mixed-race kids. During the day, while he's at work in the nearby headquarters, the woman and children stay in the room next to mine, or they play outside in the quadrangle's garden. From time to time I encounter them, whom I presume are his family. Neither the mother nor the children speak any English, so our meetings are only a few nods and smiles.

One morning, as I'm leaving my room, the neighbor major is standing outside the door of his room, and calls to me. "Say, have you got a minute?"

"Sure, what's on your mind?" I reply.

"I've just received orders to return Stateside and I'll be leaving here in three weeks," he says.

"Well, it must be good news for you," I answer.

"You'd think so," he says, "but I have a family here you've probably seen sometimes outside your room, or in the quad."

I nod. "Yes, I've seen and acknowledge them sometimes now and then. What about them?"

"Look, I have a family back home in the States, too, and I can't get another extension here. I have to do something about this, or rather, I mean for my family here. I care about them and want to leave them with someone to look after them."

"Well, how do you see that happening?" I ask.

"I thought you would like to have her. She's a good woman and a good lover. I'm sure you'll like her." He's now almost pleading. "And the kids are very well behaved."

For a few moments I stare at him in disbelief. He's talking about them as if they're pets or commodities. I can't believe he thinks I'd want his or have any other family given to me. Regaining my speech, I tell him, "No, there's no way I'll take over your family. I'm sorry about your situation and theirs, too, but I can't help you. I'm really very sorry for all of you." As I leave him standing there, I'm shaken having just been offered human beings for my own use. Though, I really shouldn't be so shocked, as I've already come to learn there are other situations like this one taking place in Vietnam. And right away, I'm reminded of my friend, Ralph's situation, in Saigon. This is just another variation, but this one's with children.

As the senior team advisor for the II ARVN Corps area, Colonel Ted Mataxis, from time to time, he travels to visit each advisory team site for informal inspections and to hear about their needs and other problems. But as the U.S. military presence in country continues to grow, demands increase on him and the time for such visits becomes scarcer. As the end of his tour approaches, he wants a comprehensive review of activities and the conduct of subordinate advisory teams in the ARVN II Corps area. Without much explanation, after notifying each team chief in advance of my mission, he assigns me to visit each of the teams on their sites. Though as I'm known as an intelligence advisor, my visit is intended to be a deviation from the norm. So, I can see why some of the team leaders might regard me as a spy. Some may even consider me as a hatchet man, rather than a formal visitor on behalf of our advisory leader. To carry out his orders, I make up a schedule and forward it to each of the team leaders, hoping to ease their suspicions.

The team leader at Kontum, located a few miles north of Pleiku, its officer, also a major, welcomes me as I drive into his compound. He's forthcoming about his team's activities, and doesn't seem to hold back as I question and take notes. I depart with a basket of fruit, one I've bought in a nearby market, not one I've asked from him could be considered nor taken as a bribe.

To reach the next team, I'm having flown in to Ban Me Thout, a settlement in the southwest near the border of Cambodia. This group is much larger, and led by an Army colonel. The team works with the Montagnards, native mountain folk. When I land, leaving my pilot at the airfield, I'm met by the team leader. He acts as though he and his staff are under the headquarters' suspicion, and I've been sent to find what he's been up to. It isn't long before I have the feeling he doesn't get along with my boss, Colonel Mataxis. In short, he acts as if I'm there to spy on him, and makes no effort to hide his resentment to my presence. No amount of my assurance to the contrary why I'm visiting changes his mind. Nonetheless, he continues believing I'm there to make a critical report, rather than about his needs and normal activities. With a grudging attitude, he does show me around and provides a briefing by his staff. At the conclusion of my visit, he and his personnel watch me take off, I guess to make sure I've gone.

My welcome at the next stop, near the beautiful resort mountainous area of Da Lat, is the exact opposite. This team leader, a major, goes all out to make me and my pilot feel welcome. Leaving the pilot in the care of his staff, he also provides me a briefing and a full tour of the installation. What's unusual is the presence of an attractive, curvaceous young Vietnamese woman on hand, who follows us around. Her unexplained presence suggests "other comforts" may be available for me. The offer is so obvious, I'm convinced the Major is trying to compromise my visit and influence my report. I leave wondering what he fears I might have discovered, much less what my report will include. I guess he also wonders whether and how I'll include the presence of the Vietnamese buxom beauty. After all, he'll never know whether and how I include her in my report, which I simply don't.

The last two team leaders I see are in Ninh Hoa and Tuy Hua, both captains. They're welcoming and prepared with lists of pressing needs.

Being senior to both of them, I hope I let them feel I'm there to help, rather than be critical, or spying on them. As I leave, I still find it curious some of us choose to be suspicious of each other's motives, despite being within the same organization and carrying out the shared mission.

Chapter 29

THE ENEMY'S EVIDENCE

AS AN INTELLIGENCE OFFICER, MY ORDER OF BATTLE TASKS are mostly well defined. Included, I need to know whom we're fighting, the composition of the enemy's forces, where they're located, in what strength and their tactics. As U.S. forces are continuing to grow in the highlands, captured enemy soldiers also begin arriving at the II Corps interrogation center. Captured enemy by ARVN and increasingly by U.S. forces are as likely to be northern Vietnamese soldiers as they are Viet Cong. And with U.S. Army operations also mounting at an increasingly rapid pace, the capture of NVA or VC fighters have become commonplace. Sometimes, the corpse of an enemy soldier is dropped off at the nearby military airfield for special identification, and to be studied for evidence of new units fighting in our area of operations. Such evidence is usually forwarded to Saigon, but its importance is also becoming routine.

On assignments to investigate dead enemy casualties, I usually accompany Colonel Nghia, whom I supposedly advise, to examine the corpse. But in some cases, he seems to consider the case is already closed. Yet, despite the ARVN G2's such decisions, Colonel Mataxis sometimes believes such a body may be of MACV command interest, and orders me to go on alone for an examination. In this particular case, the body has been dropped off next to one of the defensive timber-lined foxholes spotted around the perimeter of the airfield near Pleiku. To examine recently killed soldiers we have to get to them before the vultures, the rumored occasional roaming tiger and inevitably by the maggots.

My being in the presence of death, enemy or not, is always awe-inspiring and commands respect. After driving in a jeep there alone, I come to this body in question. It takes me a few minutes to work myself up even to touch the corpse, before examining it in more. Because he's in an NVA uniform, there should be little to differentiate him from any other soldier similarly clothed. But, in this case it's his body size and facial characteristics are so unusual, such differences being critical for ethnic recognition. A nose can be a little flatter or shorter, and sharper or longer, the cheekbones a little higher or flatter, the eyes set farther apart, squinty, more slanted or rounder. It is these stereotypical features can help us identify the ethnic group of the soldier is a part, but it isn't always so easy. First impressions can be misleading, especially when a hurried identification is demanded, such as it is with this one.

It's how I've come to see this particular face, the one belonging to a young man, in his late teens or early twenties, with a body strong and muscular. His eyes are open, likely surprised when shot, so it wouldn't be right to say he looks back at me. It would imply life, but his stare is blank, the eyes have become dry and their shine gone dull. It's a glow in the iris, now absent, would signifies life. Nonetheless in the late afternoon light, his startled expression is haunting. His mortal wound, probably in his back, isn't evident from my cursory once-over. But, it's not what I'm here for.

My mission is to determine whether he's just another North Vietnamese Army troop, as his uniform indicates, or a Chinese People's Army soldier in disguise, come to reinforce an ally. This very real concern is a carryover from the Chinese intervention in the Korean

Conflict of the previous decade, which had such devastating consequences for U.S. forces. I'm suspicious of the man's origin, not only because of his features, but especially his size, noticeably larger and taller than the usual Vietnamese male.

As an intelligence officer I have to make this judgment, though my expertise really goes little further than my job description. I'm well aware of the substantial ethnic Chinese presence in country. Chinese migration into Vietnam even dates back to the era of the 2nd century BC, when northern Vietnam came under Chinese rule. Chinese soldiers and fugitives from Central China had migrated *en masse* into northern Vietnam from time onward, and brought Chinese influences to Vietnamese culture. Chinese merchants, sprinkled throughout the country, north and south, have been present in Vietnam for centuries; as a matter of fact, they've been and are through all of Southeast Asia. So, it's quite possible this Chinese youth could and would be conscripted for service into the NVA, or the Viet Cong. Earlier, I tried to describe this I.D. problem to Colonel Ted, but my explanation has fallen on deaf ears. Command nervousness about missing an important development in the war demands immediate resolution. OK, I can't argue it.

Now kneeling beside the body, I gaze at his face for another long minute or two, before gently try to close his eyelids. I can't help thinking of him as someone's son, brother or even, like me, a young father. The rough cloth of his dirty, mustard-colored outfit is the uniform I recognize worn by NVA regulars. Whatever he carried with him has already been removed and turned over to a U.S. unit Intelligence Officer. His documents, letters, photos and a notebook, were then delivered to my office in Pleiku, where I've already examined them with my Vietnamese counterpart. It's those papers prompted our direct, immediate look at his remains. Nonetheless, I go through his pockets and backpack again for the sake of thoroughness. As expected, they come up empty.

As I can handle his remains as I wish, it embarrasses and gives me an unwelcome feeling of power. In death he demands a respect he would not have received were he alive. Indeed, ARVN intelligence personnel routinely beat captured NVA and VC soldiers, ostensibly to force disclosure of military secrets. And after all, he is the enemy; never mind the talk one hears about respect for a worthy opponent.

A report on my observations is still due to Colonel Ted, and this will be sent on to MACV headquarters in Saigon. In my notebook I fill in a prescribed list of "facts." The report requires my informed judgment of the soldier's identity details. I limit my conclusion to his ethnicity, probably Chinese, but I don't want my boss or intelligence personnel at MACV to jump to conclusions and take this as evidence of the presence of the Chinese People's Army forces.

If it were true, I suspect my boss would want to be the "first" to give the alarm. It would then reverberate all the way to Washington and possibly be grounds for escalating the war effort even faster. I want no part of it, but I have to be careful, ready to resist any pressure to change my evaluation. I also know he doesn't want to be embarrassed by being wrong.

Finished with the report, I'm anxious to know how it will be used. There aren't enough hard "facts" in it to make it newsworthy. I suspect my honest conclusions are likely to disappoint my boss.

Colonel Ted is soon to be re-assigned to the First Brigade of the 101st Airborne Division, recently arrived in country. His deputy, another colonel his junior, can hardly wait for Ted's departure so he can take over the US Pleiku advisory team. Known for his size in fatigues as the "Jolly Green Giant," he jockeys, whenever he can, to gain recognition with the MACV staff in Saigon. As Colonel Ted's deputy, he tries to direct my work with Colonel Nghia, and to embellish, without basis, my reports to Saigon. On a number of occasions, I have to demand we take our differences to our team leader for resolution. After a few of these confrontations, Colonel Ted, as the team leader, finally tells "Jolly" he will be the arbiter of any changes "Jolly" will have to justify. Not surprisingly his number of proposed changes fall near to none.

As previously mentioned, after four months I'd taken my turn for five days of Rest and Recuperation, or R&R, in Bangkok. While away, the newly arrived Ist Air Cavalry Division launches its first major operation in relief of the siege of Plei Me near Pleiku, by a North Vietnamese Army regiment. The pursuit of the withdrawing NVA forces culminates in the major Battle of the Ia Drang. On my return, Colonel "Jolly" accuses me of having planned my R&R to avoid the combat, as if our advisory staff would have had any role in it, or I'd had some inside information about the anticipated encounter. None of his accusations are true. In fact, I'd submitted my R&R request more than a month earlier, well before we even knew of the Air Cavalry's planned operation. It still didn't seem to dissuade him. I see his accusation as just another way to try control me.

My interaction with the "Jolly Green Giant" is frequently contentious. The issue is over what I'm willing or unwilling to report to higher levels. I'm guessing behind it is his eagerness to enhance his reputation as an important role player. Our relationship only worsens as the day of his command of our advisory team approaches. But as long as Colonel Ted holds the top post, I know I'll have support for standing my ground.

Office politics anywhere, are as rampant in our advisory group as in private businesses. Egocentric senior officers are particularly keen to get the next assignment putting them in line for promotion, or for a coveted billet. With tours in the country limited in length, time is short to make the right move, to impress the right senior officer, or a review board. Some believe being in a war zone increases the opportunity for promotion. "Jolly" is determined not to miss his chance for promotion to general grade.

Apart from maneuverings, like his, others want to log flight time for air medals, or accrue points to gain service and combat ribbons, both American and Vietnamese. Jumping with Vietnamese Special forces a few times can earn one a Vietnamese airborne parachutist's badge;

repeated or extended tours are undertaken for the same purpose. I don't try to evaluate an officers' commitment to the war, but the effort to win may be hampered by minds marinated with ambition.

Only after I return to the States, I'll discover the true nature of, "Jolly," the man whose attention has been so focused on me at Pleiku. On a Sunday afternoon, my wife and I are attending a party in a Washington, DC apartment, where I'm surprised to meet Jolly's wife. She's intriguing and seems eager to relate her story to the group around her. As part of the cluster of partygoers we're listening to her relating how, shortly after her husband's return from Viet Nam, in the bedroom she'd come upon him in bed--with another man. And how, as she stood in the bedroom doorway, stunned at the scene, he's surprised and jumps, naked from the bed, and flees through the bedroom window. It's then I suddenly see his constant badgering of me in a completely different light.

Chapter 30

AIRBORNE DUTY

IN FEBRUARY 1966, MY TOUR ENDS AS THE INTELLIGENCE
advisor to the G-2 of the II ARVN Corps. Meanwhile, Colonel Ted
Mataxis, the MACV Advisory Group team commander at Pleiku, agrees
to arrange my request for a transfer with him to serve with the combat
airborne infantry. Our new unit will be the 1st Brigade of the 101st
Airborne Division, then conducting combat operations in the highlands. He'll be taking over as the Deputy Brigade Commander, and I
as the brigade's intelligence officer. We've become friends while serving
together as advisors, frequently helicoptering to ARVN and Vietnamese
Special Forces outposts and to the US advisory detachments deployed
in the II ARVN Corps area.

The day when I arrive at the brigade headquarters, one of the first
things I notice is its motto: "Stay Alert and Stay Alive," painted on a
wooden panel posted outside the command tent. The slogan is above
the 101st Airborne Division's shoulder patch image of a screaming
American eagle's head, over arced by the word, "AIRBORNE." I'm
thinking how apt and this advice is critical, though not always seriously observed.

Once our transfer is completed, Colonel Ted still has a problem accepting the fairly new Army Intelligence Branch insignia I'm now wearing on my collar. I'd recently transferred to the branch before shipping overseas. He tells me, since I've been reassigned to an airborne infantry brigade, I should wear its infantry crossed rifles insignia. It suits me, I tell him, having already worn them for many years before. But I tell him the change will have to take place back at the Pentagon between the two branches. Apparently, he has arranged for the change, for a couple of weeks later I'm surprised to receive a communication authorizing me to wear the infantry insignia as long as my assignment lasts with the brigade. The temporary transfer also authorizes the awarding of the Combat Infantryman's Badge, once I have had enough time in the assignment and exposure to combat. Colonel Ted and I celebrate the transfer by toasting with some of his vodka martinis, though warm, since ice is scarce and difficult to come by in the field.

After meeting with the brigade commander, Brigadier General Willard Pearson, I have less than a day to meet with my assistant, a lieutenant, and the enlisted intelligence staff. With my experience as the ARVN II Corps intelligence advisor, I'm well prepared for the job. The next day, as in many to follow, I'm in a helicopter airborne with the brigade commander on his daily inspections of our battalion units deployed in the field. At the time of my arrival, elements of the brigade are making sweeps of paddy rice fields and the surrounding jungle probing for contact with Viet Cong and North Vietnamese Army units. Before taking off with the general each early morning, I scan the reports collected the day before and during the night, so I'm able to analyze them and brief the general during our next flight between stops.

On one such morning, a couple of weeks after joining the brigade, my analysis of intelligence indicators strongly suggest an impending attack aimed on our troops involved in another sweep currently in the field. The telling clue is the absence of workers in the rice paddies, who are normally present each day for work just after dawn. On this morning, I learn the workers are nowhere to be seen. I immediately alert the operations officer of possible danger and request he notify the commander of our airborne battalion then deployed in the field. The warning reaches the unit's commander in time for him to shift the orientation and re-deployment of his troops and mount a surprise-spoiling attack. The successful maneuver routs the VC enemy and inflicts many casualties on them. A short while later, Major David Hackworth, the battalion's acting commander, bursts into the Intelligence tent demanding to know who predicted the impending attack on his unit. The following success of his operation establishes our mutual respect, and the timely warning starts off my tour with the brigade on a solid footing.

I'd met David Hackworth, also known as "Hack," previously in Pleiku. He'd been there with a group of the airborne brigade officers who'd come to the II ARVN Corps headquarters to plan a possible operation. Dave had acquired a mythical reputation as a "Warrior Soldier" preceding him wherever he went. A Warrior Soldier has the connotation of one, who "Loves War," and seeks out war fighting opportunities. Such a soldier is only fulfilled when in combat, and then is also at his most effectiveness. A reluctance to plunge into the possible peril of battle, most soldiers have a natural tendency to survive, and if possible, avoid combat's inherent danger. It takes a soldier's determined effort to overcome his fear, though I can't say it's true of Dave. Still, this impression of an overriding exuberance for the impulse of combat can inspire men around him to overcome their own fear. True or not, Dave's special quality is rumored to have the same effect on his airborne soldiers.

When I get to know him better, I learn we've both come from impoverished backgrounds. To get beyond his, he'd run away and, lying about his then age 14, started his military career as a sailor in the Merchant Marines. The mariner's life apparently isn't enough exciting for him, he transfers to the Army a year later. When the war in Korea begins, he volunteers to go and, once there, quickly moves up in the ranks, first as a sergeant, then winning a battlefield commission to second lieutenant. He volunteers for a second tour and, before the Armistice stops the fighting, he's become the war's youngest Army captain. These experiences have won him a whole string of medals to which he adds a number before leaving Vietnam.

The brigade commander, General Pearson, is a scheduled man, whom I find fitting to my own tendencies. When possible, sunrise finds him and other members of his staff, including me, running for exercise on the pierced steel planking of the nearby makeshift airfield. Then, the best part of every day I spend flying with him to check in with the brigade's three battalions deployed in our sector. Our chopper is fairly flying at a low altitude, sometimes at treetop level. On occasions upon return to the base, our pilots point out bullet holes in the fuselage result from enemy attempts to bring us down. I realize we'll have to be aware being shot at and possibly injured, or worse. We also maintain contact with outposts manned by Vietnamese Army units. Native mountain people, known as Montagnards, are often manning some of the high-land outposts. Known as ferocious warriors, they fight off VC or NVA attacks.

The Author is the Major on the right, assigned as the Intelligence Officer for the Ist Brigade, IOIst Airborne Division, at a North Vietnam Army combat field in Central Vietnam in 1966.

In one instance, a call comes in to our brigade for assistance to repel a larger attack then underway. By the time we get the necessary information and clearance and move out to the scene, the battle is over, and the living remnants of the attackers have withdrawn. Later in the morning, the general, the operations officer and I arrive to find the battlefield strewn with mainly bodies of NVA soldiers. Many of them with abdominal wounds having their intestines already ballooning in the morning rising heat. The horrific reality of the death spread all around us is numbing as I have to accept the reality of such death.

It's even harder to control my mental and physical reactions, especially when I see the numbers of black body bags showing up daily at our headquarters. I know they hold our own dead soldiers killed in battle, now laid out awaiting transport to graves registration. Seeing dead enemy fighters is bad enough, but seeing those of our soldiers is much worse. Though I'm grateful at least having the bagged-bodies of our casualties hidden from view, it's still impossible to avoid the thought of their deaths being passed up the chain of command and on to their families. It doesn't take much imagination to see myself in one of those body bags. Or worse still, it shakes me to imagine being informed that the body in one of them is of my son's. It's then I'm so grateful he's not a soldier.

Though I'm not directly involved with our airborne infantry soldiers, I'm nonetheless greatly impressed with their evident positive attitude. My past involvement commanding infantry soldiers back in the states now reveal the comparative decisive enthusiasm manifest in airborne troops. It's understandable, since they are all volunteers and are imbued with the airborne pride and history. I sense the aura and it inspires me, too.

After settling in and conducting operations in a given location, the brigade receives orders to move to different operational sites within the II ARVN Corps area to engage the VC and or NVA units. The brigade sets up a temporary headquarters and assigns areas for its battalions. On occasion our units and the headquarters receive sporadic enemy fire. Even though it may not be directed at the headquarters, at such times I may find myself rolling out of my cot and spending the rest of the night on the ground, and occasionally in a shallow foxhole.

When not with the brigade commander, I brief at our headquarters on the enemy situation to high-ranking visitors, both military and civilian, including the press. All hours are working hours. To perform my main job as intelligence officer I have to do my review, study and analysis at night. It's when I can read incoming raw information from electronic intercepts, aerial photography, interrogation reports, captured materiel and an occasional live prisoner. From all these sources my staff and I write intelligence reports, some of which are sent daily to MACV in Saigon.

It's a critical job and often I feel like I'm contributing significantly to the effort. But what I don't like is being ordered to develop, or identify targets, however sparsely documented, for our Navy ships stationed off the coast. Equally deplorable is our being pressed to identify targets deeper inland for B-52 Bomber runs. Flying in from the base in Okinawa, these raids are known as Rolling Thunder. Though the targeting data are shaky at best, I suspect the Air Force and Navy mainly request the targets to claim credit for Vietnam combat duty. Despite the absence of anti-aircraft fire, these bombing runs may qualify the airmen for combat pay, medals and service ribbons. When I argue I have little basis for identifying a target, or the target information is already cold, our operations officer often insists I must recommend it, anyway.

As if a bit of Navy diplomacy will encourage us to act as a targeting agency, our commander, the operations officer and I are invited to visit a battleship anchored off the coast in the South China Sea. It's all very gentlemanly, but in the end, we're committed to provide targets for the Navy's big guns. All I can do is gnash my teeth knowing the targets, if any, are hardly worth the massive ordnance being launched and wasted to blow them up.

I suspect a higher authority has lent a sympathetic ear to requests from our sister services to bless their operations and credit them as combat. In my estimation, most of the bombing and naval bombardments amount to a huge waste of money and materiel, not to mention the wonton destruction of what are often can be innocent people and their property. The B-52 bombers often fly very high beyond sight and sound, but what they are delivering suddenly becomes visible as we're watching the target area. Without warning, all at once there's a long line of monumental earth bursts where the string of bombs are impacting and exploding. Later, flying with the brigade commander it's possible to review the effects of such attacks. The visible remains might have include villages pulverized out of existence. The bombing destruction is awesome, but it's also discouraging and upsetting. I'm left wondering if there's any reaction to these bombings on the emotions of the crews delivering them.

Months afterward, I have trouble erasing these scenes from my mind, and regretting whatever responsibility I share in the unnecessary massive destruction of life. We're demonstrating our overwhelming power and its wonton devastation, yet still not getting any closer to winning the war.

Chapter 31

ELUSIVE TARGETS

THE AIRBORNE INFANTRY BRIGADE IS DESIGNED TO CARRY the battle to the enemy. But the targeting often continues frustration like a Catch-22 in which the effect is the opposite intended. There's also one situation in which we're meant to find missions for an ad hoc unit assigned to the brigade. This unit is known as the Long-Range Reconnaissance Patrol, or LRRP, a 15-man team of airborne troops commanded by a captain. Rather than parachuting in, the force is to be taken by choppers deep into a presumed enemy-held territory. The mission is mainly for reconnaissance and surveillance, but if it encounters a target of opportunity and discovers enemy which could possibly impact on our brigade, the leader has a decision to make, either to avoid or engage it.

Though the LRRP unit is under my nominal supervision, its mission assignment is left to the approval of the operations officer and the brigade commander. My role is to identify possible target areas for the patrol. Yet, even when I can't find sufficient evidence to define a target, I'm still not allowed to recommend the patrol should stand down. I'm reminded of paraphrasing Mark Twain's line saying: *When eager to use your hammer, you go in the search of a nail;* and that pretty well summarizes the unit's mission we're trying to put together without an identified enemy target.

The day arrives, while the LRRP unit is ready for an assignment. It is when the operations officer and I pick target areas about we brief our commander. The general's question to me is, "Major, what enemy evidence do we have?" Then, I recite a list of indicators and their date of discovery, concluding by adding there's really no firm intelligence on the target area itself. I'm well aware why the general doesn't ask for my recommendation.

Following the decision for deployment anyway, the captain commanding the LRRP is summoned early in the day and briefed for the operation set up for later in the afternoon. The brigade operations officer starts his briefing the patrol's leader. "Captain, in the evening, the mission will be launched, and your 15-man patrol will be flying in to the two HU-1 choppers. Then, they'll be inserted into the supposed enemy-held occupied area. Any questions so far? The patrol leader shakes his head, and replies, "No sir."

The briefing continues. "OK, your troops in the choppers will be flying just above treetops and be feigning a number of touchdowns in the general target area before actually unloading your soldiers in one of them."

Since no questions are raised, he briefs on, "This tactic is meant to confuse the enemy as to whether, where and when your force has landed, and how many number of airborne troops it might have." Then he continues. "Up to this point, your patrol has the advantage of secrecy and surprise. But once your men are on the ground, your team will lose advantage when it continues its reconnaissance on foot in an unknown area to them and possibly held by enemy."

The patrol captain finally raises a hand and asks, "And keeping radio silence is necessary, isn't that right?"

"Yes, at least until you make contact with the enemy," the Operations Officer concludes. The LRRP now in its first effort, is briefed on possible enemy encounters, properly equipped, prepared and is finally launched.

With each day following passes without contact or receiving from the patrol, it begins increase our concern and it continues to rise. Finally, after nearly a week passes, we feel forced to break radio silence in an effort to determine if the team is still operational, or if its members are even alive and free. Despite attempts to continuing contact, there are no responses. As our concern rises even more, we follow launching aerial searches during days for the unit in the target area. Then, in the complete absence of contact visual or radio, we are forced to consider the patrol may have been captured, injured or may have been destroyed. Finally, what we're now left with is having to accept the patrol's devastating possible total loss.

When realizing their possible demise, I chastise myself for not arguing more at the outset against the mission's ambiguity, even as if my evaluation of the mission would've been accepted. Still, if the unit may have found and has engaged the VC or NVA, we have to accept the mission's risk as being inherent. There's little solace, as I won't have to be the one writing condolence letters to the families of the long-range patrol's lost men.

With the brigade's constant movements and operations throughout the highlands from one combat area to another, time passes quickly. In May, along with Dave and another brigade major, I take five days off and fly to Hong Kong for rest and recuperation.

Before we leave, Dave suggests, "You'll have a better time if you're slightly high while awake," he tells me and he assures me he's not joking. To establish and maintain a slight buzz, he recommends carrying along a bottle of Mateus, a pink, sweet Portuguese wine to sip from. He then produces a bottle and offers me a drink. The wine's odor is pleasant enough, but when I try taking a drink, it almost immediately makes me feel sick, and I reject it. It's then I'm thinking how combat exposure can make a man lose his reason.

Shaking my head, I say, "Dave, for me drinking during those days would be a waste of time, and they aren't going to work for me anyway. Instead, I'll be going on with the shopping I've already planned. "Why don't you come along with me?" I suggest. But he declines and I can detect his anger as we part ways during the next few days of our time in Hong Kong.

My main R&R purpose there is a mission to find a few gifts for my wife and plan to have ordered a tuxedo and two other made-to-measure suits. I'm to be measured for the clothes within hours of arriving in Hong Kong, and fitted twice during the next two days with time for them to be completed before my return to duty. On the commercial flight from Vietnam, one of the Chinese-American stewardesses agrees to connect me with a dependable tailor, she knows and agrees to show me around in Hong Kong for a day. After declining to drink with Dave, I decide to contact her and decide she's important and could also be interesting company. She speaks the language and really knows her way around the city, where to shop and especially where to eat, and of course, I treat her to dinner before our parting.

Once the shopping is done, my remaining days are alone, but they're given to sightseeing Hong Cong's popular features, relaxation, exceptional dining on wonderful food. The tailored clothes are finished on time and I pick them up as planned.

While waiting at the airport for our return flight to Vietnam, I meet Dave there again. He's apparently still upset I hadn't spent the R&R break drinking with him. His evident resentment seems to continue even after our return to the brigade and once again on duty it clouds our relationship. Each time we run into each other it's clear he still holds a grudge. In staff meetings, ordinarily he's outspoken and doesn't hesitate to contradict and argue with other staff members. Regularly, he usually challenges assessments presented to the brigade commander made by other staff officers and including me.

But, after returning from our R&R, following one of the first staff meetings, he's obviously angry and later accosts me outside the tent. I can't tell whether he's opposed to the issue we've just been discussing, or it's his lingering resentment from our trip to Hong Cong. Whatever it is, he's obviously furious I've opposed one of his proposals. His visible upset now takes the form more challenging with his fists clenched, as if ready to fight right then and there. I try to convince him my position was based on factual judgments, not assumptions and certainly not meant to demean him, or to boost myself before our commander. In any event, it strikes me as ridiculous two field grade officers would settle such a disagreement, or anything else, with a fistfight. We're about the same height, but he's more muscled and has said in past he's well experienced in brawling. I haven't fought with my fists since elementary school and certainly I have no intention to start again now. Even so, I'm determined to stand my ground.

"Dave, is this how you think will solve your problems?" I ask, indicating his clenched fists. He recoils, but says nothing, still glowering at me. I add, "Understand, I'm not going to fight you," I tell him, "I don't doubt you're well brawling experienced. But I can tell you it won't solve your problem, won't change my mind, or the position I've presented, if what's bothering you so much." Still angry but saying nothing, for a few moments, he finally un-clenches his fists. Glowering, he lets out the breath he's been holding, and says, "Yeah, you're right," before he walks away. Though his angry attitude has entirely yet to dissipate, within days, his tour with the brigade ends. I have to admit I'm not unhappy to see him go.

As spring turns to summer, I'm nearing the end of my tour with the brigade assignment and beginning to think more about returning home. I want to do some shopping for souvenirs in Saigon and gather my personal belongings stored at our home base on the coast. After a little shopping in the city, I hitch a flight north up the coast to Phan Rang, the brigade's home base. I spend most of the next day there preparing my stored belongings for shipment home. Late in the afternoon, after finding a place to eat, I call our brigade operations officer to let him know shortly I'll be catching a flight back up north. I'll be landing at an Army airfield near the brigade's deployment and ask to be picked up there.

Having finished dinner, I arrange for a ride to the Phan Rang airfield. But when I arrive, the last cargo flight for the day is already rolling down to the far end of the runway. I can see it will be about to turn, make its during increasing run and takes off. I ask the driver to make a dash for the control tower. Arriving there, I climb up into it for an attempt to have the controller hold the flight for me. But I'm just a bit too late and my attempt is futile.

"The plane is loaded with 105 mm artillery shells and it can't be delayed," the control officer explains. "Come back early in the morning tomorrow, major," he says, "and you can catch the first ride out."

After an early breakfast the next day, I catch the first sunrise morning flight out as planned. Landing after flying for an hour, I commandeer a jeep ride and finally arrive an hour later at our brigade's headquarters. I stick my head into the operations tent and sound off. "What the hell happened to the ride you agreed to have meet me at the airfield?" I ask the operations officer. For a few moments he seems unable to talk and stares at me incredulously. Then he blurts. "For God's sake," he expels, "last night's flight, with a load of artillery shells, blew up in mid-air.

We thought you and the chaplain had both blown up and gone down with it."

For a few moments, I stare at him silently and stunned, my mouth partly open. It's then I'm learning about the loss of the aircrew and the chaplain, and especially how closely I came to my own end, too. The operations officer and I agree, despite our planning, ultimately fate is in charge of our futures. This time it's an invisible hand seems to have intervened in my survival, chosen for me to return home safely, alive and hang around on earth a while longer.

In the final weeks of my tour with the brigade, one of the battalion commanders, a lieutenant colonel, seeks me out. "Major, I know your tour is about to end, but I'm wondering if you'd be willing to extend it?" he asks.

"What for reason and for how long are you asking?" I reply.

"If you're willing, your return stateside will be delayed only four more months. I'll make you my executive officer, my second in command," he says.

I know this colonel has made a name for himself leading his battalion in combat. The tactics he has developed in fighting the NVA are by now well celebrated.

"Exactly what do you have in mind?" I ask.

"I'm intending to reorganize the battalion's three companies into two taskforces, one of which you'll command," he says. "I've been impressed with your assessments of the enemy's strength and tactics, and I can use your experience." he says.

At this point I'm flattered and intrigued with the idea of commanding an infantry airborne force in combat.

"It's an important opportunity and I'll really give your offer some serious thought," I tell him.

"Yes, please do. If you'll get on board and accept, I'll see you'll get a fast promotion to lieutenant colonel." Then he adds, "I've already been informed of my own promotion to full colonel and reassigned to the infantry promotion board when I'm back at the Pentagon."

Again, I'm flattered by his praise and promise. But on my return to the states, I know I'll revert to the Army Intelligence Branch, and doubt my promotion would be any faster, despite even considering his effort.

But it isn't my primary concern, anyway. Audrey and I have kept up correspondence through exchanged tape recordings; each delayed ten days to two weeks en route, in each direction. When she learns of the light colonel's offer, she's immediately furious at the idea I might consider extending my tour, even if just for a few more months.

Her reaction comes as no surprise. She's quick to let me know an early promotion is of no significance to her. "I don't care about the promotion, at all," she says. "Robbie and I have already suffered enough with your leaving us alone, and worrying every day you might be wounded or even killed."

"But it's only for four more months," I argue, for the moment ignoring her correct evaluation.

"Don't you think you've already tempted fate enough?" she says, "The fighting is increasing there every day now. It could happen to you on the first day of your added four months. Just how much longer do you think your luck will hold?" She won't have me risk my life for a promotion, especially one I'm likely to receive anyway. I'm left with a choice: Do I want another feather in my Army hat, or a divorce, never mind the possibility of my injury or death?

In the end, I turn down the battalion commander's offer. As a life-long bachelor, maybe he doesn't understand what I could lose, if my wife were to leave me and take our son with her. Such a loss could never be worth the promise of a fast promotion, or anything else.

Chapter 32

PENTAGON DUTY

LIKE MOST SOLDIERS LIVING FOR MONTHS IN A HAZARD-
ous combat zone, I'm trying to shake off the constant feeling of vulnerability. Often, I also dream of coming home to be reunited with my
wife and son. Our designed new home, then under construction, gives
my anticipated return an added sense of yearning and excitement. In
my absence, my wife has found and bought for us two acres of land
in Fort Washington, Maryland, a DC suburb. Across the circle of the
cul-de-sac she sees a house of unique design and its construction nearly
completed. She learns from its owner the architect/builder's name and
phone number.

After we've had a number of detailed discussions, we decide, if
possible, she should go ahead and hire the neighbor's same architect
to get our house designed and get its construction started. Unlike the
other sub-division homes, ours will be built according to our architect's unique contemporary design, and be somewhat larger than other
houses in the neighborhood. She especially likes the two and one half
acre lot of land for our new home giving some sense of intimacy facing
into a cul-de-sac. On the opposite side of the property, situated on the

cul-de-sac's northwest arc, includes a panoramic view of the Woodrow Wilson Bridge spanning the Potomac River. Farther just beyond is the skyline of Alexandria, Virginia. The building site is a jewel and leaves us wondering why it hasn't been previously sold. For a few months before my return, we correspond about a few changes in the plan. It has me so involved; I wonder how I could ever consider extending my tour in Vietnam for even a four-month longer.

On the lengthy return flight to the States, I experience a mixed sense of anticipation and anxiety. I'm wondering how, if any, our 14-month separation has brought changes in each of us? And if it reveals, then how our relationship has evolved? For my son, Robbie, I also expect the reunion could possibly be especially difficult.

In reunion, almost immediately I sense changes in our relationship. Her anxiety for my survival, coupled with all the child caring and house-keeping responsibilities, has not only aged her, but also is depriving our getting back together for genuine happiness. Our love making, very soon after returning to our Bladensburg temporary apartment, lacks the passion and enthusiasm we had known and so desired before I left. While she accepts my stored-up yearning, our lovemaking seems like an obligation, almost more a chore for her than a pleasure. It's obvious to me our realized estrangement isn't going to be overcome quickly, or even very soon.

And when it comes to five-year-old Robbie, no matter how many times I remind him I'm his Dad, he simply doesn't seems agree to accept me. I'm aware how he's acting as if not caring who I am, and he now has to share his mother's attention with me. His attitude is understandable, but it also adds to my general feelings of frustration. Overall, while hopeful and grateful to be home, the reunion atmosphere leaves me somewhat depressed. I realize in part it's due to my exaggerated expectations. The thrill I'd felt earlier about coming home is failing to match up with the actual situation I'm now experiencing. Still, I'm determined to recapture and bring our cohesiveness and happiness feelings back into the family.

During the thirty days of leave, I work with the carpenters on the house and continue trying to get re-acquainted with my wife and son. I soon realize things aren't turning out as I'd hoped. After 14 months without me, Robbie looks only to his mother for direction and ignores any from me. I know in time his behavior will change, but it still annoys me to have him snub my authority. I know Audrey is doing her best to make me feel at home, but she's still somewhat distant in her acquired independence, acting almost automatically in the routine she has developed in my absence.

I confess to some distance in my own behavior. It will take more effort on my part to achieve the compatibility we'd known in the past. While I was away, Audrey has been working part time in a day nursery. Then, more recently her application has been accepted for work as a qualified occupational therapist at D.C.'s St. Elizabeth's mental hospital. Her new position is satisfying for her and adds to her sense of independence. On the positive side, our shared interest in our new contemporary house, whose construction is nearing completion, helps a lot to draw us back together.

Despite her concern about my attitude, I don't agree I'm suffering from post-traumatic stress disorder. Yet, I'm very aware of the frequent thumping sounds of helicopter's flying over and along the Potomac River near our home. Their flybys each time still making my abdominal muscles tighten in reaction, as they have done so regularly in Vietnam each time I had to fly in choppers. Any increase in stress automatically affects my bowels and evidence now and then they can't be ignored, and I have to check in with a doctor from time to time.

As weeks pass, I have to admit my exposure to combat has affected me both physically and mentally, and my relationship with Audrey. I'm convinced she is genuinely sympathetic when she tells me she believes I need the help of a psychologist or even a psychiatrist. But I wave it off, suspecting it's mainly her Occupational Therapy schooling at play. In her job at St. Elizabeth's, a large part of her work is patient evaluation with psychological testing. I think it's certainly appropriate, but I'm angered when I realize she may be secretly subjecting me to the same type of scoring. Though I don't know it for a fact, I'm also suspecting she's discussing my behavior with her St. Elizabeth's colleagues. If so, I regard it as a betrayal, and wonder about the professional hospital staff on which she's leaning. It suggests I'm being viewed as a lab specimen for them. I'm having such troubling thoughts and feelings could also be possible, and it may have begun to undermine my trust in her. For the moment, I try to brush aside the warning signs could threaten our future together and the disintegration of our family.

◆◆◆

The Author is a Lieutenant Colonel assigned to the US Army Intelligence Branch, at the Pentagon, Washington, D.C. in 1968.

When I tell Audrey my first job at the Pentagon is learning how to find my office, she laughs, thinking it's a joke, until one day she goes there and experiences it herself. The term, "Puzzle Palace," is no exaggeration for someone new to the enormous building. I'm assigned to a Section of the US Army Intelligence (G-2) Branch dealing with Special Warfare and Assistance to the Latin American armies. I'm feeling completely in over my head, when preparing or reviewing studies on subjects in which I have no insight, background or contribution. There's little comfort in learning for newly arrived officers who're sharing the same frustrating experience. The other major in my office has been there a few weeks before and helps me to learn my way around the huge edifice. He's especially helpful dealing with the studies flowing in and out of our office. It wouldn't surprise me, once such a study is returned to its origin, it probably may be buried and forgotten. I wonder if many of them are mainly designed just to keep us busy? Apart from endless staff studies, my assignment takes me to a number of other U.S. military posts.

I hear an assignment to the Pentagon is one most officers deplore, and my experience there is no different. The workday begins before 7 AM and often continues well into the night. I find some relief at the Officers' Athletic Club, in which I use every possible weekday noon-hour for the physical exercise, which also releases my mental condition as well.

My military records show I speak Spanish, so I'm also assigned to accompany the G-2 Army Chief of Staff, a major general, to occasional conferences in Latin America. During his attendance he might have to deal with Spanish-speaking officers, who can't or don't care to speak English. I try to explain to my section chief, a Colonel, I only spoke Spanish until I was five years old. After entering the orphanage, where I lived for ten years, the policy only allowed children there were to speak English. Whatever of my Spanish remains, it's most likely now as spoken by a five-year-old. The Spanish I took in high school emphasized grammar and was oriented to its examinations. It also did nothing to improve my fluency, nor add much for my vocabulary. And later, nor did it help living with my mother and stepfather, though they spoke in Spanish to each other, they only spoke in English to my siblings and me.

I tell all of this history to the colonel, if he insists on the Spanish-speaking assignment, pointing out I'll need a crash course in the language. It's really the only way I'll be speaking Spanish at a high enough level to do the job for our General. At least, the colonel has the good sense to authorize my attendance three afternoons a week at a language school in Washington, D.C. There, I'm soon working with a Peruvian woman language instructor whose Spanish is some-what different the version spoken in Mexico. So, she warns me I may encounter some difficulty in whatever Spanish-speaking countries I'll be visiting. To speed the process, two evenings each week during the following months I also attend a group in a private home in Washington. The current events there are discussed entirely in Spanish, in which I'm expected to contribute. Through both efforts I'm hoping to gain a sufficient level in Spanish, though I'm aware I'll still not always be able to translate correctly and quickly.

During the next few months, I struggle with the language, and sometimes have nightmares in which dreams I embarrass my boss and me for my inability to recall certain Spanish words, much less the correct ones to use. Yet, despite these problems, my travels to confer-ences with the intelligence Army Chief of Staff are generally successful. I'm also charged to write his thanking letters to the army commander hosts, at least they are in English. I perform well enough to enjoy the travel involved to Panama and including four other countries in South America.

The first of them is Bogotá, Colombia's capitol, where my boss and I are toured to their military headquarters and lectured to about the mili-tary's support needed from the US. An official luncheon is later held at Medellín, in a mountain resort with the entire route guarded along by soldiers protecting us from armed guerillas. Upon leaving the country, we're given gifts, mine being two gold coins imprinted with images of the country's original Indian leaders known as the powerful Caciques.

In the second country, we participate in a meeting with the Venezuelan Army staff, which is mostly consisting of lectures and an official dinner with native entertainment. Afterward, one of its Army majors is assigned to show me places of interest around in Caracas, the capital city. My guide, apparently trying to show memorable places of excitement, it includes visiting a house decorated with blue lights. Once inside, I'm presented with a group of women, partially dressed and looking inviting. It's then I suddenly realize I'm in a whorehouse and carefully decline to any activity there and manage to get extracted without embarrassing my guide.

The next two South America countries, Ecuador and Peru, I travel on alone to where I'm met by our respective US Army Attachés and tour me to memorable unique sites. In Quito, Ecuador's capital, I encounter some difficulty breathing in the thin air at its elevation of 2,850 meters, or 9,850 feet high. The other memorable event is the discovery of having the earlier two gift gold coins in my baggage are stolen even before I reach my assigned room. Lacking proof, I decide not to make the theft an issue. In Lima, the capital city of Peru, the stay is interesting but the time is so short, I'm unable to stay long enough to visit Cuzco, the famous center of the mountainous Incan empire, I've long wanted to see and experience.

An assignment to the Pentagon is one most officers deplore, and it's no different for me. I find some relief at the Officers' Athletic Club, in which I use every possible weekday noon-hour for the mental release as well as physical exercise. During the assignment to the Army Staff my promotion to Lieutenant Colonel comes through along with a few more decorations awarded for service in Vietnam. Each time I'm to be pinned with another medal, my wife and son are invited to the Pentagon to participate in the presentation. Apart from endless staff studies, my assignment takes me to a number of other U.S. military posts.

As part of my pentagon duty, I'm also assigned as a member to the Organization of the American States in Washington, D.C. I attend their functions, including social, and thus meeting their member military attaches. When the group is assembled, the two Soviet attaches seem to hover near me, who finally joke I'm spying on their behavior. My colleagues and I believe the opposite is more likely and true. I make a few friends among the group, one in particular, an Indian Army major, whom I will later sponsor for immigrating to the US with his family.

I'm also detailed as one of three escorts for the annual attaché coast-to-coast tour across our country. The most dramatic stop is in Houston, Texas, where Dr. Denton Cooley and fellow surgeon Michael E. DeBakey pioneered in heart surgery during the 1960s. The group observes and briefed about the operation room, though now empty, it is still sobering. Our international group is also invited to a nearby ranch to observe the artificial insemination of cows by human arm and hand. This time there's rampant joking, while watching this operation carried out and hearing the cows baying while being impregnated mixed with the group's laughter.

With my wife and son, during the second summer, we take a two-week vacation and decide to travel to Greece, and Turkey, parts of the world unknown to us. One of the Turkish officers, I've met in Washington during the attaché tour, suggests if we ever visit to Turkey, he'd be happy to show us around in the famous and remarkable city of Istanbul. During our summer vacation, it's his invitation decides us to make the trip there. First, flying into Athens, we spend three days exploring some of its Athena Temple ruins, sampling the Greek unique food, its inspiring music while struggling with the language. Yet, we all enjoy the people and its musical atmosphere. Adding to our tour there includes a day trip to Piraeus with a boat trip around the harbor. Seven-year-old Robbie's interest, for a change, is suddenly inspired by the boat ride, for which we're pleased to see him climb out of his recently grumbling pit.

The next hop is to Istanbul where I contact the Turkey Army Officer, I'd met in Washington, DC, and his suggestion we meet in a restaurant. During dinner, before I can ask him for suggestions or guidance, he appoints himself as our host and wants to take us in hand.

Meeting with him the next morning, we find ourselves especially exploring the interior of the Great Hagia Sofia Mosque, its floor covered with hundreds of hand-woven rugs. But even more intriguing is his leading us on to visit into the Grand Bazaar. It's also known as the Covered Market, one of the world's oldest and largest. He tells us it has more than sixty covered numbering streets, and contains over 4,000 shops. He also warns us to stick closely together, since we're joining the more than 200,000 visitors who go in there every day. Though we have no desire to buy anything, somehow, we still come out of the labyrinth owning two small prayer rugs. In the massive market one could also easily get lost in its corridors.

Our vacation so far has been interesting and challenging. Two days later, I rent a car and we begin driving south along the coast toward Izmir. Along the way we stop to explore a number of ruins, especially at the ancient City of Ephesus. For Robbie the rumble of piles of the building's great stones is a challenge to see if he can climb to near the top. While Audrey and I are busy taking photographs and touring around the grounds on foot, we hear from distance and above us is Robbie's voice fairly high up on the temple wall. He's yelling about how proud he is for have climbing so high. But it's getting him back down to the grounds without injury and safely, it takes the rest of the visit is keeping him under control.

But it's at our arrival in Izmir where our other troubles begin, we've hardly expected. Because an International Fair event is in full sway, the first problem is the lack of available hotel rooms, and we spend most of the rest of the day searching for one. We finally are forced to end up in an old dilapidated building with small rooms including mirrors on the ceilings above the beds. When Audrey asks the clerk about them, in his matter of fact explanation it turns out we're in a whorehouse where the rooms are usually rented by the hour. Despite the despicable environment, because it's getting very late, agree we must have someplace to sleep and we're felt forced to spend the rest of the night there. It comes as no surprise hearing grunts, squeals and muffled other human noises suggesting the kind of activity for which it exists. We simply have to ignore it long enough to get some sleep.

In the morning, in a nearby cafe and shortly after a typical breakfast of cheese, dates, small dry cakes and thick black coffee, we decide to start driving back to Istanbul. But before getting very far back along on the road, Robbie begins vomiting and develops diarrhea for which we soon become desperate for a medical facility. We're directed to a nearby military facility, where we hope for help, but arriving there we're not allowed to enter and are turned away. Furiously arguing at the gate with the policeman, I'm finally able to get a doctor on the phone, who directs me to a Turkish clinic fairly close by. We have to spend two nights in a small town outside of Izmir while Robbie is being treated at the clinic to stop his excretions. Recommended by the doctor, we stay for another full day to allow Robbie's further recovery. During the whole time we're worrying we might lose him. By the third day, he has lost weight, but apparently recovered well enough, and with medicine given us in hand for him, we return to Istanbul. Upon arrival there, as soon as possible, we're able to get on the first available flight and take it back to the States. Our main memories of Turkey will mainly be about the unfortunate overnight facility and of Robbie's sickness attack there.

In early October of 1968, at Walter Reed Army Hospital our daughter, Suzanne, is born. Like her brother, she enters the world healthy and with a full head of hair. Her birth brings a burst of joy in our family. By this time, my relationship with Audrey has also returned to a mostly happy state. We have both agreed to determine it's very important our marriage is stable before bringing another child into our world. We know well enough having a child to disguise a marriage's unhappiness, or try to make it seem right, not only often fails, but could also may leave the child damaged thereafter.

I'm kept so busy during the two-year assignment to the Army Staff it passes quickly. As the end of the assignment approaches, I'm surprised receiving new orders to redeploy unaccompanied once again to Southeast Asia. I immediately react claiming a return to a combat zone seems much too soon, and argue strongly the new assignment is also unfair. The last thing, I argue, my marriage needs would be another separation. Finally, we're both pleased when my request is approved and the assignment changed for another one stateside. This time, the job is to the Defense Intelligence Agency, or the DIA.

My new activity begins with a four-month-long orientation course at the Washington Naval Air Station, located just east of the Potomac River. Most of the students in my class are senior civilian men and women, all career intelligence analysts. My assignment also includes traveling to other intelligence installations around the country, coast to coast. The purpose seems to be for our awareness of the Air Force and Army intelligence activities charged with other aspects in missions with which we may need to coordinate.

Of this new assignment to the Defense Intelligence Agency, I won't really understand its meaning until I'm back in the Pentagon.

Chapter 33

IN A LABYRINTH

THE FOUR-MONTH DIA ORIENTATION COURSE COMPLETED, I'm back once again at the Pentagon, and feeling swallowed up in the maze of its warren halls. This time I'm assigned to the Southeast Asia Branch, supervising intelligence analysts, mainly civilians and a few Army, Air Force and Navy officer personnel. Many of the civilians are recent college graduates, and I'm pleased to think, despite the elapse of the past two years, my combat experience and insight from the Vietnam War might actually be useful to them. But I soon realize my experience has been too low at the troop level, and has little to offer this elevation, which is well beyond ground combat action. And meanwhile, the in-country situation has changed immensely, since I was in Vietnam. Nonetheless, I still feel like I've gained and retained an insight these analysts working in the Pentagon's basement lack in experience.

If I thought the pressure on the Army Staff was high, it pales by comparison with duty activity in the DIA. The weekday usually starts at 5 AM and frequently lasts well into the night. With the war is still underway in Vietnam, the Southeast Asia Branch is on the hot seat for supporting the office of the Defense Department's Joint Chiefs of

Staff. There are daily briefings "upstairs," which our part is prepared the evening before and updated early the next morning. Our portion is presented as a briefing first to our major general, the branch chief, and after making "fixes," then it's sent upstairs to the Joint Staff. The briefings have to be coordinated with the corresponding office at the Central Intelligence Agency, or CIA, mainly by the means of facsimile equipment, or FAX. Our interpretations are often at issue with the CIA's counterpart analysts, but in any case, arguments over the differences have to be resolved. Against deadlines, the briefing-preparation arguments and counter arguments may reach seeming madhouse volume before a report is finally produced and considered ready for presentation. I often find myself reviewing analyst drafts working into the night before the agreed piece is ready for final coordination. The discussions often get heated, the high tension further aggravating the upset with my bowels. Coupled with insufficient sleep, I also begin to lose weight and worry about giving my latent encapsulated TB bacilli the chance to break out again.

For a while, my assignment seems un-anchored and I feel I'm not contributing much to the daily effort. But no situation in the Pentagon lasts for long. Soon, a new but rather white-haired aged, Army colonel arrives to take over as the section chief. He's obviously in his years and on his last assignment before retirement. He changes my ambiguous role by assigning me as his assistant. Now, I'm obliged to investigate, find answers to and deal with daily problems for him. As his surrogate, I'm finding myself seen unwelcome as an intruder in our sub branches. The Colonel would normally resolve problems himself and render decisions to them coming down from higher offices. But he rarely does so and instead I'm assigned to deal with other officers and civilians from offices and organizations outside of our branch. They are usually concerned with issues beyond my knowledge and in which I also lack any authority.

It's not long before the Army colonel section chief receives his retirement orders and is replaced. The new Chief, a navy captain, does away with my ad hoc job and assigns me as chief of an office of analysts, who are mostly civilians. Our office's responsibilities are to cover China and south Asia, especially focusing on India and Pakistan then threatening mutual renewed hostilities. The analysts' work produced strikes me a waste as their finished articles rarely seem to go anywhere else than within the section, or to any other offices.

It's a unique assignment for me to be working among a number of civilians, and supervising a number of young men and women. To act as a buffer, I have an African American male assistant, who is the senior civilian among those who make up the office of some dozen people. A few are enthusiastic about their work, while some simply seem to be putting in time. For the most part, when engaged directly they are bright and capable. Yet, there are a few who avoid involvement and resist my efforts to get them to produce any useful intelligence in their areas of responsibility. The three Army majors assigned to my office at least make me feel I have some sense of command and control.

The assignment at the DIA must have interesting aspects, and include some talented people. But to me in general, it feels more like a dead end, and I'm beginning to sense my career is coming to a close. Though I learn I'm on the list for promotion to full colonel, I haven't been, nor will be selected to attend the War College. I wonder if this may have had to do with my request to be temporarily assigned to the Infantry Branch while serving in Vietnam with the 101st Airborne Infantry Division. If so, I'm being penalized for seemingly having abandoned the Intelligence Branch during an intensive combat period. Though I've hardly ever imagined myself a general grade officer, at least I still want to feel be in the running for it. Though not being selected to attend the War College also tells me where my career will end.

During this same period, I receive a call from my former friend, Klaus Martin, whose Tacoma, Washington house-building operation by now has become well developed. He advertises his construction company specializing building the "Workingman's Dream" home. The slogan strikes me as tinged as sarcastic and limiting his ambition. Visiting us a year earlier at our home in Fort Washington, Maryland he said he was in search of construction managers. If and when I leave the Army, he wants me to consider such a position. Despite not caring much associating more with him, it did sounded interesting and I said so at the time, but I'd never followed it up, and certainly made no commitment.

On this current visit he surprises me while being in Washington, DC and with an invitation to join him for lunch at a downtown restaurant. Ostensibly, he says he just wants to renew our friendship and to bring me up to date on his progress back in Tacoma, of which he sounds quite proud. His invitation seems simple enough and doesn't require any preparation on my part for the meeting. From the Pentagon, I arrive in uniform at the restaurant and join him at his table. He introduces me to two men he describes as potential "investors" in his company whom he hasn't prior mentioned are included in the luncheon. But their presence immediately raises my suspicion for being introduced into a meeting he and his investors have already planned and discussed. During the lunch we all chat about life in the Washington, DC area, and they ask a few superfluous questions about my military experience in Vietnam. During the lunch, my suspicions continue to grow and I'm waiting to see them unmasked.

At the end of the meal, when coffee arrives, one of Klaus' guests finally turns to me, and asks, pointedly, "How soon will you be leaving the army?" Then quickly he adds, "More importantly, when will you be moving to Tacoma, to take on one of the manager positions?"

Having unanticipated such requests, I'm caught by surprise. But to be sure I've understood him correctly I ask him to repeat his questions. As he does so, I glance at Klaus and read the guilty grin expression on his face, as he nervously pushes his glasses up on his nose. I'm sure the guest can see I'm caught unaware, and I make no effort to hide my displeasure. This is just like the Klaus of old whose business tactics were always seemingly less than honest.

"I don't know what you've been told," I reply to the guest, "but I haven't decided to leave the Army any time soon, and when I do, I have no plans to leave the DC area. I've built a designed contemporary home nearby in Maryland and my wife has an important position as a therapist at Washington's St. Elizabeth's Hospital. So, you can understand we'll be continue living here well into the future."

Following my statements, on the guests' faces there are sudden changed expressions. It's obvious Klaus not only hasn't cleared anything with me about a future job, and it's now apparent he has also misinformed and misled his guests. I guess the hopeful half-grin now on his face must have been I'd play along with his game. Instead, no sooner I've finished answering his guest's questions, he and the other "investor" turn their chairs to face each other. Now ignoring Klaus and me, they deliberately begin a conversation about an unrelated subject. Their act of turning away clearly shows their displeasure, and I can hardly blame them for being misled and misinformed.

Based on my past experience with Klaus, I should've been forewarned. But it shouldn't be surprising he'd play the "big shot" role like this one. I've no doubt this is his usual way of doing business and treating people. Apart with excusing myself, without another word to him, or the others, I push back my chair, stand, button my uniform and depart without looking back, only stopping to pick up my cap on the way out.

Driving back during my return to the Pentagon, Klaus' disreputable conduct lingers on, and I decide to put a final end to my association with him.

Meanwhile, returning to focus on my future, again I'm faced with the familiar dilemma: duty to home and family, versus a return to an assignment in Asia following with the expected next promotion to colonel. But in mind having visited it there, this time my choice is not as difficult. A two-year assignment to Bangkok might not be so bad. My family, as I've learned could live there with me and even find it interesting, except it would be now with two underage children. Yet, on the other hand, I feel certain my wife would not leave her position at St. Elizabeth Hospital. It's her career, so why should she?

Then, worsening the assignment possibility, I'm further informed it most likely wouldn't be to Bangkok, but to a site in northern Thailand, where I'd command a station and its troops in a jungle outpost. Though little detail is provided, it's not difficult to analyze what would be involved. First, being isolated in the northern jungles, where none of assigned troops would find it enthusing. The opposite would be more likely. Secondly, discipline would also be a major difficulty to be maintained, not to mention the growing widespread use of drugs. A variety are even more easily obtained in the country's economy and have already become more widely used among our troops. Though I'd be allow to visit home twice a year, and with Audrey dead set against this path, I would probably have no family left after returning from Thailand.

Presumably, I'd return from the two-year stint for promotion to colonel, then serve in grade possibly in command or various staff assignments, to the end of a thirty-year career. Facing this prospect stirs little enthusiasm in me. She has her own career and my promotion would make no difference to her. Another separation would most likely lead to divorce, and its negative effects on our children. So far, having been dragged around to my assignments, there's no denying Audrey's position I know is logical and justified.

Now, retirement is the alternative I'm facing, an uncharted route into the future. I enter consultation with the Veterans' Administration, which offers guidance in career choices after military service. At age 42, I could probably work for the available options for older retirees. I take a series of aptitude and vocational tests whose high scores indicate good potential in a variety of fields. Even so, these beg the question of what field might interest me. I'm discovering I don't really want to be employed for the rest of my working life in any one of them.

Retirement now staring me in the face, it completely baffles me about what should come next. I'm wondering what other government agency could take advantage of my military rank and experience. My bi-lingual ability, assuming it could be improved, might also be useful. For a while I consider joining the fairly new US Drug Enforcement Agency, or DEA, which is looking for recruits for its intelligence operations. But after reading about its short history, tactics and results, I decide it's not for me.

I've finally come to the conclusion: my Army career is finished. Regardless of the unmapped road ahead, I know I've reached the end of this one.

Chapter 34

RESHUFFLING THE DECK

———•◆•———

FINALLY, MY LIFE AS SOLDIERING HAS REACHED ITS LAST stop, and I realize it can go no farther. Now I'll have to start considering other directions, one of the paths I'll have to take. These thoughts have already started beginning, but at the moment they are all still hazy. Meanwhile, first things must come first, and at this moment, on this morning, my attention is fixed on my retirement ceremony. Also retiring with me are eight soldiers, three other lieutenant colonels, two majors and three master sergeants. All nine of us are now waiting for the order to march out to what normally would be a reviewing stand on the Fort Myer's parade ground. Usually, we would be honored as the reviewers, but because of this day is rainy, the parading troops won't be out in the open air this morning, nor will we. While it could have been a mixed time of exhilaration and regret, instead it's now more a longing for the event to be over with and done.

My gloom matches the rainy day and forces our retirement ceremony from the parade ground to the inside of Fort Myer's gymnasium. Instead of a live marching band, our music and the cadence are to be delivered by recordings. Also, there will be spectators in support of this ceremony, but they won't be doing much if any cheering for us nine soldiers marking the end of our respective service years. In the place of troops parading for us, only the hardiest of office colleagues, a few friends and family members have come to the stands to salute our service and to watch our bid farewell to the U.S. Army. For me, who has always loved a parade, it's clear there won't be one for us to review, and I'll miss and regret it. Consequently, there also won't be a very large crowd this day, either. On this wet gray morning, the usual parading troops are absent and are in their barracks, or somewhere else to stay dry. I doubt they'll miss this opportunity to stay in, as they don't have so often. The significance of the event is downgraded even further, as our group's highest military grade is a lieutenant colonel. My guess is why the post commander, a Major General officer, has dispatched a full colonel in his stead to provide the Army's official farewell ceremony.

After the National Anthem recording concludes, and our audience take seats in the stands, the unseen band starts with delivering a quieter version of John Phillip Sousa's, *The Washington Post March*. The sound of this marching cadence music is the signal for the senior lieutenant colonel in our *ad hoc* formation to call us to attention. At his subdued barked order, we march to our appointed spot on the gymnasium floor, where he halts us, orders us to face the crowd in the stands and orders us to assume parade rest.

The reviewing Colonel then strides out and takes command of our small formation. Again, our ad hoc leader calls us back to attention, then returns to face the Colonel. They exchange salutes, and our leading member rejoins our formation. The Colonel orders us to parade rest. Then, one by one, as a name is announced over the Public Address system, each soldier comes to attention without an order, as the Colonel arrives before him. Then, he and the reviewing officer exchange salutes and shake hands. While, still before each soldier, in a *sotto voce*, the Colonel also gives to each of us, on behalf of the U.S. Army, thanking for our years of service and expresses its farewell. In a few minutes it will take for him to work his way down the line to me, nearer the middle.

Clustered with the few of my former office colleagues and other observers are Audrey and our children. I notice Robbie and Suzie seem more impatient than prideful, or even very curious. They are also sitting among the friends and family of the other retiring soldiers. Silently, I tell them all they won't have to wait much longer. Though I may have brought some impatience with me, I will still stand at full attention for the last time in uniform. The choice I've made to retire than continuing active service, it reminds me and fits with Omar Khayyam's warning: *"Ah, take the cash and let the credit go, nor heed the rumble of a distant drum."* It's what I've now chosen, a new life on the barely imagined new path I'm to follow.

As I wait to be saluted and thanked for my years of service, my mind flashes back to where this ending all started. We're told it's in every seven years new ones replace all the cells in our bodies. Consequently, some believe, when our cells are replaced, we're remade into an entirely a new person. True or not, still I do know I am not the same person who volunteered to avoid the draft 22 years ago by joining the U.S. Air Force. According to medical science, the cells in my body have since been transformed or replaced at least three times, maybe even more. I also can't relate my physiological transformations to seven-year periods, but I do know I've shucked off the old ones and replaced them each time with a new me.

With the first cells exchange, I learned not to let my childhood define the rest of my life. At an early stage I could have stayed with my mother and stepfather after the ten years in the orphanage. And then I might even have gone into the restaurant business with them, as they planned and wanted, but if so, I probably wouldn't have broken out of my cocoon and taken flight. Yet, I was determined to break free from their plans and unrestricted myself from their control.

Just now, it's difficult to remember clearly my 19-year-old self at the Los Angeles train station, about to depart on my way to Texas for the U.S. Air Force. I'm certain the teenager I was then is a stranger to the man I am now. My first concern at the time was to avoid combat, to stay alive and remain whole. It came at the cost of giving up four years of my youth to military service. Then, less than a year in the U.S. Air Force already deeply disappointed, I decided for the chance to shorten my service by trying to become an Army officer. It was the deal offered by the Army, despite the possibility of being injured or killed in Korea. Nonetheless, I was then ready to reshuffle the deck, even if it meant being sent into combat, though, what at first, I'd tried to avoid. With this decision was beginning the effort of transforming myself.

Winning my commission and the gold bars of a 2nd Lieutenant did come with an unexpected profound change. The surprised make-over of my self-image produced a brand new confidence, especially after competing and making it in the top ten percent of my 160-man class in the Officers Candidate School. At the same time, this started shucking off of the second-class status imposed on me at the orphanage. Now I knew remaining at home with my parents I might've given in to our sense of minority status. But, by now I also knew I had to change who I am. Despite the prospect of being sent off to Korea, possibly to die, then as an officer I was still satisfied I'd made the right choice. Then more pleased with the new man I was becoming than the old one I'd shed, and left it behind. The military draft by itself might have freed me to an extent. But it wouldn't to the degree by being commissioned as an officer. To my mind, the new status was a true transformation.

For once, and for the first time, I had brought a weighty change in my life through my own efforts. And for the first time I felt the playing field of life was flat in the arena provided by the Army. Now I also knew, though in battle, I had to accept I might end up just so much cannon fodder left on the battlefield.

Indeed, the military cared little about my impoverished background, or the second-class status I'd felt as a Mexican American. It mattered profoundly I'd competed in a large sample of American males and had come out near the top. In less than two years, I'd earned the rewards of self-respect and dignity. If the feelings of inferiority had plagued me for so long may have not been entirely erased, I knew now they would be gone in time. It wasn't just a matter of self-respect; I recognized other people now had a respect for me I'd not seen before.

My performance, following in the various Army units to which I'd been assigned, continued buttressing the new self-image. I earned the regard of my commanders, acceptance by my comrades and civilians, men and women alike.

Now in my mind, as in a movie reel turning too fast, scenes from Army life flicker by rapidly. There were so many assignments, so many stations, so many people I met along the way, and their effects on me both positively and negatively. It's like watching a stone skipping across a pond, each surface-touching splash leaving a smaller concentric circle, one merging into the next before the stone sinks and its evidence entirely all disappears. Admittedly, at the outset, with a war underway in the Far East, if possible, I would have avoided the service entirely. But it wasn't likely, and here I am at the other end, so different from the teenager who left home on the train bound for Texas so long ago. On sober reflection, it was not only a good experience, but also a discovery of myself and achieved a new self-image with self-respect, a necessary prelude to all was to follow.

Wrenching me loose from my reverie, the Colonel suddenly arrives before me, as my rank and name are being announced. We salute each other, and with a firm handshake and his nearly whispered thanks, my two decades-plus years of service and a life as a soldier come to an abrupt end. Yet, despite this event in my honor, I still have a sense of being cast aside, as no longer important to the organization has ordered all the years of my adult life. Following the end of the retirement ceremony, a few of my now former office subordinates remain waiting around for a few handshakes and some quick goodbyes. I know they'll fade into the past, as I will in their memories, too.

With rain still falling, while I'm driving us on the way home, my wife and children are surprisingly quiet. I guess there wasn't much in the ceremony to arouse their imaginations, or have any questions. While my five-year-old daughter, Suzie, is silent and watches the road going by, my son finally asks, "What will you do tomorrow, Dad?" I answer and tell him, "Rob, you've just read my mind. That's exactly what I've also been asking myself."

I'll have time to reflect, if I have the courage to do so and do it honestly. Looking back, I believe I played out my military life as best I could. But it's the future will now be on my mind. I'll also have to be thinking about how to use my time and to find my way ahead.

Once again, as if on cue, Omar khayyam's verse of his shrewd understanding comes to mind and says it best:

> *The moving finger writes*
> *And having writ, moves on.*
> *Nor all your piety nor wit*
> *Shall lure it back*
> *To cancel half a line,*
> *Nor all your tears*
> *Wash out a word of it.*

Omar has it right, there's no point in rehashing and regretting what is past. It's time to face the future.

Words After

◆◆◆

FOR A FEW WEEKS FOLLOWING THE RETIREMENT CERE-
mony, I'm left feeling completely lost, rejected and somewhat useless.
Considering and trying some possibilities, I should have learned by now
I'm not a businessman. A brief trial as a car salesman quickly teaches
me my new career will not be happy in sales, either.

Yet, it doesn't take long before a new life begins to coalesce in a
different direction on a road waiting to be taken. I've done art in some
form since childhood and while in the Army, even now and then, I've
also done so. I stop looking for a job and decide to use my available GI
Bill to enroll in the Corcoran Museum's Art School in Washington, D.C.
My art preference is for figurative sculpture, but first I'm required to
take a year's worth of drawing and design. Despite some initial disappointment, my efforts still turn out well. A year later, transferring to
The American University, also located in Washington, D.C., it requires
more drawing, but now I'm also sculpting in clay and working from live
models. To my great pleasure, I discover a natural talent in the three
dimensional art form, as well. A year later, I apply for the graduate visual
art program at the University of Maryland, where I'm accepted and
continue figure sculpting, stone carving and studying art history. The
older instructor there teaching stone carving sculpture also impresses

me with the importance of expressing myself in my art in any form. It has been a goal ever since. Two years later, now with a Master of Fine Art degree, the art school environment has given me purpose, hitched my talent and showed me the direction for my life.

While still in school, through a local nursery I receive my first commission to create and produce unique hanging flower containers for a mall. Pleased with my work, the owner recommends me to a Washington, D.C.-based company; one it builds shopping malls in many states. My proposal wins a commission for a 20-foot-high metal fountain sculpture for a shopping center in Louisville, Kentucky. Due to my inexperience, while the project succeeds, income only covers the cost and produces no profit. Yet, I still gain vital experience and begin to acquire the credentials for success in similar future projects.

The Author is creating "Trio," a bronze and copper sculpture, outside his studio in Leesburg, Virginia, in 1998.

270

With my reputation growing as an artist, I help to organize an artist's cooperative gallery in downtown Washington, D.C. At the Touchstone, as it becomes known, I have my first solo exhibition there. The show not only produces sales, it also adds further to my reputation as an artist. Eventually, I'm elected president of the Washington, D.C. Chapter of the National Artist's Equity Association. A member there puts me in touch with her contractor husband, who is responsible for two re-development projects underway in Philadelphia. The City financing construction, its law requires a public sculpture must be included in all its projects. I apply, compete for and receive both commissions. These monumental size concrete sculptures are both successful and well received, leading to two more similar concrete projects for a Maryland County Park and for a concrete products company in Virginia.

During these first few years in retirement, I've been keeping track of Saigon's fall to the North Vietnamese Army. I learn the thousands of South Vietnamese soldiers have managed escaping capture by evacuating to Thailand. When I learn our State Department there has established centers for evacuees, I register as a willing sponsor for my former friend, Lieutenant Colonel Nho Tan Nghia, with whom I served as his advisor at the II ARVN Corps Headquarters at Pleiku, Vietnam. To my surprise, I'm shortly notified, thanks to my willingness to sponsor him, he is on the way to the United States and I'll be contacted when he arrives.

It's no surprise Colonel Nghia is highly regarded and has had many US Army and civilian friends in Vietnam. Now, many of them are also in the Washington, DC area, and I'm among them. Shortly after he arrives, rather than accepting our invitation to temporally reside in our home in Maryland, he asks my wife and me meet him at a Chinese restaurant he has selected in the Chinatown section of the District.

There, we spend an afternoon with him dining and learning about his escape from Vietnam with his son, a lieutenant. He tells us how they both had to hide in a fishing boat for a while, before eventually escaping by going on sailing to Thailand.

Colonel Nghia relates how, before leaving Vietnam, he first tried to corral and reorganize fleeing retreating ARVN groups of soldiers to fight off the invading North Vietnamese Army, or NVA forces. But soon, when he could see the cause was hopeless, they fought their way back to Saigon, only to discover it was already in NVA hands. From there, they first went into hiding and then managed escaping to Thailand in the belly of a fishing boat.

Colonel Nghia, still a leader, tells us of his new mission in the U.S., which is to gather and organize resettled Vietnamese fishermen in the coastal areas of Houston, Texas. He also tells us of his plans to establish a Vietnamese restaurant there to be managed by his wife, who is also on the way to follow him. He has obviously planned his future well to live out his new life in our country. Later, I learn, as part of his future in America, he has also taken on a new name. With his new identity, he has also moved into our American population and to settle among us.

Meanwhile, though my artistic success continues, my marriage frays. Despite a mutual effort to revive our earlier closeness, we instead grow farther apart. A four-year struggle fails to improve our relationship and it ends in divorce.

Meanwhile, through the Touchstone Gallery I meet a new member, a painter, who'd recently completed her master of fine art degree at The American University. I seek her insight about a thesis for my master of art graduation at the University of Maryland. In a few meetings, we discover our respective marriages have separated from our spouses, and we both love ballroom dancing. We dance well together, are compatible and our relationship leads to love and marriage. Since we want to live in a new venue, we decide to move to Virginia and buy ten acres of country land. There we plan to build a home and studio to be designed by the same architect who had done my home before. To prepare myself for the task, I take a two-week design-build course in Vermont, return and assume as the main contractor and carpenter to build our contemporary house and studio.

Sherry also encourages me to write about my background growing up in a California orphanage. "Stewing in The Melting Pot: The Memoir of a Real American," the biography is finally published in 2001.

We share more than 25 happy, productive years. Until three years later, cancer relentlessly overtakes her life.

Her passing leaves me in my life of its eightieth decade, profoundly sad, my career in suspension and while I execute her will. I inherit the large body of her unique paintings she leaves for which I attempt to find homes through sales and mainly donations to institutional organizations. Shortly after her passing, my life is further diminished by the deaths of my brother, my son and then my younger sister.

While now alone, I live on getting back into my passion for sculpture, write and publish a novel. Now, this memoir of my life as a soldier and discover who I am. If not solace, it provides understanding and at least distraction. Though the experience of my life and its unfolding may have been new to me, Hippocrates' life lived long ago, he summed it as:

Life is short,
Art is long,
Opportunity is fleeting,
Experience is treacherous,
and
Judgment is difficult.